Healing at the Harbor

Book 4

The events and conversations in this book have been set down to the best of the author's ability, although some names and details have been changed to protect the privacy of individuals.

Copyright © 2013, 2024 by Keri Dangerfield Stone
All rights reserved. No part of this book may be reproduced or used in any manner without written permission of the copyright owner except for the use of quotations in a book review.

Cover Design © Diane Mower
Cover Illustration © Celia Roberts
Edited by Keri Dangerfield Stone

Second Edition, Expanded and Updated published January 2024

First Edition published 2013
Published in the United States of America

ISBN: 979-8-9885607-0-8

Please direct all correspondence and book orders to
hello@keridangerfieldstone.com

Proceeds go to bringing awareness, reuniting adoptees with their families of origin, and keeping families together.

www.keridangerfieldstone.com

HEALING
AT THE
HARBOR
Book Four

A Memoir By
Keri Dangerfield Stone

How can we even begin to comprehend, honor, and acknowledge one love on a soul level in the Heavenly Realm if we can't even comprehend, honor, and acknowledge one love on a cellular level in this Physical Realm? We are who we are. It is what it is.

-Keri Dangerfield Stone

Dedication

Dedicated to the Lahaina community. Lahaina Harbor received me as part of their family at a time when I felt like I didn't have one.

I currently have the time to finish this book. The Lahaina town fire on August 8, 2023 displaced many, including myself. I, like many others, have been laid off from work after the entire town burned down.

I feel so honored to have been a part of the community and to have known Lahaina before August 8, 2023.

Moving forward, I am praying for a sustainable city, bringing the community even closer in Unity.

Table of Contents

Family Tree ii
Introduction iv
Author's Note x
A Perspective from Kanyon Kale' Stone xiii
Prologue xvi

AUGUST 2011 1
Let Us All Be Real 2

OCTOBER 2011 5
October Season 6
Inviting All Witches 8

NOVEMBER 2011 13
Zila Moves Out 14
Thanksgiving 15

DECEMBER 2011 17
My Connections with Jesus 18
Christmas 24
A Christmas Love Letter to All 25
The Sangraal 28
Goodbye 29

JANUARY 2012 33
Madonna Is the Man 32
My Beloved Son 34

FEBRUARY 2012 39
Astrology 38
Suzi Enters Our Life 40

MARCH 2012 43
Dawn Visits from Vegas 44
My Army Arrives 46

APRIL 2012 49

    The Healer Down South 50
    Lots of Sistahs and Brothas..52
    My 42nd Birthday 54

MAY 2012 57
    The Storm Rolls In 58

JUNE 2012 61
    June 1st...62
    Viva Las Vegas...68
    Time for Take Off..69

JULY 2012 71
    Let Us Start with Lenny 72
    Oh Yeah... a Baby Was Born 79

AUGUST 2012 81
    The Day of My Father's Death..82
    My Job Found Me...85
    I Love My Job..87
    Spiders in the Space 93
    Tyler Moves Out...95
    Kandi Moves In..96
    Dawn Arrives to Maui...99
    Cousin Kimber Arrives to Maui 100

SEPTEMBER 2012 103
    A Text from Kai..102
    Sweet Messengers in Maui..105
    What Did We Do in September?..108

OCTOBER 2012 111
    Homeless in Olowalu 112
    Infested Home...114

NOVEMBER 2012.. 119
    Facebook Messages with Kai 120
    Mother's Update Letter from Utah...123

 Thanksgiving and Kylie's Arrival 124

DECEMBER 2012 127
 Casper, Wyoming Makes the Maui News 128
 Kai's Birthday Month 131
 Monk Seal 135
 Santa Sent Sapna 138
 Christmas Eve Whale Watch 140
 Christmas 141

JANUARY 2013 143
 New Years, Hawaiian Style 144
 Kai Announces New Arrival 145
 Letter from Mother 152
 Kandi Moves Out 154

FEBRUARY 2013 157
 Whale Season at Its Peak 156
 Letter from Mai 157
 Stoney McStonerface Stone 159
 Sharks at Work 160
 Scott Gets Arrested 161
 Truth Be Told 163

MARCH 2013 165
 Rachel Comes and Goes 166
 Jr. Pays Us a Visit 168
 Word from Scott 170
 Cardinals Everywhere 171
 JC Inquires 172
 Laundry Gets Lifted 173
 Messaging Mai about Kylie 176
 Kylie Hates It Here 179

APRIL 2013 183
 Letters with Scott 184
 Boss Almost Pays Me Salary 188
 Easter Sunday 190

- Personal Reference Letters for Scott...................191
- Dan Moves In 195
- Marie Checks In 198
- James' Birthday...................201
- Let's Break It Down:...................203
- Kylie Goes Home/Kandi Moves Back In 203
- Lizards Thick in the Space 208
- My 43rd Birthday 210

MAY 2013...................213
- The End of Whale Season...................210
- Scott Writes His Kanyon Boy 212
- Mother's/Victory Day...................214
- Family Letters 218
- My Perspective These Days...................226

JUNE 2013...................231
- Scott Faces Sentencing...................230

JULY 2013...................237
- Scott Writes 238
- Jasper Arrives 246

AUGUST 2013...................249
- Girlfriend in the Hood 250
- Thoughts... Feelings...................251
- Kanyon and Scott Write One Another...................252

SEPTEMBER 2013...................257
- I GOT ARRESTED...................258

OCTOBER 2013...................277
- Scott Gets Sentenced 278
- First Days of Incarceration 283

NOVEMBER 2013...................289
- West Maui Parasail...................290
- Messages through Dreams and Nature...................292

 Heart to Heart 294
 Kai's Visit 305

DECEMBER 2013 311
 Utah 310

JANUARY 2014 315
 Telling Scott All about It 316

FEBRUARY 2014 327
 Kanyon Stays in Utah & I Go Home to Maui 328
 Back in Maui!!! 332

MARCH 2014 337
 Making the Best of Our Situations 336
 JC Checks In 340
 Last Letters from Scott 342

APRIL 2014 345
 Last Letter to Scott 346

APRIL 2015 351
 Final Words 352

Family Tree

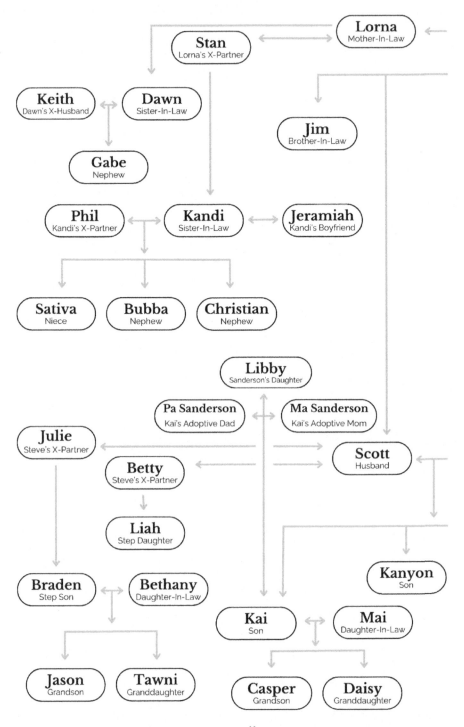

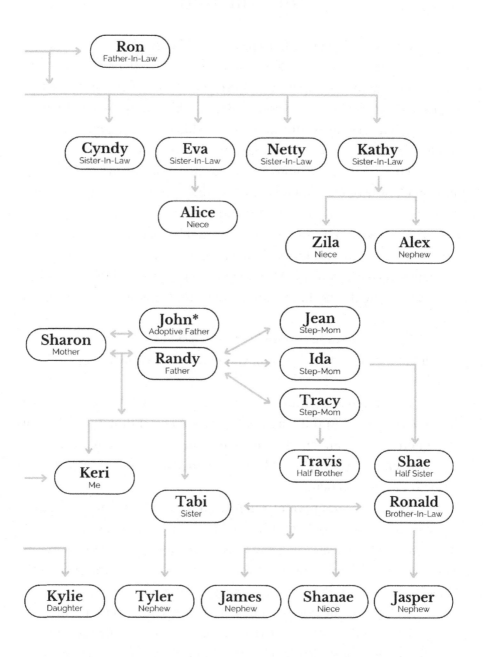

*Not shown: John's children from a previous marriage, David and Mike. David's wife is Helen. Mike's wife is Georgia and their children are Hilary and Jessie.

Introduction

Where do I begin... Let's just say, *I MADE IT!*

It's been a journey and not an easy one. It has been scary, strengthening, and eye-opening. I have gone from a *perfect* little life to a highly *dysfunctional* life, to a *homeless* life, to a life I only *dreamed* I would be living. The details of the *dream* are nothing as I imagined, but the comfort and bliss I found have made the journey all worth it.

There are a few things I have always disliked *(hated)*: Chickens and eggplant, riding a city bus, missing out on family functions, being away from my children, driving old cars that are not in pristine condition, cockroaches, using coin-operated laundry machines, having to hang your laundry, camping in a tent, ballerina buns, country music, wearing miniskirts, and FISH. Crazy how now that I look at the list, these are all the things that I had to adjust to, living this life of mine in Maui.

I have always been taught, *to hate something is to love something*. If you didn't love it to some degree, you wouldn't use any energy on it to hate it.

I used to tell my husband, *"Feel lucky I hate you right now. It means I must still love you!"* And it was true. Near the end, I didn't hate him at all. There wasn't an emotional charge at all. One day, when he repeated his behavior after **23** years of marriage, the energy I held towards him was so neutral.

Sure, I was disappointed in his behavior, but I finally didn't take it personally. Instead of hate, I just held compassion toward him... *"It's too bad he doesn't grasp this family love he has at his fingertips and enjoy the love we have to offer him."* Which brought more compassion into the space of... *"That's too bad he doesn't feel comfortable with a stable family life because he never had one."* This took me back to a few of my first memories with him...

Scott and I got married in 1988 (two years after losing our firstborn to adoption). My uncle, who is a doctor, said, *"Scott will never forgive Keri for giving his son away. It will be a very rocky relationship if it lasts."*

Well, being 18 and so in love, I thought, "What does **he** know? Our love is strong."

To some degree, I had pretended the adoption never happened. I had a brick wall up all around my heart, helping me with the facade that *My baby died... My baby wasn't meant to be mine... I'm not good enough to be a mother... Life goes on... Get over it... I did the right thing...*

Well, in the two years we were *moving on*, Scott developed a liking for drinking. By 1990 Scott had gotten into trouble, alcohol-related, and was faced with jail. The judge ordered rehabilitation treatment. In this rehabilitation treatment, I was confronted by the counselors/doctors regarding Scott... *"This man has been so neglected by his parents and so violated as a child he will never be capable of trust or love in any relationship. We advise you to leave this relationship while you still haven't brought any children into the world with this man."* Little did they know, it was already too late for that.

Well, that was the saddest thing I had heard. I hated thinking these counselors/doctors were saying this man was unlovable and doomed to live a life without love. In my opinion, he was already the father of my child.

I took the challenge to prove them wrong and committed to loving this man for better or worse 'til death do us part, just as I had promised on July **23**, 1988, in those vows of marriage when I said, *"Yeah"* (*I do*). For you see, in my truth, this *WAS the father of my child*, even if I didn't actually have that child with me. It didn't matter if our baby had died, was kidnapped, or was placed for adoption... The loss was the SAME. In my head, Scott was the father of my firstborn child. When I allowed myself to think of my son as alive, living with someone else... there was always this conviction in my heart that I would meet him as soon as The Universe allowed... Obviously, that factor played a huge part in my loyalty to the father of my child.

Being raised a Latter-day Saint (LDS) (Mormon), I was solid with the beliefs, "Families are Forever" and "Cleave to your husband." Coming from a divorced family, having lost my father and then losing my son, I obviously wanted to hold strong to this programming.

I knew so much loss, and I didn't want any more of it. I was committed to Scott from that day forward. And let me tell you, it was NOT a pleasant union most of the time.

Scott provided well financially, and he didn't physically abuse me. In my eyes, the relationship wasn't dysfunctional enough to give up on him, and the good times made up for the bad.

In 1992, Scott and I moved from Salt Lake City (SLC) to Boise, Idaho... After one month, Scott came to me and said, *"I think this was a bipolar move. I want to go back to Utah."*

My mother (a graduate in psychology) has, in the past, tried to help me understand this man I married. She had explained "bipolar" to both Scott and me... bringing awareness... helping us, "help Scott."

After packing up the whole house in a semi and moving a 65-gallon saltwater fish tank to a different state, just to have Scott say after one month, *"Oops, I want to go back"* ... I made an appointment with a psychiatrist to get Scott on Lithium, a drug used for bipolar disorder.

After hearing our story, the Dr. turned to me and said, "There must be bipolar in your family for you to have put up with this behavior for as long as you have, as well as you have. How many times has your mother been married?"

"Twice."

"How about your father?"

Well, at the time, he was on his 5th wife and has since married a 6th time before he passed.

"Okay, there it is. That explains it."

After prescribing Scott lithium, the Dr. warned, *"Scott may not like being neutralized. They like their manias."* And boy, was he right!

Scott did not like his thoughts being shut down. I remember watching TV with him after lithium. After ten minutes of watching, Scott turned to me with such concern and asked, *"What are you doing?"* He was concerned that the lithium was affecting him, maybe in a bad way.

I asked him, "What do you usually do while you watch TV?"

Scott answered, "A billion things... Usually my mind is constantly racing with thoughts and ideas, problem-solving... while I watch TV."

So, I asked him, "How do you like sitting here, just watching TV?"

"I don't know."

Well, obviously he couldn't stand it because we packed up our house in a semi and moved our 65-gallon fish tank back to Utah after only three months in Idaho.

It had been nine years since we lost our first child. It was 1995, and I was still childless and married to Scott. We then pursued fertility treatment.

Subconsciously both Scott and I wanted to replace that baby we lost, and when no "oops" happened after seven years of marriage without using any preventative action (knowing the combination worked so well the first time), we went to find out why.

The doctor found my fallopian tubes totally blocked, having too much scar tissue from an earlier infection. My doctor had concerns about a tubal pregnancy, so he suggested in vitro fertilization (IVF). Scott and I sold our fifth-wheel trailer, four-wheelers, and wave runner to invest in a baby.

On October 8, 1996, Kanyon Kale' was born with Kylie Dawn two years later, on March 21, 1999

By the time Kylie was born, Scott and I had been married for eleven years. It was always a rocky road, but it was doable, and I never pursued divorce, no matter how bad it got. As far as I knew or wanted to believe, Scott wasn't cheating, and he wasn't abusing drugs. He worked a lot, drank a lot, and was gone a lot. But he would always make time for the vacations I demanded, and he always provided a nice home for me with financial abundance.

After Kylie was born, we invited Scott's family to my family's cabin up in the mountains for a Stone family reunion. My father was there, and this was the first time Scott's mother would meet my father. I looked over at my mother-in-law as she witnessed her son interact with my father for the first time. Her jaw hanging, she said to me, *"I now know why you have stayed with my son as long as you have."*

Yeah, you could say I married my father.

Being married to Scott was always challenging and brought me sadness most of the time.

I was able to be a stay-at-home mom, signing my kids up for

everything that was offered: Music Together, Little Gym, lessons for instruments, dance, horseback riding, skateboarding, skiing... You name it, we did it, and I made sure the family went on one trip a year to spend quality time with their father. Scott worked so much, and when he did come home, he would not interact with us much, pulling a Brian Wilson (of the Beach Boys), glued to the TV in our room.

I'm glad I stayed with Scott as long as I did. My children know their father, and in knowing their father, they know themselves. I also cannot imagine reuniting with our eldest son in 2006 if we hadn't been together. It was such an emotional roller coaster ride with tons of drama as it was. I cannot imagine riding that ride if Scott and I had not been together. I have heard about other reunions where the Mother of Loss and Father of Loss are played against one another to such a higher degree than what we were dealing with. The degree of drama that we had been living in was so much... I could not imagine Scott and I not having had each other to make sense of the madness.

After the reunion with our firstborn son, we moved back to Utah from Texas to salvage our marriage... *again*. Scott had started drinking heavily, adding pills to the mix. Our entire marriage had been one that was always in counseling, in church, striving for Scott's sobriety and happiness. He would succeed at sobriety off and on. It seemed that each year, October till February were his hardest months. It made sense... At the young age of seven, Scott's father left his mother on Christmas Day. Ten years later (*to the day almost*), on December 26th, at the age of seventeen, he was coerced into signing away his rights for his firstborn son.

It was now 2007, and we were back in Utah with the goal of healing our family from that thing called adoption. At the time, Kai was rejecting me... we are at that part of the roller coaster ride in reunion. There is the *Honeymoon*, the *Reality*, and now *Subconscious Rejection* from the adoptee... but I had read (and it stands true), "*Be patient because the 4th curve on the ride is*, 'Can't Live Without You,'" putting you back in the *Honeymoon* phase again, basically surviving the emotional development between mother and child. The relationship starts in the infancy stage and continues on a fast-paced crash course of emotional development to adulthood.

On and off the roller coaster ride we go... Kai was coming around. By 2008, Scott was sober again, and the family was going to church again. By 2009 Kai went on his LDS mission, and the following Christmas was ... *Story of Mother Mary, Kai's Birthday, Anniversary of Loss*; my emotions hit hard with my eldest son being away from me... separated once again, triggering all the emotions I hadn't yet faced head-on. And that's when I wrote book one, *Life Goes On* (basically the *Honeymoon* of the story). It was very therapeutic. Everyone wanted to hear the story, and I just couldn't tell it anymore. Retelling the story kept me there energetically. Little did I realize that book two, *Letters to My Missionary*, was unfolding (the *Reality* of our relationship as mother and son). Of course, book three, *Mothers of Loss*, followed (based on an emailing support group for mothers in reunion facing *Rejection*). And now let me present book four, *Healing at the Harbor*, which of course, is the last curve of that emotional roller coaster ride, the realization of, *Can't Live Without You*. And that brings us full circle back around to that beautiful curve of *Honeymoon*, coming together again. The never-ending story continues...

Author's Note

Before I continue with my story any further, let me tell you a little bit more about myself. I am a hippie's daughter. My mother divorced my father when I was four. My mother remarried a well-established man 18 years her senior. The lifestyle of my immediate family changed drastically. I went from living under a young hippie's roof to living under a very structured, disciplined, religious roof.

For a few years after the divorce, my sister and I continued to see my father. In 1976, my mother decided to get married in the temple with my stepfather, and part of the requirement was that my stepfather had to adopt my sister and me.

My father, having been adopted from birth and raised with this Mormon theology, understood the rules and regulations, if you will, of the ordinance requirements of the religion. My father signed his rights away for his two girls and basically ran away from his home in Salt Lake City, Utah. The added loss and rejection were too much for this adoptee. I didn't see or hear from my father again until 1984; that story is in the first book I wrote, *Life Goes On*.

I have always been very familiar with marijuana. Remember, my father was a hippie. I had been around the medicinal herb since birth. I had witnessed firsthand the effects of it (more good than bad, by far). I even have young photos of me and my sister looking a little blitzed. I have memories of my sister and me sneaking, against my mother's will, to sit in the circle with my daddy and his friends. I have memories of weekends with my daddy where Daddy let me, and my sister be the leaders! Being in charge of directing the adults where to go, handling my daddy's money for him so he wouldn't lose it... basically being the lady of the house, taking care of my daddy and my baby sister. I LOVED WEEKENDS AT MY DADDY'S. They were what I looked forward to. And then he was gone, out of my life, mistaken for dead after being absent for four continuous years without any contact with anyone.

Anyway, by the time I was in 6th grade and some 9th graders asked me and my good friend Wendi if we knew what a bong was, it was a no-brainer to take a rip. I pretty much smoked regularly from then on. Well, as regularly as a junior high student gets it offered to them back in those days, which isn't as much as these days.

So just to set the record straight, by the time my father returned to Utah, *and* my life, when I was 14, I was already smokin' the ganja. So, when my sister and I had our next visit with our father, when he smoked, we smoked. It was so healing smoking weed with my father.

1984... My father had returned to his Salt Lake City home for a short time. One of the first things he did was pick me and my sister up for a visit. We would always go to my grandparent's cabin, lighting up the moment we pulled out of my parent's driveway. We would get to the cabin stoned out of our minds, unload the car, and pack in multiple trips of groceries and bags of things up this steep handmade steppingstone staircase path. *I rarely mention the names of each and every grandchild that were etched in the cement surrounding the stones that you had to step on with each step up. Mostly because it rubbed in the fact that my father is the adopted one. For you see, all the grandchildren's names are represented, with the exception of any of my father's children.*

My daddy taught me how to smoke the herb and get shit done, eat, think... basically live life more peacefully, and enjoy this thing we call life. My favorite part of smoking together with my father and my sister was the philosophizing that went on while hanging with my father in this way. We would study everything; music, history, math... I found it so amazing how much this stoner hippie guy, that I am getting to know as my father, knew about the scriptures. And for the first time, I liked the translation. I would have to say this is what started my own spiritual journey.

In my eyes and in my truth, I witnessed how much better my father did when he was medicating with marijuana instead of alcohol. In my true opinion, my father's downfall was when he quit medicating with marijuana. Wife #6 requested a temple marriage, which meant going to a medical doctor and giving up the herb. My father changed. I think he found a good woman. My father wasn't the man I knew... he had sold out. Our relationship dwindled. My father OD'd on those prescribed pills in 2009, and they revived him. In 2012, a few weeks after I moved to Maui, my father's wife found him dead at the family cabin. My opinion on marijuana??? Do I even need to say more???

When I got pregnant with Kai, I quit smoking (I never really smoked cigarettes, just weed). But of course, I am going to turn to the herb that heals the most after placing Kai up for adoption. I was a total Stoner until I married Scott Stone and became Keri Jean Stone... a lot of my friends said, *"Yeah, that name fits you soo much better."* I had always had a hard time fully letting go of the Dangerfield name I was born with and rolling with the name from the stepfather. Poulsen never clicked with me. I was delighted beyond belief when I first found out Scott's last name... STONE.

Very soon after marrying Scott, I had a front-row view of how alcohol affects a person. I had been drunk a few times in my day. I always hated how out of control I felt, and it definitely was not worth the hangover the next morning. My daddy had taught me to stick with the natural stuff, *"Be a Stoner, never a Juicer."*

I knew Scott had a problem with alcohol, so I requested he stop drinking. I quit smoking weed once again... I am not a hypocrite, and if I was going to ask Scott to quit, I was going to quit my "drug" of choice too. All that we can ever be is a good example. After all, we are only in control of ourselves. I stayed pretty damn sober and straight for fifteen years.

The next time I started medicating with weed again was in 2004 when my husband of sixteen years got caught cheating and was expecting a child with another; she was ten years younger than me. Both my father and my sister, who were both married in the temple, came up to me separately, suggesting that I start smoking some weed because I was having a hard time processing in my head **WTF** had happened.

I was concerned about not being a good mom, so I tested out *half* of a little blue *legal* pill (valium or something) that many of the "temple-worthy" Mormons are prescribed and had the worst trip I've ever had. It was like being drunk and stoned at the same time... *"I can't be a good mom on this shit."* I have been smoking the herb ever since.

A Perspective from Kanyon Kale' Stone
Desert Rocks
June 2011

Watching my dad use and abuse alcohol and pills has saddened me since the age of six.

To cope with the hurt of my father's drowning of sorrows, the affairs, and Kai coming back into our lives (who was also a disappointment to me with such imbalanced chakras), my mother started smoking marijuana.

My father was abusing legal painkillers and alcohol more than ever around the time when my brother moved in. Kai would go to bars with my dad. Kai was also on prescribed medication with me following suit, *which flared the Tourette's more than ever, bringing rage into it*. I decided at nine years old, *I'm not doing that chemical shit anymore*!!

During this whole time, my mom was smoking pot (the "illegal" medicine that Kai always criticized so much). Kai, my older brother who I was meeting for the first time, was stealing, bringing a hooker home, and letting his woman friend smoke cigarettes in the house, or he was off vandalizing somebody's belongings, which would lead to a fight with my mom.

My mother would be so hurt she'd smoke a bowl to calm down. I witnessed my mother use the medicine of her choice ... marijuana ... no slurring of her words; seeming like the same person but much brighter, happier, and peaceful; matching the energy the smoke session provided for the whole house; calming us all down from her interaction with Kai. The only side effects I have seen to this day from her smoking the herb is her red eyes, and sometimes she has minor forgetfulness. I saw all sides of each so-called medicine.

At the age of fourteen, my natural high off life had started to fade away. My emotions and thoughts manifested a worsening case of Tourette's and a horrible case of leaky gut syndrome. The illnesses stemmed from undealt issues of the past and new issues on the rise. In trying to decide what the best medicine was for me; I had been asking everybody I felt comfortable with about their medication.

From the information and energy, I got from people's experiences with every drug, legal and illegal (never even having met "Mary Jane" in person), I decided that the natural herb was the medicine I would try the next time it was presented to me.

Two weeks later, my family went to Desert Rocks (a music festival in southern Utah). My dad was assisting a friend with putting on a festival in Moab, Utah. By this time, I was fully aware of my mom's usage of marijuana, so when my mom was going to go on a "walk," I said, "*I'll join you, Mom.*"

Hesitantly, my mom allowed me to join her on her walk. With us both knowing what she was doing, we walked to the middle of the forest from our hotel room.

When my mother turned her back to me while lighting the pipe, she said, "*Don't look at me.*"

I laughed and said, "It's time for me to find medicine for myself."

Shocked, she said, "I can't! Kai used it against me, and people will think I'm a horrible mom!"

I then told her, "It's not your decision, it's mine. It's time mom. If you don't do it with me, I'm going to have a bad trip with my friends."

So, I took my first hit. I was so shocked to find an astonishing, skunky citrus aroma filling my mouth, seeming too good to be just a plant. I took two more hits. I had smoked the same amount as this heavyweight veteran. When the high hit, it was intense. Everything was so beautiful as if I was seeing everything for the first time. The trees and nature looked so vibrant and vivid; it was like nothing I had ever felt.

A sudden security came to me when I realized that life wasn't going to be nearly as stressful as I had been anticipating/experiencing up until this point. The constant chase of the destination had shifted to the journey now being the destination. I knew that with this herb, I'd appreciate every life moment for the miracle it is. It really showed me the beauty in life, which I somehow knew I would need for the trials awaiting me.

My whole perspective and appreciation of life from that point forward would continue to greatly improve, my mind, body, and spirit.

The ganja got my mind thinking more deeply than it ever had gone, with a vivid imagination to go along with it.

Marijuana really helped me get out of the linear left-brain thinking that is pushed on society. My mind was balanced with the right brain's creative, intuitive thinking. I soon pursued meditation, yoga, reiki, tai chi, organic foods, exercising more, and grasping the things that truly matter in life. I dropped out of school. The Internet (limitless information), much too complex to be coming out of a middle school teacher's mouth, became my new source of knowledge.

This thinking also brought frequent excitement, saying multiple times a day, *"I can't wait for Hawaii."*

Prologue

"*I can't wait for Hawaii,*" Kanyon repeated continually until we were on that plane on July 21, 2012.

"Kanyon, I don't know about this Hawaii thing you are so excited for. Things are looking bad. I don't even see a vacation anywhere in the near future, let alone Hawaii," I would repeat back continuously, until...

In March 2012, when I took Kanyon tanning, the tanning salon lady introduced herself as a medium and told me many things but most importantly... "*You are supposed to be in Hawaii... next to Wayne Dyer, wherever he lives.*" And with that, she continued to instruct me to go see her healer friend down south in Mapleton, Utah, to help prepare us for what was to come.

This beautiful, gifted woman named Suzi continued to give us messages explaining what was going on at home. Scott was using heavily, the worst I had ever seen.
Kanyon had known Scott was using "Black." Kanyon is a Crystal Child; he has always had a sense of all-knowing. Even though he didn't know what Black meant or was, he just knew. Kanyon had insisted we catch Scott doing whatever this Black was, and in October 2011, we did... Black is HEROIN.

August 2011

Let Us All Be Real
BLOG POST

Folks, I saw two movies in one day! It was my husband's birthday on Saturday. We honored my husband's birthday on the 26th instead of the 25th this year. For you see, through Numerology, we discovered that the passport officials were correct, and his parents *had* remembered his day of birth wrong.

My husband has always loved going to the movies. I, on the other hand, have a little problem called ADHD, so I don't like to frequent movies as much as him. Since it was his birthday, I let him dictate the day. We woke slowly and went to the theater to see *The Rise of the Planet of the Apes*. I'm not even sure if that is the title, but I am a huge *Planet of the Apes* fan! I remember the black and white and then color TV episodes. Loved it!

WOW WOW WOW!!! I cannot rant and rave enough about this movie!!! Of course, that is how it all started!!! How did we not all already know!!! Right!

And the preview for it... *TIME*... OMG!!! Cannot wait!!!

Caesar has identity issues, and because of his intelligence, he is able to rise above it (accept it), find his identity (heritage), and help his kind (species of origin) rise above for a better life together as One.

After this amazing movie that I truly want to see again IN the movie theater, we came home, and I cleaned the house until around six. My husband thought another movie sounded good. This time we went to see *Idiot Brother*. Loved it!

Scott was getting frustrated with the brother, who kept being too honest for his own good, a trait I have that has gotten me into trouble many times as well. Our problem? We are so REAL. You ask us a question, and we tell you our truth; we believe in everyone, we see people at their highest potential of who they can be, and we trust everyone... We are incapable of lying.

The movie was great. The sisters in the movie get so annoyed with their "idiot" brother for innocently speaking the truth and being incapable of cover-ups, making them own their truth and face their reality... until the end (when he had to go back to the slammer for saying too much and being too REAL with his probation officer, who he had mistaken as a sincere person who cares). The sisters, who at first were so annoyed with him for innocently making them face their truth, bailed him out because they realized his honest integrous self is a great way to be. TO BE REAL with oneself, owning your truth, facing reality, acknowledging it, accepting it, and loving it... IS TO BE LOVING YOU.

October 2011

October Season

It was October 2011 when the shit really hit the fan. Kai had returned home from his mission, married, and moved away. The adoptive parents' behavior had gotten so possessive over that boy of ours they adopted... Seriously, the mom had called the police on me because Kai was storing his things at our home while he was away for the summer.

I can't say for sure what it was that pushed Scott to go from churchgoer to heroin user... but he apologized at one time in the middle of this madness that it was too much for him to be addressing issues around the losses he has incurred in the name of adoption.

I had been attending adoption conferences, bringing awareness about the loss involved in adoption and bringing awareness that fathers have rights. Being quite the radical, I was sharing with anyone that entered my space. You could say it's how I dealt with the loss, rejection, and madness revolving around this adoption reunion. I was dragging Scott everywhere, speaking out, bringing awareness, and talking about it out in the open, addressing issues that Scott did not want to address.

Scott was legally prescribed pills for his injured back. Along with his occasional drinking, which escalated to more drinking, prescription drugs became an added demon, also acceptable in today's society.

Back Problems

Cervical C1-C7: Fear. Confusion. Running from life. Feeling not good enough. "What will the neighbors say." Endless inner chatter ... Rejection of wisdom. Refusal to know or understand. Indecision. Resentment and blame. Out of balance with life. Denial of one's spirituality ... Accepting blame for others. Guilt. Martyrdom. Grinding oneself down. Biting off more than one can chew ... Guilt. Repressed anger. Bitterness. Boarded-up feelings. Stuffed tears ... Fear of ridicule and humiliation. Fear of expression. Rejecting one's good. Overburdened ... Burdens. Overload. Trying to fix others. Resistance. Inflexibility ...

Confusion. Anger. Feeling helpless. Can't reach out.

Thoracic T1-T4: Fear of life. Too much to cope with. Can't handle it. Closing off from life ... Fear, pain, and hurt. Unwillingness to feel. Shutting the heart off ... Inner chaos. Deep, old hurts. Inability to communicate ... Bitterness. A need to make others wrong. Condemnation.

Vertebrae T5-T12: Refusing to process the emotions. Dammed-up feelings. Rage ... Anger at life. Stuffed, negative emotions. Fear of the future. Constant worry. Lack of self-love ... Storing pain. Refusal to enjoy ... Obsession with failure. Resisting your good ... Feeling let down by life. Blaming others. A victim ... Refusal to take charge. Needing to be a victim. "It's your fault." Blaming others for your problems ... Low self-image. Fear of relationships ... Disowning the right to live. Insecure and fearful of love. Inability to digest.

Lumbar L1-L5: A crying for love and a need to be lonely. Insecurity ... Stuck in childhood pain. See no way out ... Sexual abuse. Guilt. Self-hatred ... Rejection of sexuality. Financial insecurity. Fear of career. Feeling powerless ... Insecurity. Difficulty in communicating. Anger. Inability to accept pleasure.

Sacrum: Loss of power. Old stubborn anger.

Coccyx: Out of balance with yourself. Holding on. Blame of self. Sitting on old pain.

Scott has been hard-working from a very young age. Yeah, we could credit his back pain to the concrete forms he packed on a daily basis or blame the guy in church basketball... but bottom line, there was an energy leak in the areas in which his back felt weak to not endure the pressure or impact. It would be interesting to me to read Scott's medical charts and see exactly which areas were his affected areas... reading the list, I have a pretty good idea.

Inviting All Witches

Things were getting worse and worse. Bills weren't getting paid. Scott and I had met with the bishop to help with our utility bills... well, any bills they would assist with. Here we were, living in a 5000-square-foot home with outrageous bills... I could understand the silliness in asking for help for our abundant/lavish lifestyle. But Scott made sense of it, justifying it and saying, *"Do you know how much money we have paid in our tithe over the years? Thousands, hundreds of thousands... We can ask for help once in our life."*

I'm telling you about this part of the story only to explain what exactly the final straw was to push me to leave the LDS church...

I love the holidays. I love being able to celebrate them. They can be so magical.

For Halloween this year, I just wanted a night out with my hoodoo-voodoo sistahs... Folks no need to fear. We do not practice black magic. We just love educating ourselves about energy and how the Universe works. Learning how to keep our chakras open, healing in the process. I love pretending I am Samantha Stevens on *Bewitched*... Halloween is a good, fun time for me.

Well, I sent out invites to my hoodoo-voodoo sistahs and extended the invitation to some of my gal neighbors. I have just moved into the neighborhood and have befriended a few. Well, for those of you that don't know, I live in Salt Lake City, Utah... all but two of my hoodoo-voodoo sistahs are committed LDS Mormon women who have an open mind about the gospel and believe it goes hand in hand with how the Universe works, including chakras.

Another tidbit that I think speaks a little loudly as to what my ward is like... I live in Boyd K. Packer's ward. Boyd K. Packer is rumored to be the next Prophet for the LDS religion. He is an apostle for the church, and his son, who also lives in the ward, is a member of The Seventy, which to my understanding, is the step before becoming an apostle... Not that they have anything to do with my story, but let's just say, this ward had more of a stuffy feeling than other wards I have belonged to. I must say, it is the most reverent sacrament I have ever sat through. I do enjoy the *"you can hear a pin drop"* stillness.

Well, I think I have scared them with my purple hair, stiletto nails, and now... My invitation to a "Witches Council".

The ladies and I had a great night playing intuition games. But my new neighbors? I haven't really heard from them yet.

I have never cared what others thought. I have been sporting violet hair since 1999 and *Tis the Season* (Halloween). I was wearing acrylic stiletto nails... beautiful claws. I guess some would say I looked like a witch. But I am a good witch, lol. Bottom line, I scared the neighbors by talking about energy healing and teaching others to clear their chakras...

I had started taking classes about energy and alternative healing in 2004 when I found out my husband had been cheating on me and was expecting a child with another woman. At the time, I was so upset with my personal life... I had dedicated myself over and beyond, putting everyone else's needs before mine, and I was very disappointed with where that had gotten me after living life in such a way. If you had invited me to a shoelace party, I would have shown up early and left late.

This energy class was held at my good friend Tiffani's neighbor's house. It was with a small group of ladies, young and old, Mormon and not Mormon (but being Salt Lake City, Utah, most in attendance were good 'ole Relief Society ladies), gathering together to learn about essential oils, crystals, energy clearing, chakra clearing, and the benefits of healthy eating and living as taught by the talented Ms. Sylvia.

I had always paid for psychic readings since I was seventeen, continually needing reassurance that I did the right thing by placing my baby up for adoption. About once a year, I had to hear that the oldest boy of mine was safe and happy... How else to do that except through a psychic, medium, sensitive, gifted, *witch*... whatever you want to call it.

I have met with this specific group of ladies over the years, continually sharing our life stories and findings on how this world works. I credit this intervention to my successful healing as much as I do marijuana. God bless my hoodoo voodoo sistahs (that is what I like to call us). The ladies and I have never toked together. They all know I do, but they don't know when I am stoned and when I am not, nor do they care.

My appearance didn't help much with the neighbor's fears. By the time we asked the bishop for assistance, I guess a buzz was going around that I might be a practicing witch. The bishop helped us with our utilities for one month, but then he called me into his office to address my witch-like behavior. *On behalf of the bishop... Tis the season. Yeah, I wore my goddess dress to church, accessorized with my combat belt & boots... and had sent a few invitations for a Halloween party, girls get together at my home...*

After being confronted by the bishop over his and many others' fears of me being a practicing witch, I never went back to the church for any kind of help. I just continued to talk to God, Spirit, Universe, Source, whatever, whoever y'all want to call it. I just knew that the help I was to get had to come from outside of this physical realm.

The Invitation
(from *Sabrina the Teenage Witch*)

The Witches Council is a group of high-level and powerful witches and warlocks that preside over the magical societies in the Mortal and Magical Realms. They also ensure the proper use of magic by witches. The Council is the highest governing body for magical creatures in either realm, and all magical beings answer to them (on occasion, so do mortals when they become entangled in magical affairs).

But mostly, they are a tyrannical group that creates foolish and nonsensical laws and rules to suit their own desires. Their primary goal is to ensure magic is not abused (although some members take great delight in the sometimes barbaric and outdated lessons, which they often force young witches to learn).

Join me at my Fairylicious Castle to discuss the magical realm in our lives.

November 2011

Zila Moves Out

Before finding out what Scott was up to, I started praying fervently, "*I need help. I need an army. I don't know what is going down, but it is big.*"

My niece Zila was the first to move in. Zila and I had always been close. Zila is Scott's niece. My relationship with Zila started when she was three. Zila was a challenging child for many, but being a Mother of Loss, you tend to collect children. I didn't have any children of *my own* to raise, so I was always available to help with all of my nieces and nephews. By the time Zila was four, her mother had moved in with us, and I had Kanyon. During this first year of Kanyon's life, Zila was a huge part of ours.

It was a huge blessing to have my eighteen-year-old niece call upon me for a place to stay. It's a hard transition, becoming an adult. I warned her about her uncle saying, "*Scott isn't doing well. We don't know what is up, but as long as I have a roof over my head, all are welcome.*"

Not long after Zila showed up, we caught Scott smoking heroin in his home office. It was good to have an extra "adult" in the house to help Kanyon and me hold down the fort, distract Kylie, and keep the vehicles out of Scott's reach on multiple occasions. Kai was in Hawaii for his employment, and we really didn't have any contact (I got a little upset about Kai's mother calling the cops on me after Kai had asked us to store his stuff in our home). In fact, Scott, in his delirium, would always threaten, or shall I say, *attempt* to fly to Hawaii to be with Kai.

Scott's behavior continued to get worse. In November, Zila moved out. I had the holidays to focus on and to distract me from Scott's usage (that he was claiming wasn't going on).

Thanksgiving

I had been spending extra time with Mama Jean during this time in my life. Mama Jean and I had always kept in touch after she divorced my father back when my kids were babies. I had told her, *"Once a grandma, always a grandma. You can't divorce grandmas."* I was very grateful for Mama Jean in my life. It seemed that she was the only one who understood soo many things that I was saying. Everyone else wanted me to pretend and live The Program. I loved the wisdom that Mama Jean offered. My favorite, is *"God Knows."* To this day, it still brings me comfort.

I was not in the mood to have Thanksgiving with any *pretenders*, if you will. I wanted a Thanksgiving with *REAL* people. I know that statement will offend a lot of my family... But I don't think they even realize how much they are pretending. I take full ownership of how loud my make-believe story (the story of me pretending nothing happened and life is perfect) has gotten... so loud I cannot ignore reality... *anyone's*.

Along with Jean and her hubby, the only other person that came over was one of Kanyon's buddies, Kenny. I enjoyed the very untraditional Thanksgiving Day.

December 2011

My Connections with Jesus
BLOG POST

I haven't written for a long time and feel a need.

My son Kanyon struck up a conversation about his older brother Kai. He said, "*Looks like Kai's curse to himself is playing out.*"

I said, "*What do you mean?*"

He replied, "*Kai had said, 'I wish God would quit blessing me so much. I have been slacking on my religious duties.'*"

"*Oh wow! Kanyon, you see wisdom.*"

Let me fill you all in on what has transpired and share how I have connected so many things in life this past week.

This holiday season, we are broker than broke. As a mother, friend, and relation to anyone who loves gifting to all, I have been blessed with ah-ha's and wisdom as an outcome of our despair.

In the shower, I can't help but connect the dots to the order of events that have transpired...

Out of my desperation to give gifts to all, writing love letters to family and friends, I think I am about finished when I realize I have left two people out... Kai and his new wife, Mai. I write to my son explaining my failure to acknowledge him and how I had forgotten about thinking of the two of them, continuing to say...

> *Yep, I do try that hard to shut you out of my space, but then I will get this feeling, like something is missing, and the memory of you floods in with the familiar ache. I'm sorry I am incapable of being what you want me to be. I'm all or none. Maybe one day you may understand the power of a mother's love that starts in the womb. Until then, I have to distance myself. Enjoy your holiday season. Love your mother, yep, your mother.*

...and then signed it, *Keri*.

Well, let me tell you what I have just heard through the grapevine... Just recently, Kai and his new wife were on a cruise ship. They went off the boat on an excursion and didn't make it back to the ship, missing their ride in Mexico. I can't help but see the similarity of my having forgotten about them when preparing holiday gifts, that literally happened at the same time the cruise ship forgot them. Kanyon and I just sat there and connected the dots. We were holding Kai in our hearts and prayers, hoping that he would join this family one hundred percent. We are sick of the ache when Kai continually chooses not to be. So basically, after our wishes and prayers, we cut the cords and surrender for it to be whatever it is meant to be... and look how his world has been rocked, if you will.

Getting ready in the shower, I continued my thoughts, optimistic about how the neglected relationship with our son/brother will turn out. As I am connecting the dots, I am thinking about all my newfound knowledge from studying the people in the Bible. My interest in studying the Bible came about due to my own newfound knowledge about my own immediate ancestry.

When my grandparents died, my mother gave me all the journals and photos that they had. I cherished these and dove right in; reading my grandparents' hand-written journals and typed memories takes you on a journey of their lives, which I totally relate to. It brought me such compassion for my ancestors. Not only a better understanding of them but a better understanding of my own self... understanding why I am walking in the shoes I am walking... leaving me excited to not only heal for me but to heal my ancestors and my posterity by learning not only from my experiences but from theirs as well.

This understanding of my ancestry, the recognition of the pattern of cycles repeating themselves... gives way to a better understanding. To find a better way of doing things and bringing compassion into my space by being able to relate to them and by knowing the madness or dysfunction of their situation and of the ancestors before them... it seriously got me excited to learn more history.

Magically, books about Jesus kept coming into my space in all sorts of ways. I dove right in and started studying and learning about Jesus and his ancestors. I have connected so many dots that resonate with me on the theory that everything cycles through a full circle in order to gain full knowledge... To know up, you need to know down.

Being a Mother of Loss, I hugely connected to many stories and scenarios from the Bible; mostly to the stories surrounding other Mothers of Loss, such as:

- *Jochebed*. She was Moses' mother. The Pharaoh ordered all males under two years old to be killed because he was afraid the Hebrew slaves would overpower the Egyptian empire and outnumber them. Jochebed, desperate to save her son, made a basket and sent Moses down the Nile River to spare his life, an act that ultimately delivered their people out of bondage.

- *Mother Mary*. A young virgin mother, who I am sure was questioned about her immaculate conception and therefore judged. Plus, all those other young mothers, but just to name one...

- *Hagar*. Hagar is Sarah's maiden. Sarah is Abraham's wife. Sarah was Hagar's infertile boss, an older, affluent woman with a husband to take care of her... Sarah ordered Hagar to sleep with her husband, Abraham, to conceive a child. A child would guarantee Sarah financial support and importance because Sarah was allowed to own Hagar's child, Ishmael, as her own. Abraham regarded Hagar as a petty servant, in service to Sarah until she was no longer needed. However, at 90 years of age, Sarah was blessed with a child of her own, Isaac. Sarah no longer needed Hagar or Ishmael as a guarantee of financial support and survival. She kicked Hagar, along with Ishmael, out of the concubine, banished to the desert to fend for themselves. Remember, there was no welfare or jobs for women back then. Most women had no other choice than to serve as a prostitute, desperate to be owned by any man in order to survive.

Well... let me tell you, I am a Mother of Loss who has always connected with Mother Mary, the 15-year-old virgin mother of Jesus, a mother from royalty... Being that I myself was one month shy of turning 16 when I lost my virginity and became pregnant the very first time (as was the case in many biblical stories with those young maidens).

And I came from an affluent family myself... but instead of keeping my baby and watching my son be sacrificed as a man like Mother Mary, I sacrificed my son at birth.

My firstborn son's birthday is December **23**rd, two days before Christmas.

I have taken my loss, my feelings of sorrow, grief and anger, ... and have taken an interest in getting to know Mother Mary, her mother Anna, and Jesus, with extreme interest after finding the connection with my own ancestors. My great-grandmother on my mother's side was left in an orphanage at age one with her siblings for 13 years until her mother was able to come back for them after finding a husband that would have her... *"A Meal Ticket."* I also have a grandmother on my father's side who lost a son to adoption - my father.

My interest in Anna and Mary and Jesus, as well as their ancestors, became personal when I was able to connect that I have traveled a very similar road as they have, and that my relationship with my second-born son is very similar to the relationship of Mother Mary and Jesus. My discovery has opened my eyes so much. I am shocking people with my new belief that Jesus did not die on the cross.

For you see, people, we were not ready for my interpretation. Remember, back in Jesus' days, the mentality was totally *an eye for an eye... "Oops, sorry I bumped into you," "Oh, here, let me shove you back, and we will be good."* In order to save mankind, that mentality needed to stop because, after all, the main message... lesson... we are meant to learn while down here on Earth, is the importance of family... Oneness... and to gain full knowledge of the Creator within ourselves. So, Jesus had to come set an example and be crucified and teach God's Word of being the God of Mercy. The old interpretation of Jesus being resurrected from the dead is what the people of the ignorant masses of those times needed to believe. After finding out how evil men of ancient times were and how wrong men have always treated women... Even the "good" men, like Abraham, who, out of his own fear of a more powerful male harming him in competition for his beautiful wife, Sarah, lied and said, *"Here have my sister for your concubine,"* not only once, but TWICE. These ignorant men did not like the respect Jesus gave women... and even in today's dictionary, Magdalen means a reformed prostitute... When in all actuality, the Disciples were jealous and did not understand the forgiveness and respect Jesus gave Mary of Magdala and did not like that she got most of His attention because she understood His Word. They first needed to understand that there is life after death, so we better make good choices and try to be as good as we can be.

Nowadays, well actually, never with me... I just never understood that *eye for an eye* mentality. So, when I learned that one of the translations says Jesus did not die and the Atonement is about walking the walk of forgiveness, everything made much more sense. Along with that wisdom rolling, I am connecting the madness of cycles completing full circle... gaining full knowledge and becoming aware of the Creator we ourselves are. I can see the pattern of how ancestral behavior is life balancing and our returning with full knowledge from knowing the down, in, and out of it.

My newfound knowledge totally validates that these are the times to LOVE ONE ANOTHER AND '*ADOPT*' THE MOTHER. Sarah of Biblical days should have adopted Hagar and loved her child as a grandmother loves a child, loving one another, '*adopting*' the mother.

I am so grateful for history and my understanding of it. We are people of full knowledge; we are the creators of this life we have created for ourselves, believe it or not. When I see life from this perspective, I yearn to love and serve others. I see mothers in need, a need for ALL to learn from the past.

BUT ... mostly right now, I see the power of love and what manifests out of fear and desire. I see how I, for one, desire a better future, and I am now a true believer in what the meaning of the Atonement is: to save our souls. I appreciate the story of Mother Mary and Jesus and how much it now means to me.

Now, how do I connect all this with my present circumstances, you ask...?

Well, knowing Jesus and all those other powerful, beautiful mothers of old... bringing them and their stories into my space, I am comforted with the knowledge to have faith. We always get what we desire or fear, so get fear out of my space, let my desires be known... then surrender to God's will, be patient, serve, and love others, and it will soon come around. After all, when we are serving and loving others, we are serving and loving ourselves.

With that said, I look forward to Kai becoming 100% a part of our family.

Christmas

Scott is sweating profusely from the heroin usage. We are functioning as best we can, pretending everything will be okay. I loved having Kandi and the kids over as often as they were. The kids gave me more reason to do my traditional holiday baking. I spent most of my days in my sitting room studying and reading.

Kylie somehow caught on film the obvious discomfort while at my mother's house for a family Christmas party. Kai showed up because he thought I wouldn't. I didn't think he would show... I was sick of being at the party, and my own emotional bullshit got a little out of control. I kind of started yelling at my mother in her garage and carried it on into the house before leaving the Christmas party. I left the kids with other family members who would bring them home later and headed home on my own. I was so in my thoughts processing my f***ed up life that I passed my exit and drove an hour south beyond my house, all the way to Santaquin before I realized where I was. When I finally turned around and headed back north to home, I had cried a good cry.

My mom sent me home with a care package of all of my favorite things, which also happened to be the color of my hair, red violet. I loved all she gifted me and had to take a photo of gratitude and send to her. I don't like it when I yell at my mother.

At Scott's family Christmas party at his mother's, there was similar energy going on. Kai showed up at my mother's, thinking I wouldn't be there, and now, Scott's sister Kathy showed up here because she thought we wouldn't be here. Guess you could say we spoiled a lot of people's holidays. I behaved myself at this party and didn't yell at anyone, lol.

A Christmas Love Letter to All
From, Keri

What a year we have had! We had a missionary come home, a wedding, and the biggest storm I have ever survived. The great thing about storms... when you ride it out the best you can... when you get through it... you are much wiser from it and become a better sailor for it.

My book is about to explode!!! Thanks to this last storm I have sailed, I am ready! Bring it on. I have learned many valuable lessons with the help of many of my loved ones supporting me on this ship of mine, acting like a mighty sailor's crew.

The lessons from this last storm... *GOD KNOWS*!!! Yeah, buddy, God knows, and I don't need anyone defending my honor, nor do I need to defend my honor, 'cause *God knows*!

LOVE ONE ANOTHER!!! No matter who enters your space, be it friend or foe, love thy neighbor as thy sister. I passed with flying colors. For those of you that are not familiar with my dear sistah Julie, my foe... (Julie is Scott's ex-girlfriend who lost their son to adoption and lies.) I had a confrontation with her that I handled with absolute sincere love and forgiveness for my fellow woMAN. When you know the shoes that people have walked in, there is such love and understanding, no matter how horribly they may behave. I can only imagine walking in her shoes, God bless her. I had a hard enough time walking in my own shoes that I thought to be pretty bad... There is always someone who has worse shoes than yours.

I honestly just learned that Jesus declared to his disciples that Love One Another is the 2nd most important commandment, along with Love Thy God. And ultimately, it is these two commandments that Jesus focuses on most.

WALK THE WALK OF FORGIVENESS. My truth about the Atonement... Jesus did not die on the cross. He was only on the cross for three hours without broken legs when he was sedated by the sponge of water (opiate) and rushed into the tomb Joseph of Arimathea had made so he wouldn't die from suffocation when buried in the ground. With the next day being the Sabbath, Jesus was taken off the cross and rushed into the tomb with Mary, his mother, and his wife, Mary Magdalene, where they were waiting with essential oils to address Jesus' wounds and dress him with water and bread that was hidden in the dressings.

They all exited the tomb with anticipation, waiting for his "resurrection," with soldiers guarding it so no one could steal the body. Joseph of Arimathea schemed a plan to have a beautiful lady with a wine jug (with some kind of opiate in it) entice the soldiers to drink until they passed out. Then he and two of the disciples moved the stone and helped Jesus get out. They took him to Mary's (the mother of Mark ~ there were so many Marys!) huge room suite where they were all staying during the whole Passover, Last Supper, and Crucifixion time. When Mary Magdala came to Jesus to hug her husband with gratitude that he survived, Jesus pushed her aside because of his sore wounds. Earlier transcribed as, Go, lady. I need to focus on God's work...

The Atonement of Christ is a subject I have never been able to make sense of. My old interpretation of the Atonement... If I flip someone off, it's alright because I can ask for forgiveness, and God will forgive me without any physical punishment because Jesus has bled and died for my sin. Okay, whatever...

Well, my firstborn son, whom I have sacrificed to the world as did Mother Mary, that sweet mother that delivered Jesus two days after I delivered (or so we celebrate) challenged me to learn the Atonement. I thank him for the challenge. I have studied all the books in the library along with the LDS scholar historian's teachings about our dear older brother, Jesus, who did not die on the cross.

With this new full knowledge, I indeed understand the Atonement of Christ as being an example of the WALK OF FORGIVENESS. Those people called him every name in the book and tortured an innocent man, believing him to be something he was not, lying about him... while HE walked the walk of forgiveness throughout his whole entire life.

Well, being someone that just went through a storm of people calling me every name in the book, believing me to be something I'm not, such as a witch and whore, just to name a few... Jesus, Mary, Mary, and all the Essenes were always being accused of being witches and warlocks, with Mary Magdalene constantly being accused of being a whore... I am prepared for anything this book exploding brings with this walk of forgiveness and love... and this new knowledge of *"God Knows."*

Understanding the Walk of Forgiveness ultimately means if everyone walked this Walk of Forgiveness, we would have world peace... the shift to a perfect world.

Great, great lessons I have acquired. Christmas is here to celebrate the birth of this amazing guy, Jesus... my older brother, whom I, for once, can really connect to as a tangible being. Not only have I gained more love for HIM, but I also adore his mother, Mary, his grandmother, Anna, and his beloved wife, Mary of Magdala.

This year has been humbling and may be the most memorable ever. We usually spend thousands of dollars gifting to all of my favorite people and celebrating big by trying to gift as fabulously as we possibly can! I love to find gifts for others. But this year's storm has been quite the hit, and thanks to the many people in our lives, we are surviving this storm amazingly well. Because of the story of Jesus and my understanding and love for the Lord, I can celebrate big, giving all my favorite people a little note, sending my love to them.

BUT CHEERS TO NEXT YEAR!!!! I am very ready to be done with this one! Lol, Love KERI

The Sangraal

A connection is sometimes drawn by Grail scholars between the word Sangraal and *grades*, a word that seems to have meant cup, platter, or basin in the Provencal language. But it has also been suggested that if one breaks the word Sangraal after the g, the result is *sang raal*, which in Old French means "blood royal." This second derivation of the French Sangraal is extremely provocative and perhaps enlightening.

Suddenly one is faced with a new reading of the familiar legend; Instead of a cup or chalice, the story now states that Mary Magdalen brought the "blood royal" to the Mediterranean coast of France. Other legends credit Joseph of Arimathea with bringing the blood of Jesus to France in some kind of vessel. Perhaps it was really Mary Magdalen, under the protection of Joseph of Arimathea, who carried the royal bloodline of David the King to the Mediterranean coast of France.

Could it be that the royal blood was carried in an "earthen vessel" (2 Cor. 4:7)? What if that earthen vessel was a woman? The quest for the Holy Grail is a mystery that is centuries old. I gifted Kai a goblet with this letter:

> *Kai, may this goblet remind you of the vessel you see me as. It can be the connection of blood in a cup with really no value, or it can be the connection of the divine blood carried in the earthen vessel of a divine mother carrying a divine child ... a child to continue the teachings of Jesus in a faraway land... to not judge and to love one another, walking the walk of forgiveness. Everyone carries their own truth. What is yours?*
>
> *Love your earthen vessel, your goblet of blood, the vine that is your mother,*
> *Keri*

Goodbye
BLOG POST

Well, the horrid season of December is over!!!! Don't get me wrong, I love Jesus, but along with the month of celebrating Jesus and his virgin mother, Mary, sacrificing her son for the world to better understand the law of repentance AND forgiveness... I am in mourning for my son, who I lost to adoption. His birthday is December **23**rd. I had him at my bedside until the 25th, Christmas Day, 1986. Saying goodbye. Leaving to try to forget and pretend it never happened.

Well, every December since, I haven't been able to forget and pretend it never happened. I have continued to hole up in the safety of my home for the month of December, only seeing my most favorite people.

When I reunited with Kai, I thought, *"Oh, I finally have him back! I will never miss a birthday, Christmas, holiday, moment, etc., ever again!"*

The sad reality: I have yet to spend a birthday, Christmas, holiday, moment, etc., with him.

The first year, we were invited for his birthday and sent home on Christmas Eve... the adoptive parents wanted him all to themselves like they traditionally have had him. I have never seen Kai on his birthday since... Scott and I have celebrated Christmas one day late (with young children) just for him, and we have had the blessing of one late afternoon visit on a Christmas day a few years back. This year Kai said he dropped in at 6:00 in the evening (on his way to his wife's family party down south that started at 6:30), but we were at the movies... I know... most Mothers of Loss have it so much worse. I should be so happy I am graced with his visits. Kai lives minutes away. His parents moved to Utah, where I live, to make it easier for him to see us. I should be grateful for their sacrifice, but I feel it's like dangling meat to a dog, making him sit and behave for a lick.

This has been an exceptionally hard December for me. For once in my life, I opened my heart to the story of Jesus and his dear virgin Mother, Mary, and allowed myself to sit with the feelings and not ignore the feelings that are always triggered when hearing about their story. I am relating in so many ways... I have finally accepted: it is what it is, we are who we are, I believe what I believe, and no one can tell me otherwise unless they have walked in my shoes.

The *Salt Lake Tribune* is about to publish an article on me and my family about the loss of adoption and what it has done to us... How divine that the article is to come out this Christmas season, the 25th anniversary of my loss. I am owning my truth and speaking out. I am upsetting a lot of people, especially my mother. Her new fear... I am going to be excommunicated from the Mormon Church!!!

Well, you know what? I have a better relationship with Jesus and know that I will not be damned if the church kicks me out for bringing awareness, speaking out, teaching others how to love unconditionally, supporting unwed mothers in need to keep their children, and fighting to bring father's rights, along with women rights, to full attention... accepting others, loving everyone as a whole, not judging who is better than whom, as in who would be a better mother and father for the child... *The* mother and father *are* the mother and father of that child, and *we*, as a whole, need to love one another and mentor any person in need, especially a person with a child.

If people realized the *apple doesn't fall far from the tree*... If you are looking at this apple and find fault, you need to look at the generation before them. And if you don't like it, move further back another generation... keep moving back... see the pattern.

Bottom line... we aren't *saving* anyone by adopting infants. It is just creating more problems of conditional love and independent thinking... dissecting families as if born to another. And honestly, I don't care to be sealed in the Church records to anyone on my made-up genealogy chart with a messed-up roll call that was most likely made up in Adam and Eve time, just to remember everyone and to not leave anyone behind. The way Mormons and many others have taken this adoption to a whole new level does not interest me.

Let's learn from our ancestors and honor them by preserving our families and loving one another unconditionally with acceptance and forgiveness in our hearts. We shall not covet what others have... Let us reach out and offer our love, service, and acceptance to all that come into our space, without fear or expectations. Just LOVE... after all, *IT'S ALL YOU NEED*! I love John Lennon!!!!

January 2012

Madonna Is the Man
BLOG POST

Madonna never ceases to amaze me! I have always admired her bravery to be true to herself and be who she is, no matter what *anyone* thinks.

The other day, Friday the 13th, my dear friend called me and asked if I could be her designated driver. She had to get a crown at the dentist.

"*Of course!*" I was delighted to take a day off from my life and serve a dear friend! I dropped her off and came home to wait for the call to pick her up. The call came and I jetted off to go pick her up, entering the dentist's waiting room right at the exact moment *ABC 4 News* was advertising the *20/20* interview with Madonna. Folks, I honestly don't make much time to watch TV, so for me to just happen to catch these 15 minutes of TV time at this moment was soo divine!

I was excited to be updated on Madonna! What is that girl up to!? To my amazement, she was working on a movie, *W.E.*, which she co-wrote and produced, coming out February 3rd. It's a great story about Edward VIII leaving his throne of Britain to be with the woman he fell in love with, an American divorcee, Wallace Simpson.

The thing that amazed me most from the interview? The interviewer, Cynthia McFadden, challenged Madonna's position of believing the accusation that Edward VIII was a Hitler supporter, plus other rumors about the couple. I loved Madonna's confidence in her truth about what she learned while researching the couple and that she challenged Cynthia right back, telling her she wouldn't find any information that supports otherwise. WOW!!! Madonna, you are one smart lady that I truly admire! I've always heard that knowledge is powerful, but boy do I love witnessing Madonna living the concept and being a great example to me. Especially because, just like Madonna said to Cynthia in the interview about Edward VIII's love for Wallace Simpson, "*She has the ability to survive against all odds... is deeply misunderstood by people.*" Madonna, being a true survivor as well, is notoriously deeply misunderstood, having been judged her whole life, I'm sure, as not being very intelligent because of her unconventional choices, when in all reality, she is most likely one of the most brilliant people amongst us.

The second thing that amazed me during the interview was the part about Lady Gaga. WOW!!! Madonna's vocabulary has always impressed me, but I must say, today was a day to remember! Not only did she think of the best word to describe how she feels about Lady Gaga's song, *Born This Way*, being a copy of her song, *Express Yourself*, but she also stumped Cynthia McFadden on the definition of the word reductive.

"*Is that good or bad?*" Cynthia asked.

Classic Madonna, full of grace and beauty, reaches for her coffee mug for a sip and says with such eloquence, "*Look it up.*" I LOVE IT!!!

Reductive: simplified or crude. I even found a scientific definition: lower-level entity.

By the end of the segment, I had an outpouring of love for Madonna after her comment when questioned by Cynthia McFadden, "*Do you feel more authentic when you are without makeup?*" Madonna replied, "*As long as I'm doing what I want to do, whether I am done up in makeup or not, it doesn't matter. That is when I am feeling most authentic.*"

CHEERS TO MADONNA!!! Exactly!!! "*As long as I am doing what I want to do.*" Madonna... a woman we can all admire and learn from to live in our truth and be who we are!!!

It is no wonder Madonna Louise Ciccone was named after her mother, Madonna Louise. After all, the definition of *Madonna (name)* is: a name from the 16th century, originally used as a respectful form of address to an Italian woman. It comes from the Old Italian phrase, ma donna, which means "my lady." It was later adopted as one of the titles for Mary, the mother of Jesus, in the Roman Catholic tradition in the 17th century (Wikipedia, 2023).

MADONNA... a woman who has truly lived up to her name and will definitely go down in history like the amazing ones before her, such as Virgin Mother Mary, Mary Magdalen, Jesus, John Lennon, Bob Marley, Harriet Tubman, and Dr. Martin Luther King Jr., just to name a few!

My Beloved Son
BLOG POST

My son Kanyon and I have been going to an amazing healer. No pretending with her... she reads energy and your mind. She is absolutely amazing. My son and I have been having a hard time with the realities of adoption and reunion. He lost a brother just as I lost a son. I never realized that relinquishing my firstborn son for adoption would also hugely affect my 2nd born, first-raised son. Kanyon has suffered from a phobia of being kidnapped his whole life, and he still suffers, often not feeling safe, even now at the age of 15.

Kanyon was nine when Kai, who was nineteen, entered his life. In the beginning, it was just as hard for Kanyon as it was for me. Kanyon, being the "oldest" in our raised family unit, was demoted to middle child. Instead of his dad asking *him* to go places, this new older brother was being asked, and he felt like his spot as the oldest son was taken. Kanyon was also worried that my love wasn't big enough to share with this new older brother. He was afraid he would receive less love from me with Kai moving in on the turf. To top it off, Kylie, his little sister who has always treated him poorly because of her bossy ways, was kissing this new older brother's ass, even though Kai was treating her more poorly than *he* ever had. Not to mention the grandmothers and grandfathers that went gaga-goo-goo over this new older brother who was getting all the attention now, even though he had been right under their noses the whole time. But it was all worth it... he now had his older brother in his life.

As conflicting as it has been, wanting Kai 100% in our space/not wanting Kai in our space at all... we had to seek out professional help. We had to allow ourselves to grieve the loss of Kai in our family and accept it for what it was because we cannot change the past. We needed to clear our energy so we could have a healthy relationship in the future since our relationship was traumatized by adoption... my "choice" as a 16-year-old mother. I know... I will live with that "choice" for the rest of my life.

It has been a huge blessing to have my son Kanyon on this

journey of healing with me. He teaches me as much as I teach him. It's crazy, he will process an emotion, be upset, react, scream, and rage... and then, shortly thereafter, I am processing those same emotions. It was so great to have Kanyon to look at, find comfort, and laugh, saying, "*I pulled a Kanyon. Kanyon knows what I mean.*"

Well, this last upset we processed... I went first. Not on purpose. It just happened that way. It was good to be able to help Kanyon through this process. By helping him through it, I was able to further heal and strengthen *my* emotional charge on the upset. And in return, I was able to further heal and strengthen Kanyon with his emotional charge.

I feel Kanyon and I have been able to shift, accepting that it is what it is. Kai is who he is, and we are who we are. And with that, Kanyon said chuckling, "*Because after all, Mom, Kai did not ask for this, and ultimately he is just making the best of it the only way he knows how. Because mom, if it were me that had to be raised without you in Wyoming, I'D BE PISSED.*"

After these wise words from my beloved son, who I refer to as my dessert... my reward for my obedience, having sacrificed a son to the world in the name of adoption so I could help others heal, my reward from above to help me heal first and foremost so I could help others heal, my reward from above to support me and help me heal others, my cherry on top. I could not help but feel his words penetrate my soul. "*Kai did not ask for this, and ultimately he is just making the best of it the only way he knows how. Because mom, if it were me that had to be raised without you in Wyoming, I'D BE PISSED.*"

I have finally accepted 100% that *it is what it is*, and I think I can accept that I didn't fight hard enough for my motherhood back in 1986. I can honestly say that I have fought hard to prove my love and try to earn my motherhood when in all reality, *it is what it is* and *I am who I am*. And honestly, nothing can take my motherhood away because it just *IS*. With that reality, I can let go of all the energy of grieving and trying to earn the place of *mother*. Whether Kai wants to accept it or not is up to him... and in all reality, why should he when I haven't been the one to be there. Like Kanyon said, "*... I'D BE PISSED.*" So, in all reality, I owe my firstborn an apology. An apology that he has never asked for... an apology that I have just realized is needed, thanks to my beloved son, Kanyon.

February 2012

Astrology
BLOG POST

I've done it! I have dived into ASTROLOGY! And do you know what my favorite part about it is? It doesn't give a rat's ass who you were born to or what the heck your heritage is anyways! LOL

Don't get me wrong, I am so grateful for the half of my heritage I *have* and *know*. But I think I am finally done giving a rat's ass who is *not* choosing to be a part of my heritage through loss of adoption! If I never meet or know my paternal grandmother or my paternal cousins, uncles, or aunts, I can rest assured that I have researched pretty much every aspect of decoding this thing called *my* life, and how everything works from a(n) *energetically, spiritually, physically, emotionally, scientifically, historically...* you name it... side of it.

I can honestly say I know myself well enough from knowing half of my family, history, and all...
Knowing how:

- o Everything is energy, and we hold energy in our DNA that passes down our dysfunction magically through the air until that energy of dysfunction is healed and not spinning any longer.
- o Emotional upsets manifest physically, and healing emotional upset is how we live to obtain perfect health.
- o History repeats itself. Even if you were not raised anywhere near your family, you are a clone of two... a combination of two people who are your parents, whether you have been adopted or not.
- o Babies are born with 100% use of their brain, all-knowing straight from heaven, trapped in this little helpless body that has to trust their mother to provide them with the best outcome, so they can fulfill their mission in this life that they themselves have chosen.
- o To live, to gain more hands-on wisdom, or shall I say, in these last days especially, to bring awareness and healing. We are going to take all the information in the **23** chromosomes from

each parent that will create/program this vessel of a human body, that they will utilize and develop strongly before the *thickening of the veil*, when parts of this human brain shut down surely and slowly unless stimulated. It is constantly judging, creating aspects and perspectives... "*a spiritual being having a human experience.*" Continuing blindly, equipped with the energy we were born with, genetically, as well as Universally.

- o DNA is so important to our soul group; to live, and learn, and conquer our way to full awareness, knowing that LOVE is the most powerful energy, and it's extremely magical. This knowledge has been obtained from living through history, all the way back to Adam and Eve; All as a whole, learning as a whole, all one, learning certain themes as a soul group, living the down of it to KNOW the up of it, learning from the ancestors before us...

I have totally figured ME out, and I am pretty damn amazing. And as for anyone that doesn't think so, I really don't give a rat's ass. It is very freeing to love and understand myself to such a high level... I have figured out, and can even imagine, what the other half of my family must be like and how much they all look just like me and act just like me.

But back to astrology... It doesn't give a rat's ass who you were born to or what the heck your heritage is anyways! After decoding my husband, my children, and me, it was so exciting to see how well-equipped and prepared we are (including the time of our delivery!) to survive, live, learn, and heal ourselves, our families, and others just from the experiences we have. Because, after all, we all are just "*spiritual beings having a human experience*"; a human experience that has got itself wrapped up in a world of ego and apathy, a world that needs masters to bring awareness and healing to humans on this beautiful Mother Earth. And I can honestly say I have mastered some *stuff*!!!

Suzi Enters Our Life

The holidays came and passed, and that was when I started taking Kanyon to the tanning salon, and the medium at the tanning salon was giving me lots of amazing information and instruction. It was the end of February, and I continued to pray fervently, *"I need help. I need an army."* At this point, I was still trying to save Scott and keep the family together. I had been feeling a lot of rejection from my eldest son Kai. Kanyon was also feeling rejected by his older brother. We have missed so much of his life, we had dreams and expectations that Kai would return from his mission and move in with us so we could all experience being a whole, happy family.

Immediately upon arriving back from his mission, our dreams were crushed. Kai returned in February 2011, married his girlfriend on April **23**rd, and by May, he was in Texas selling security alarms for Vivint.

Kai was excited to move on with his life and have a family of his own. I could understand his rush. This juggling between the two families is awful, and I can see his desire to have his own solid family. But the rejection we felt was too much.

Kai returned from his sales job at the end of September. It was February 2012, and our family was doing a nosedive. Scott was using heavier by the day. I was taking Kanyon tanning, trying to keep his spirits up because something was going down with his father, and it was such a bummer about that older brother of his (again, our own selfish reasons for wanting him in our life). I was so down on life, not wanting to talk to anyone. I made sure I had my nose in my book.

As soon as Kanyon walked back to tan, I heard someone say, *"More and more Crystal Children are coming."*

Well, that got my attention. I looked up from my book, and this cute little pixie (woman) was staring my way with her big beautiful blue eyes. I offered, *"My son is a Crystal Child."*

"Oh yes, I know." Suzi explained that she was a medium and continued to inform me about Crystal Children because she noticed I had one.

Suzi told me many things, but most importantly, she said, *"You are supposed to be in Hawaii,"* confirming what Kanyon once again knew. Suzi described what was going on at home with Scott, and what the rejection was all about with Kai. All she knew was that I needed to go see her healer friend in Mapleton because I needed to get my butt to Hawaii. *"You are going to live near Wayne Dyer, wherever he lives."* (I ended up in Lahaina, which is very near Kaanapali, where he lived).

March 2012

Dawn Visits from Vegas

By now, I was homeschooling Kanyon, again. Kanyon and I were having a hard time dealing with the man of the house using heroin. I got creative with homeschooling. Kanyon built a hut next to the river in our neighborhood while I would read to him about science.

By now, Kanyon and I were partaking in the medicine regularly. "Mary Jane" was the only thing I could bribe Kanyon to get out of bed for. I would use the herb to get him to do his chores and studies. It got around quickly that Kanyon's mother approved of marijuana, and eventually, Child Protective Services (CPS) was always stopping by with cops wanting to investigate our house, checking to see if I was providing a safe sanctuary for my children. Rumor had it so bad; I was the supposed dealer for the junior high.

I passed all the surprise house visits with flying colors. They could tell I knew how to deal with my children and that I was an intelligent person. Plus, I'm sure they are experts at reading the energy in a home, and I bet they read people even better. The only real problem we had to conceal was the dad that was on heroin. If only they knew, they would have totally taken my children away, when in all reality, my children were right where they needed to be. And I had a handle on things, taking care of other people's children as well. If society wanted to really help, they could have offered food. But I was fighting to keep society out of my business so that I could take better care of my children.

These surprise visits were getting more frequent, and along with the bishop stopping by, the foreclosure people stopping by, Scott's collectors stopping by, etc.... If you didn't do the secret knock, everyone in the house would hide and whisper, "*Shh quiet...,*" sneak to the door, and peek to see who it was. It was kind of fun, but a crazy way to live.

During this time, Dawn and Keith (her husband at the time) came from Vegas for a visit. I had been practicing my meditation skills and had been showing others how to clear their chakras. Marijuana is a great medicine that helps with the resistance to sitting still and allows one to quiet their thoughts and slip into a meditative state. I was grateful for my niece, nephews, and their many friends who frequented my home for advice and wisdom. They encouraged me to practice my healing skills on them to help them get through their hard times.

After one of these healing sessions with Dawn and Keith, we emerged from downstairs to find a woman from the Division of Child and Family Services (DCFS) and the cops knocking at the door once again. Dawn and Keith couldn't believe that this was how I was living... in such fear energy. Dawn, being the wise woman that she is, took action and told me how to handle it. I was to honor my Medicine Woman healing ways and tell that DCFS woman exactly what I was doing; *"I was in a healing session with a couple that had driven up all the way from Vegas, and I won't answer the door during sessions."* Dawn then made sure we had a, *"Quick, hide the paraphernalia,"* drill.

Dawn always magically arrives at the right time, preparing me for what's to come during her lovely warm visits.

My Army Arrives

March 2012 was an eventful month; My army arrived. Within a week, I had six young adults living in my home. James was the first to arrive. Having turned 19, with many decisions to make, feeling pressure to go on a mission, and feeling unhappy about his life in a huge way, he called up his Auntie to see if he could move in.

When James moved in, he had never touched any liquor or smoked any herb in his life. He was a good Mormon boy who just wasn't sure if he wanted to go on a mission but wasn't looking for a party by any means.

My sister had a huge fear that her son would start smoking weed if he moved in with Aunt Keri. I have always owned my truth, and it was no secret that Kanyon and I were smoking the herb.

Tyler, 20, was the next nephew to call.

Tyler explained it like this, "*My mom is so angry with James that she has kicked me out.*" Now, Tyler has tried marijuana, but he tends to like alcohol better, which scares me. I get confused about the acceptance of alcohol when it continues to ruin so many peoples' lives, yet it is legal. Tyler is another Crystal Child. He struggles with never knowing his father, having come from a split/joined family, and figuring out who he is, who he wants to be... typical adoptee identity issues.

I have always been very close with Tyler. My sister wasn't in much of a relationship with his father, and with me having been married and childless for a few years, I was very involved in theirs.

Crazily, three days later, their brother Jasper called me explaining that his mother had kicked him out because she found out he was dealing weed. "*Well, Jasper darling, you are an answer to my prayers.*"

No, seriously, Kanyon and I hated our lives so bad that if it were not for marijuana, we would have just given up and DIED. I seriously had run out of money and did not have any more resources to get any more medicine.

Going down this downward spiral, I got a clear understanding of the order of importance of the things that made me happy. We had been in such financial abundance that I was unaware of what really living within your means, means. As the money disappeared, I had choices to make... What to eliminate first? When it came down to the last things, it was a choice of, *"lashes or a bag of weed?"*, *"nails or a bag of weed?"* Thank God it did not get down to *"purple hair or a bag of weed?"* before Jasper moved in because that is one thing, I have learned about myself; I love my hair a lot. It is how I see myself. But weed was the only thing that could help us see joy in this downward spiral we were in, while the man of the house numbed his pain with heroin. My home was in foreclosure, but as long as I still had a roof over my home, all were welcome. Within a week, I had accumulated six young adults ranging from 19-20 years of age, plus their friends.

The great thing about marijuana... it brings you together. I loved our daily gatherings/family meetings, keeping up with how well everyone was doing.

Jasper brought a friend, Jr., who was kicked out of his father's home for marijuana-related reasons. Next came Scott's niece, Zila, joining us once again. Her parents didn't like her new career as a stripper. Zila brought a friend, Jasmine, who also had been told by her parents to move out.

Like I said, within one week, I had an army delivered to my doorstep. The best army anyone could ask for. I know there is no way any other family members could handle what was to come next.

I loved how full my house always was. I enjoyed getting to know everyone's friends. It was my safe haven where I felt many people had my back.

April 2012

The Healer Down South

I had finally saved up enough money to go see the healer, Pat, in Mapleton. Now that we had Scott somewhat detoxed, or so we thought, I went to get some direction and find out about the Hawaii thing. The healer informed me, "*You are supposed to be in Hawaii. You are late. The Universe has gifted you more time. You have until June 1st; Either you go voluntarily, or havoc and destruction will take you there. You have contracts with people, everything will fall into place. You will meet a good friend right from the start that will help you ease into things. There is a property manager that will take care of you. You will be volunteering with the dolphins. I see you helping a mother out. You have a car. You will be taken care of. If you only knew what is in store for you, you would have already left.*"

She continued to tell me many things that would prepare me for my departure, instructing me to start getting ready... I had a little less than three months.

After my appointment with Pat, Tyler and I went and visited Kai. After all, he lived five minutes away from my appointment, and I hadn't been over to see his new place. Our relationship was not a comfortable one for me. I hated what it was, I hated how his parents were, and I hated that he was married for my own selfish reasons. I hated pretty much everything about the situation surrounding Kai... down to his new dog!!!

Which, I must fill you in on... 1987, three months without a child, my mom saw a need to get me a dog. She could not ignore the huge void that needed to be filled. I named him Joshua. I had him with me in California, and took him everywhere I went... Until I married Scott. He hated the dog because he knew exactly what void it replaced. Scott made me give Joshua away.

Well, it just so happens that Mai and Kai got themselves a little dog (Joshua's twin brother), Riley. I could not understand this strong and strange coincidence/Universal message... but bottom line, I was not liking the situation in Utah at all, no part of it.

Tyler said I was a snot, and most likely, I was... out of hurt, ego, emotions, not having a filter... I made some comments that he probably did not appreciate. But that is a huge reason why I needed to live across seas away from Utah. I was having a hard time pretending and was not liking it.

Lots of Sistahs and Brothas

I loved how many felt comfortable regularly stopping in. I felt our home provided a sanctuary for many. I benefited greatly from having so many young adults who would listen to me, understanding the talk I talk. Always welcoming me as a mother figure in their lives, welcoming my nurturing ways, allowing me to play out my most comfortable role, Mother Hubbard ... having so many children, except I am going to have full cupboards and always know what to do.

It was also beneficial for my children to have many "older sibling" mentoring relationships that filled the void where an older sibling belonged.

Ashley is one of my favorite high school friend's daughters. During this time of my life, I had been diligently studying the scriptures, going to healing classes/sessions, and teaching others healing classes/sessions, but still didn't understand why my situation was still the same. I was willing what I wanted with my mind. It literally exhausted me... (I was doing it all wrong, begging and pleading to God, Universe, Source, whoever would listen to deliver). In freeing myself of my own limitation of a lack of belief, I threw in the towel and demanded the Universe to deliver.

Having a teenage daughter that had just had a growth spurt, I was extremely grateful that I dressed like a teen because when we did not have funds to buy Kylie new clothes, I suggested she jump in my closet.

Kylie jumped on in and jumped out, leaving only skirts behind. I was sick of wearing skirts every day and wondered how the Universe could provide for a long-legged skinny, hip mom in need of Levi's with no means to go buy any, even at a second-hand store... Levi's are hard to find that fit well, even when I go digging through many stores. I took this as my first challenge to the Universe to deliver, testing the use of intention, energy, and chakra manifestation.

Within 24 hours, my dear sweet Ashley had phoned to see if I was up for a visit. She was going to be in the neighborhood. After hearing the latest story of me supplying Kylie with my wardrobe and the "*I am so sick of wearing dresses*" story, Ashley got a smile on her face and said, "*I know why I am here.*" Ashley was on her way to Plato's Closet to sell all her older Levi's that she doesn't wear anymore when she got a sudden desire to come see me first. With that, she gave Kylie the keys to her trunk, and Kylie brought in a bag full of designer Levi's that actually fit me better than the teenager pants I had and even made me look more my age. God bless Ashley.

My 42nd Birthday
BLOG POST

It has been a grand birthday indeed, for sure... and it is only noon!!! It has been a rough patch in my life, for sure. I will skip all the details and just go straight to...

"*IT'S MY BIRTHDAY!!!*"

This rough patch I mentioned has been the biggest, eye-opening, invigorating experience... ***blessing***... in my life.

My son has reminded me I have something to say... Kanyon said to me, "*Mom, you would write good lyrics.*"

I smiled at him, acknowledging I had just gone gorillas on my parents, and when I go gorillas, I become pretty comical with what I say in a blunt, let's get to the point already, kind of way.

Kanyon chuckled, "No, I mean because you have experienced a LOT."

I laughed a little harder and said, "*Kanyon, I have too much to say. I can't keep it to a song... I have to write books about it.*" And I am telling you, this last book is going to be the best one ever!

For my 42nd birthday, I thought to the Universe, "*I would like a meal to feed all my children, who I have been blessed to nurture at this time in my life and go see The Lorax with everyone.*"

What time in my life, you ask? ... My husband is quitting heroin. He started using heroin because he could not get off prescription drugs. When no one else would step up to offer genuine help, Aunt Keri got calls left and right from her niece and nephews. Within one week, four 18-year-olds and one 20-year-old moved in, joining me on this ride of healing.

I HAVE LOVED EVERY MINUTE OF IT!!!

I needed these warriors of God. Not many... well... in my family... could have handled this intensity.

My mother heard my birthday desire (telepathically/Universally) and showed up a few days before my birthday with Kentucky Fried Chicken for all these mouths here. And then, the evening before my birthday, the kids found a brand-new cooler on the front porch filled with several meals to feed the crew!

The best part about these experiences is the joy and "belief-in-God look" these kids have on their faces when they witness the magical things that happen every day in my life.

My birthday just keeps getting better. We are all going to go see *The Lorax* (my all-time favorite little guy!) ... at 4:20.

May 2012

The Storm Rolls In

After the nephews, niece, and friends moved and settled in, Scott's behavior continued to get worse. It took the nine of us watching out for Scott, questioning his whereabouts, piecing the puzzle together. He says he is going to work but the bills still aren't getting paid. He is more and more medicated, and more and more things are coming up missing. Then one night, Scott accidentally butt-called me. I listened in horror as I heard Scott talking to another, planning a heist with weapons. I ran downstairs to the children, and we all gathered around and listened closely on speaker phone. Scott and this other kid were scheduling the heist around the kid's plans to go shopping with his mother. We all listened in, paying attention to when this would all be going down. After what seemed like an hour, Scott's phone dropped the connection.

Strangely enough, right at that moment, Scott's mother called me. She had sensed that *"Scott is about to do something horrible and is in danger."* I confirmed how accurate her feelings were and filled her in on what had just happened. Together, Scott's mother and I planned an intervention with a medicine man and peyote.

My job was to lure Scott home via phone, and when he arrives home, we will take his keys and phone away... Do everything in our power to detain him until she can arrive to start the cleanse.

I called Scott and threatened to start liquidating his furniture to pay the bills and told him he'd better get his ass home to stop me. I did not inform him about his butt-calling me. After multiple calls, such as, *"Loading up your DVDs to take to FYE* (a resale store) *for money..."* Scott arrived two hours later.

With my young army by my side, we were able to confuse Scott enough to: flatten his tire, disconnect the battery to the truck, and get his keys. Kanyon was the one who was quick and fast, standing up to his father, grabbing his phone, and throwing it over the fence onto Highland Dr., a busy road behind our house.

The endurance of this man was unbelievable. He was determined to get out of there with his truck and phone. Scott freaked out when Kanyon threw his phone over the fence and did not waste any time. Scott went to the garage and got a ladder to climb over the fence, got on top of the wood fence, grabbed the ladder, lifted the ladder over the fence to set it down on the other side, climbed down the ladder, and ran into the street to find his phone crushed.

Scott then climbed back up the ladder, got on top of the fence while teetering and almost falling onto his head, grabbed the ladder to lift it onto the other side... Together we were watching over Scott as well as trying to stop him. James grabbed onto his uncle's legs to save him from falling off the ladder and assisted Scott safely back to the yard. Once in the yard, the struggle was on again.

Finally, I had no choice but to grab my coat and follow Scott on foot to the Verizon store. Scott was determined to get a new phone that night. I knew time was on my side, and stores were closing. I followed Scott a mile or so in the rain to finally arrive at Verizon just as they were closing.

I called Scott's mother to see if she was almost in the vicinity. She arrived to pick us up 15 minutes later. Scott's mother was able to coax him into going back home to drink some peyote and start the cleanse.

I nursed and cared for Scott, with him spewing and shitting everywhere, messing sheets and missing toilets... not a pretty detox. After two weeks of that and an amazing ceremony with a Navajo medicine man, Scott was determined to get back to making money, and his new adventure was in emergency bunkers.

The boys supported their uncle, escorting Scott to End of the World trade shows and handing out pamphlets to get orders for installing bunkers. It wasn't long before Scott was making excuses to go get this or go get that, making it nearly impossible for the boys to watch over their uncle.

June 2012

June 1st

Even under high supervision, Scott was able to sneak out and use again. It was hopeless; we all were frustrated by Scott's choice to use. Slowly, my army cleared out. I was getting nervous. June 1st was almost here, and I was still in Utah.

The day came alright; I was expecting something to happen on June 1st. I was walking on eggshells, just waiting to see what June was going to bring. On June 13th, Scott came stumbling home, relapsed, and the shit goes down... in a bad way.

Scott brought his heroin dealer to the house. Upon first meeting him, I ordered him to stay away from my home. I sensed this man was bad news. Scott had always lied, introducing this man like he was a part of the business... a worker. But Kanyon and I instantly sensed **bad**.

Interestingly enough, just one hour before Scott and this dealer pulled up to the house, my nephew Jasper and a friend arrived to finish hauling his things out of the house. Jasper and his buddy were downstairs when Scott arrived.

Scott left the dealer outside while he entered the house to pack a bag. Instantly knowing that Scott was up to no good, Kanyon and I followed him. He was explaining that he needed to pack a bag (with five pairs of Levis) for a job. *"They are pouring a foundation in the mountains."* ...or whatever it was he was saying.

We were all so angry at the choices Scott had been making.

Kanyon ripped Scott's shorts off him and was able to get the pill bottle of heroin off him. It was quite a scene with mother and son against father. Scott slipped new shorts on and was angry at us for attacking him. For some crazy reason, I grabbed the Cutco scissors and put them in my pocket on the way out, following Kanyon, who was following Scott, out of the house and through the garage to the exposed driveway. Jasper and his friend were emerging from downstairs to see what all the racket was. Jasper followed us, asking if I was okay. Walking past him, confidently shoving the scissors in my pocket, I tell him, *"I got this."*

Jasper and his friend followed, with Kylie in the rear of this lineup. The dealer dude was advancing forward to get back in Scott's truck to leave to do whatever it was they were planning on doing. And I tell you what... *it couldn't be of any good.*

As we all got to the driveway out front of my house, advancing forward... those two against us five. Kanyon in the lead, me following with Jasper right beside me. The friend and Kylie stood back, holding space. Advancing on Scott's partner in crime, Kanyon grabbed a garden rake and charged the guy. Jasper, being the older brotha, took the rake from Kanyon to prevent a murder on Kanyon's hands and chased the dealer dude off, freeing Kanyon to stop his father.

Simultaneously, like a pack, I jumped in the passenger seat, finding a pile of crowbars at my feet. Before I could even close the door, the dealer dude was back. Jasper had run to Kanyon's side to be there when Kanyon needed a break ... *tag teaming.* The dealer dude was approaching the passenger side, where I was about to close the door. I grabbed this dude's soda from the middle console, threw his drink in his face, and advanced on him, charging him like a crazed mad woman with one of the crowbars from my feet.

With the dealer dude off the scene, I threw the crowbar back with the rest of them and jumped back in the passenger seat, telling Scott to give Kanyon the keys. At this point, Kanyon's hand was wrapped around his father's, grasping desperately with all his might, trying to stop his father. I swiftly whipped my scissors out of my pocket and calmly informed Scott that I was going to count to three, and then I would stab him. "*1, 2, 3,*" I counted quickly, followed by a stab in his thigh. Following another, "*1, 2, 3,*" I stabbed him in the thigh again (through Levi's... no blood). And a "*1, 2, 3,*" this time stabbing him in the bicep (through a thick shirt... no blood). That final stab in the bicep was the cherry bomb. Immediately, Kanyon was able to win the struggle, pulling his father out of the vehicle.

Kanyon was exhausted as hell. Jasper noticed and jumped in. When Jasper would take over, a crazy look would appear in Scott's eyes, so Kanyon would jump in, and the crazy look and strength would dimmer. As I jumped out of the passenger seat to join the boys, grabbing a crowbar once again, I told Kylie and the friend, "*Call the cops."*

I joined the boys who were switching off until they finally pinned Scott down with them, both laying on top of him, using all their limbs, like I have seen at wrestling matches. Scott was hanging on to his keys while Kanyon continued trying to pry his father's fingers open to get the keys. With the boys tiring, I calmly knelt at my husband's head, placing the crowbar over his throat. I once again informed Scott that I was going to count to three and then apply pressure... He just needed to release his grip on the keys, and it would be over. "*1, 2, 3.*" Kneeling at my husband's head, I applied full force down, blocking his airwave. It didn't take long for him to lose his grip and for Kanyon to get the keys.

Folks, I am one that is known to not involve cops, so my daughter has learned that when I say to call the cops, I mean... *really...* call the cops. I have resorted to their assistance only twice in my life.

The cops rolled in just as Scott lost his grip, and we all jumped up just in time for the cops to take over. Off Scott went with possession charges... Only to be bailed out by Julie, his lover from 1986.

Such craziness that Julie bailed Scott out ASAP and brought my shell of a husband, who had been taken over by his demons, over to get his things out of the house. I looked at Kanyon, apologizing. *"Kanyon, I'm sorry, but this is the end of the contract. It's over."* I then told Scott the same... I was able to let him go. Pat, the healer from down south, had cut the energetic cords, once again, that Scott had in me. For the first time in my life, I could completely walk away with no sorrow, no bitterness. Just hope for a better future.

The following week, I worked rapidly, selling furniture, gifting stuff away, advertising my 1967 Mustang for sale... Scott had always hated my asset I brought into the marriage (my car), calling it a money pit, continually harassing me to sell it. I refused, holding on to it, saying, *"Not until I need a roof over my head."* And here I was, exactly at that point.

I had run out of time to sell the Mustang. Pat told me to forget about the $10,000 that I was so set on getting for it. She also told me, *"You need to go to your grandfather's house and give him one last chance to offer information to free his soul. And before leaving, ask him if he can offer any money to assist you in your travels."* Saying almost word for word exactly what Suzi had told me.

On my way to the car lot to accept $6500 for my Mustang, I surprised my grandfather with a visit. You figure, my father was still alive at this point. The two of them were *"disgusted"* with my behavior of not letting ole dogs lie. I hadn't talked to either of them for at least a good year, and I was not looking forward to the visit. But when you are told by two separate strangers that your deceased grandmother is the one insisting, I be the one to give the message, along with information that only a truly gifted could know about my grandmother and the situation... how could I not obey?

I confronted my grandfather once again, asking for the name of my biological grandmother, who is a woman whose shoes I have walked, having lost a child to adoption myself. My grandfather avoided the question, very upset that I was bringing this up again.

For you see... after learning how this Universe works in such an orderly way and knowing that once you have walked in someone's shoes, you recognize their shoes... and once you know your ancestry stories, you see patterns, and together, there is just no denying... cycles need to be broken... energy needs to be cleared.

I know my grandfather's guilt. I recognize too many things... being a wife who has a husband that cheated and now has a child with that woman. Unlike my grandfather, instead of adopting the child with no admission to sin, and pretending there was no sin, my husband, Scott, openly owned his actions. I was given the opportunity to practice what I preach and Love One Another, *'Adopt'* the Mother... to love this child in her highest good, I needed to first and foremost love and forgive her parents and get rid of my hurt and bitterness. When that beautiful daughter of God runs into my arms for comfort, I'll be able to love that child in her highest good because I genuinely love her father AND her mother. Betty and I were able to look past the past and focus on the Now, developing a beautiful sister relationship. I always honored Betty's role as Liah's mother, and Betty respected my role as Liah's father's wife, losing romantic interest in Scott.

Anyway, Grandpa got kind of scary, speaking under his breath, saying I needed to quit bringing up what the demons made him do. And even with me pouring out my heart to him, explaining why I couldn't pretend anymore and that I was leaving for Hawaii to never come back, that this was the last time he would see me... I asked if he would like to give me any money to help me on my journey. My grandfather stiffly shook his head, no, and off I left. I haven't seen my grandfather since. But I faced my fear, faced my grandfather, and did what my grandmother had asked me to do from the other side before I left for Maui.

Scott realized I was serious about Hawaii and insisted I stop selling off his furniture. He paid me $1500 and helped me rent a car to leave Utah so I could head to Vegas and figure it out from there at his sister Dawn's house. The bank offered me $3000 to get out of the house in two weeks. I had to let my Mustang go for $6500 as I had run out of time. At the last minute, my nephews Tyler and James said they couldn't see themselves staying behind in Utah.

I asked them, *"If money weren't an issue, what would your choice be?"*

They both said, *"Go to Maui."*

"Ok, then pack your stuff, get it dialed in, and let's go."

My sister Tabi freaked out; I was taking both her boys to Hawaii. I traded my daughter for her boys. I don't think she saw it as so simple. Everyone thought I was crazy following Kanyon and other gifted people's advice. They don't realize Kanyon is my creation. I have taught him everything I know and have protected his pure spirit ferociously. I have lived with him 24/7 since the day of his birth and have witnessed the many times Kanyon predicted the future, warning me, helping me be better prepared to deal with what was to come for fifteen years. So, when one of Pat's instructions was, *"Listen to Kanyon - if Kanyon says stop, you stop. If Kanyon says turn right, you turn right. Kanyon is your compass,"* it was not difficult for me to obey. It confirmed what I already knew and gave me the confidence to do something like end a conversation on the phone after Kanyon would walk in the room out of nowhere (sensing my energy) and say, *"Whoever it is, tell them goodbye."* It was a very delicate time in my life while getting rid of the life I had known for **23** years.

And speaking of **23**... What does that number mean anyway??? I have always revered the number **23**. I thought maybe I loved the number so much because perhaps it would be my best birthday ever, and I would love being **23** (thinking, **23** must be the year that the best things in life happen). Yet as **23** came and went without any overzealous moment to hold it as a revered year, I just assumed it was my favorite number for some reason. Now that I am 43, I see all the **23**'s.... Kai's birthday is December **23**, Scott and I were married on July **23**, and ended it after **23** years... seriously, a week before July **23**, 2011, which would have made it 24 years. Liah's birthday is January **23**, my Mustang odometer stopped working at **23**,000 miles, Kai and Mai married April **23**... just to name a few off the top of my head.

Well, according to Doreen Virtue's *Angel Numbers 101*, "**23** means you are working closely with one or more ascended masters such as Jesus, Moses, the saints, or the goddesses. This is a message from your ascended master guides, who can see that the answer to your prayers is within reach. They encourage you to stay positive to ensure that you attract the best possible outcome." Hmmm, that is good stuff... If we add it up for the numerology take on it then 2+3=5. Five = "a significant change is occurring, always for the better. It's a good idea to call upon Heaven for help with life changes."

Letting go of **23** years of accumulation of stuff and memories... Leaving a marriage that I was so determined would last forever... well, at least until death did us part... was a huge step into the unknown for me, all about facing my fears and trusting in God and the Universe. My whole life was crumbling before my eyes. Saying goodbye to everything and everyone I knew... Leaving my daughter with my sister and having to say goodbye. Loading up our last belongings into the rented Suburban was another surreal feeling similar to the separation we went through seven years ago in 2005 when we left Kai in Wyoming on Christmas Eve after just coming together again. I felt like this was just temporary, but at the same time, I was nervous as hell.

My sister Tabi and I didn't say goodbye because she was so upset, I was taking both her boys. Kanyon had to leave his dog Zeus behind, and off the four of us went... to Vegas.

Viva Las Vegas

It felt so good to arrive at Dawn's and be welcomed into family arms. We had left home and driven straight to Vegas. Dawn took great care of us, showing us yoga, new healthy dinner choices, and even a system to wash dishes by hand, which became useful upon moving to Maui... I haven't had a dishwasher since I left the mainland. But most importantly, Dawn introduced us to a new way of living. Dawn was an excellent example of always doing Yoga, drinking green tea and green smoothies, and eating easy, yummy, simple meals that are healthy. We have seriously survived our journey based on her example of living simply.

During the time we were staying with Dawn, Keith, and Gabe. Gabe kept playing a song over and over. It became one of many theme songs to get us pumped for the journey ahead... *"I Can Lift a Car"* by Walk the Moon. The verse repeats, *"All by myself, all by myself, I can lift a car all by myself."* It gave me strength all by myself (well, together as one). I am going to make it all by myself. I was just leaving a familiar way of living and the only thing I had known; having a husband to take care of me ever and always. It was the perfect song for Gabe to play over and over.

We stayed with Dawn for a week, figuring out our flights and where we were going to stay in Maui. Frantically, I searched Craigslist looking for a place to stay. No one would take me. My credit sucked, I had no job, I had three teenager-ish aged boys, and I was new to the island. Finally, I found Lenny McClusky, who, for some reason, agreed to rent it to me... if I could deposit the money into his account by such and such day, it would be mine. I deposited the money, and we agreed to meet the day of our landing and go straight to our new home from the airport.

Time for Take Off

It was a good thing Tyler came with us. Kanyon, James, and I were so ADD, moseying on our way, we almost missed both flights. Well, did I mention, auntie Dawn baked us some special brownies for the plane ride?

Landing in Maui and arriving at our new home had a magical feeling like Christmas. We arrived at dusk. Pulling up in the taxi van to our first Maui house lit up like a Christmas tree. All the shutters in the house were open, and music was playing.

July 2012

Let Us Start with Lenny
BLOG POST

Everyone... Aloha! I have not had the time to call any of you, and I am so sorry. All my dear friends and loved ones, I would love to, I really would, but I just haven't the time... there really is no time after all anyway, right? Just the moment, the Now. And let me tell you all, this moment gets better and better as we go!!!

Let me tell you about this journey of mine so far. After almost missing our plane when leaving Las Vegas... Well, you know, I won the jackpot and was chosen by security to get my phone checked, and then on the way, well, you know me. I had to take pictures, and we got to the gate just after they had already closed the plane up.

"*Are you the Stone party of four?!*" CODE RED, CODE RED, bells, whistles... They stopped the plane from any further departure action, and the four of us made our way on the plane with our guitars and my purple hair.

Immediately after takeoff, the passenger on my left got up and didn't come back. Wow, how nice is that!!! I wondered, was he ill, did he have a toddler in a seat in another row??? Oh well... I had prayed that I would remember to walk around to keep my leg circulation good (I just have recently regained feeling in my shins after flying three years ago to Oahu). I just took it as an answer to my prayers.

Then, when Kanyon and I were all comfortably sprawled out sleeping, right before landing on Oahu, I woke up to some guy staring down at me. I opened my eyes, looked up at him, and said sleepily, "*There you are. Where have you been?*" I readjusted myself, moving over to my assigned seat, and he informed me he was a pilot. After flying, I guess as part of their rotation, they go under the plane where they have beds for sleeping... good to know.

We arrived in Oahu and waited three hours at the airport. There wasn't much to see while waiting to leave at gate 50. We were waiting around to board the plane, getting bored of waiting to board the plane... Well, good thing we were traveling with Tyler, who was sick of waiting because all four of us have a little ADHD and do not pay attention to overhead yapping. Tyler sensed it was time to go, or else we would have missed this plane too. Once again, we were at the tail end of loaders.

We fly our little flight, land safely, and then go get our eight ginormous suitcases. We hauled our two carts across the road to catch a taxi. After three van tryouts to see how big a vehicle this Stone party of four needed, we left the airport in a nice deluxe shuttle all to ourselves... only twenty bucks to my house from the airport! Well, that was the end of my cheaper-than-expected moments.

I used my smartphone to direct the shuttle guy to our new home. Thank God Kylie taught me how to use the navigation feature... it was my "Maui Bible." We unloaded from the shuttle and admired our beautiful home that the landlord had lit up like a Christmas tree with all the windows open (shutters that swing out all old-fashioned style.) We thought for a moment that we had gone to the wrong place. It looked so occupied... music was playing. I went to the front door and was greeted by the warmest welcoming voice, my landlord, Lenny.

Lenny... what a character, that guy. He was the sweetest thing... a little strange, but you all know how well I adore strange. After showing us the house, he showed us the shower near the back and said, "*This is the best room in the house.*" And he wasn't kidding. All three boys had something to say after experiencing it.

We all chuckled and got ready to go to the store... Our blessed Lenny couldn't believe how this freshly divorced mother with these three boys was flying by the seat of her pants, winging it, and willing to just camp out on the beach until she figured it out. And she figured she would just walk to the store... Lenny offered us a ride to go get groceries. We got back, and this wonderful character that I wish I had pictures of just came in like part of the family, got a bottle of wine out of the fridge that he had there, and asked James to open the bottle for him. Lenny witnessed how pure this kid was. James had to ask directions. Lenny poured himself a glass and sat at the tea party table in the kitchen, watching us put away our groceries. He turned on the kitchen radio and lamp and sat sipping his wine, enjoying our presence as we put away groceries. We didn't mind his peaceful sitting and sipping and didn't even notice him slip out the back. Strange, but whatever. We loved the place and were happy to be there. We went to bed exhausted.

The next morning, I was chatting on the phone with my mother, telling her how sweet this dear character Lenny was. The boys chimed in saying how amazing he was, and then we started talking about how so many people probably judged him and feared him.

Mind you, the guy lives next door in the basement. He rents out this house and the house next door that he lives in. From the moment we arrived and took possession of the house, Lenny welcomed us so well to his home. For the first few days when we got here, he enjoyed that shower... remember, it was his favorite room in the house... asking every time. He would come by every so often to rotate the sprinkler on the lawn in his underwear. He grows his hair out long on the sides so he can do the over comb with a forward action. He is very similar to a Gene Wilder character with similar curly hair. We were all going on about how amazing this sweet man was.

My mother, who knows I am going to be meeting tall, dark, and handsome, is wondering, "*Could this be the one?*" So we started explaining how he looks to my mother, with me saying, "*He has a Bozo-the-clown like quality.*"

Kanyon said, "*No, he is like the Yang of Beetlejuice. You know... Beetlejuice is the dark bad, the Yin of it, and Lenny is like the good and the light of it. But he looks like a nice Beetlejuice.*"

After I got off the phone with my mother, we noticed that lovely man, Lenny, was on the porch under the windows and had heard everything we said. Good thing we loved the guy!!!

But I put on that good ole oblivious act that I do so well and sang out oh so sweetly, "*Lenny, there you are! What are you doing today? Have you been to church? Whatcha doing?*" and joined him for a morning chit chat.

Come to find out, this dear sweet man is sweeter than we even knew. He was only living next door in the basement apartment, where he grew up with his grandmother when he came to Maui. He had a job in Oahu, and he was taking care of his mother, who is 94. He grew up with his grandmother... There is a story there, some other time, but this man never married. He didn't want to become a pig farmer, so he called off the marriage and never had children. I don't know if he has any siblings. I am guessing not. But Lenny needs a family, and we were so grateful to find family fresh off the plane.

Sunday night, I heard a car alarm going off, so I went out to see what was going on. It was Lenny leaving for the airport. *"Lenny, where are you going?"*

"Time to go back. I left some things on the porch. If you don't want or need them, just throw them out." That gracious good man had left a bag of odds and ends that we truly needed. AND, he had left a can of Kanyon's favorite flavor of Arizona Tea in the bag that he must have seen Kanyon drinking earlier.

"Oh Lenny, you are the sweetest thing. I can't believe you were going to just sneak off without saying goodbye."

He chuckled at this, not wanting to be a bother but loving the adoration. I called the boys to say goodbye, and we all hugged him goodbye.

I am so excited to be here. Maui has received us well. I am transfixed by the serendipities falling into place, bringing the perfect people in my space like clockwork.

First thing Monday morning, two days after my arrival, I walked to open a checking account at the same bank as Lenny. I got chatting with the lovely bank lady, who loved chatting with me as well. She told me, *"You have such an Aloha spirit! You are special."* I thanked her humbly and asked her name. *"Virginia,"* she said... Folks, some of you may not know about my deceased grandmother, Virginia, who adopted my father. My sister was named after her, Tabi Virginia. I have been told by multiple sources that my grandmother Virginia is thick in the space while Kanyon and I are going through this transition... WOW... right?

Anyway, we realized we needed a car. We walked to a car lot and met Sal who escorted me around allll dayyyy long, helping me get insurance so I could take the car off the lot. During our day together, I heard his story. Wow, does he have a story to tell, and he plans on telling it. I shared with him that I have written a book. I told him how

I did it, about my journey of writing the book, and then that led him to want to have a copy. You never know what will come out of it. Come to find out, his wife works at Family Services here in Maui and I had just applied for a job there to help single pregnant mothers *KEEP* their children.

And that leads me to Jim and Darrin. So, Scott, my former husband of **23** years, has a brother named Jim. Scott, Jim, and Darrin, their childhood friend who had pretty much been raised as their brother, were living on their own when I met Scott.

Well, I was sitting outside of the welfare services office to see what I was qualified to receive. I had barely pulled out a book to read when this character who was my age with a Mohawk said, *"You have the most beautiful green eyes with that purple hair."* His name was Jim, and we got chatting. Come to find out, he lived on some upcountry farm like an hour away, and he hitchhiked to this welfare center that is seriously within walking distance for me. Like seriously around the corner from my house. Did I mention... I drove there!!! I went there on the way back from getting my car, and the boys actually walked home.

As we chatted with Jim, I found out that his mother had died when he was two.

His grandparents in California adopted him, but his two brothers were left to fend for themselves at the ages of 9 and 10. They were abandoned by their dad on the northeast side of Maui, leaving them to raise themselves on the land. When Jim was 14, he joined his brothers in Maui. Darrin (spelled the same way as Scott's friend) was a friend of the three brothers and took them to his house to live, starting their brotherly bond.

Did I mention that the former husband's brothers, Jim & Darrin, were the two eyewitnesses at my wedding with Scott??? Interesting that the Universe sent me another Jim & Darrin (spelled the same), sending a clear message to me "bearing witness" once again, if you will, to me entering a new VOLUME of my life. Starting anew...

Anyway, to make a very long story short, I tend to collect children, no matter their age, and Jim tends to collect mothers. After he realized everyone adores me (not just him) and I adore everyone (not just him), and that we were going to be great friends... We had an amazing day with him being our personal tour guide around the island. The boys had a great time. It seriously was like hanging out with their Grandpa Randy, my father. So many more stories about Jim and Darrin, those Nahiku farmers that live in a wood building with nine sides, all open... farming, surfing, and playing guitar ALL day, every day.

I must say though, my favorite part about our driving around the island, jumping in fresh pools here and body surfing there, was meeting Shannon, the 56-year-old surfer chic!!! Loved it. This beautiful woman, who is a grandmother to I don't know how many surfer babies, has gotten around without a car for many years. We happened across her not once but twice while she was hitching to doctor's appointments. I can't even say hitchhiking... she was gracefully sitting on a cobblestone wall when Jim pulled over and said, "*Hey Shannon, where are you going?*" Shannon is Jim's neighbor and has been on the island since 1973 when she was 17. "*A good age to come to the island and learn this way of life,*" she informed Kanyon when she heard he was 15. This *bitchin'* grandma reminded me how *bitchin'* I used to be. I used to say *bitchin'* all the time, just like she was. She reminded me of that *bitchin'* Cali surfer chic I once was. Quite a day, quite a week, quite an adventure already!!!

Coming here has been a total blessing. It has been scary to let everything I know go and trust in God...

The eve before we flew out of Vegas, I had returned a text from my firstborn son.

> *I know I'm a wreck and make things hard... Again, I'm sorry I have stepped back and distanced myself again. You know how it is... I either suffocate you or am out of the picture. I look forward to life being simpler. I'm sure with this next move of mine, I will find it and be content with all my relationships because I have totally stepped out of the box and am now living in the moment where there are no expectations... just enjoying the Now and happy to be here. I am excited to let my strong motherly nurturing instinctive behavior be let loose in Hawaii to mother all of God's children, young and old. I have always been told who I can nurture, mother, and love, starting at 16, and when I married Scott, the restriction was still there.*

Understandably so, but like I said, I can nurture and love 100% every person who comes into my space, not having to hold back when I want to extend... being free to not have to care, be, do what anyone else thinks or wants.

Let go and let God... And folks, He has not failed me.

Love to all of you guys. I wanted you all to get the details of what's up. I look forward to hearing from every one of you. Make sure you all let me know when you are in my neck of the woods.

Oh Yeah... a Baby Was Born

Daisy Sanderson, my biological first-born granddaughter from my firstborn son, was born a month before we left Utah.

Kai was still in Texas selling security alarms for the summer. Initially, I had envisioned myself flying to Texas to be a part of the birth, but somewhere in between, there were hurt feelings after I had acknowledged the strong resemblance between pictures of myself and this newborn child. So unfortunately, I did not make it a priority to meet a grandchild of mine that will never be. How can I be a grandmother if I am not acknowledged as a mother? After a blow to my ego/self-worth, I turned cold as ice towards that son of mine. (Definition of me turning cold as ice: You no longer exist to me.) I know that sounds horrible, especially being the mother that was the first to reject him at birth, but along with that, it has become a strong defense mechanism I have become quite good at.

Over the months, Kai and I would talk on the phone, text, or Facebook here and there. I love that Kai is as confrontational as I am. Our interaction was very love/hate, hit or miss. Because of my own issues, every time Kai would want to talk about his baby, I would lose interest in the conversation. I never really allowed myself to acknowledge my granddaughter since that first initial blow.

August 2012

The Day of My Father's Death
BLOG POST

I am so very grateful that I am home in Maui. This island has received me well.

Yesterday, our new good friend, Jim, was in town. He had a doctor's appointment at 5:00 pm, so he showed up around 10:00 am to see what we were doing that weekend.

I told him, "I'm in the mood to go hiking in our backyard." ...Iao Valley.

Right at that moment, Jim's doctor called and asked if he could come right away to get his appointment over with and out of the way. Perfect! We can go hiking and play all day like locals!

By noon, we were hiking up the Needle. A great tourist spot... but... Jim knew of a "shortcut," which I have learned in my Daddy Randy's language, means a groovy, fun way to check something out. And yes, Jim does mean shortcut the same way my daddy did. We got to the top part of the tourist trail and saw a sign posted that said, *"Do not go this way! Stay on the paved trail!"* You know, one of those signs my children have always thought was posted to notify them which way they should actually go? Well, this was the shortcut Jim had spoken of. I loved the rebellious local act in front of gasping tourists.

We hiked up on a well-traveled path into the *real* hiking area like I was brought up doing in Utah.

The whole way, after we crossed over onto the local side of the hike, the boys and I kept commenting how much it felt like we were hiking at the family cabin with Grandpa Randy because Jim is so much like him, and we were hiking the type of terrain Randy would take us on.

After the hike to the top of Iao Valley, we headed to the beach near our house, taking "shortcuts" so we wouldn't have to travel the tourist routes. This Jim character is better than my smartphone navigator feature!!!

We got home, and my daughter called me and said, *"Mom, Tabi is crying badly. I don't know what is wrong. Something happened."*

While on the phone with her, James came into the room and informed us, "*Grandpa Randy died.*"

Wow, okay. We were expecting this, but wow... It really happened. I love how we felt, like we were hiking with my father, at the cabin that day. He had actually died in the cabin a short time before that day. It just happened to be the same day he was found.

I seriously was shocked by my lack of feelings. You figure, my father had already overdosed in 2009, and the paramedics were able to revive him. When I had first heard that... weeks after the fact...Ronald, my sister's husband, had run into my father at the plumbing house and he had told him, "*Hey, did you know I died a few weeks ago?*" He then proceeded to tell Ronald the story of his death and survival.

So, when my sister called me up, and had started to say, "*Did you know that Randy died? And...*"

I screamed hysterically, and it took her a few minutes to calm me down via phone to inform me that the paramedics had revived him. That wife of his didn't bother to let us know, which is a whole other drama-filled story, some other time. What I am trying to say is that I seriously processed my father dying that day in 2009. I sobbed uncontrollably and called his home, leaving a message on the answering machine about how upset I was about finding out about it all two weeks after my father overdosed... and no one bothered informing his two daughters!

Well, folks, one can't recreate something as genuine as reacting to hearing that your parent has died. When it is a false alarm, and then they really do pass... if you are like me, I made sure I apologized and tried to make things right. Even if he did not receive me, I have a clear conscience of how I left it.

Interestingly enough, being the picture freak that I am, I did not bring one single photo with me. I brought everything on my external hard drive and laptop... Two copies of my whole life, but not one single photo on paper in the physical realm. The only photograph that made it to Hawaii was Grandpa Randy's graduation picture that Kanyon grabbed at the last minute.

For you see, Kanyon is looking more and more like his

grandfather every day. Kanyon's beliefs and truths are developing more and more like his grandfather's every day. Well, the Daddy Randy's beliefs and truths that I remember them to be. My father quit smoking weed after he found a woman who wanted to get married in the temple for "all time and eternity." So... he had to take seven prescribed pills to replace what marijuana had been able to do for him. I feel like prescription pills and religion ruined him. I felt relieved when I heard my father had died. He was free.

My Job Found Me

I couldn't help but replay the words of Pat as I tried to feel my way through this journey of mine. *"You will be volunteering with the dolphins."* At the time of the reading, I seriously thought the husband would successfully rehab, and we all would be moving to Maui to fulfill my contract with the Universe. I sincerely thought I would arrive in Maui with my family intact, along with financial abundance. It just had to be that way; I had thought. How else would I be *"volunteering with the dolphins?"* So, when things went down the way they did, I was confused about this part of the message. Until my job found me.

I applied for many jobs and even went on an interview in Kula to work with flowers from the ground up, making arrangements for celebrations. It would have been a lovely job, but I had concerns that it would be very hard on the car commuting back and forth, being upcountry and all. Oddly enough, I kept missing their callbacks, and they happened to always be out when I called them. So, when Mismo basically got me a job with Hawaii Ocean Rafting at slip #8 soliciting snorkel trips to see dolphins, I knew I was where I had to be. AND upon receiving my first paycheck, I really knew I was right where I was supposed to be. Yep, this was definitely *"volunteering with the dolphins."*

I loved the new job and after being the wife of an owner of multiple concrete construction companies for **23** years, I had an employer mentality and not much of a salesperson mentality. I ran the booth with that employer mentality, creating more job responsibility for the booth person, i.e., me. But hey, it takes more energy for me to ignore things that need to be done. Plus, I loved being at the harbor, near the water. It truly has been healing at its best. There was always a good amount of dead time, perfect for meditating and clearing energy.

When my boss apologizes for my small paychecks, I would acknowledge, *"It's ok. I know I am right where I am supposed to be. I was warned that I would be volunteering with the dolphins, and here I am. I just thought I would have my family and money to support me. I look at it this way... free healing. God knows what I need, and if I am where I am supposed to be, everything will be alright and work out."* I also shared that I recognized him as one of my contracts.

Upon arriving on Maui, I quickly recognized the irony and divinity of meeting my boss, Mark Robinson, and his right-hand man, Sean. It was uncanny how these two men strongly resembled the man I had just left. It was like the two of them made up Scott Stone. Mark being the ornery one, and Sean being the tall nicer one. Being married to Scott for **23** years was the perfect training to handle Mark and his angry, defensive demeanor. I could see the soft, vulnerable side that I was familiar with, hidden deep out of their own fear of being taken advantage of. At first, I thought, *"What a sick joke. I leave that husband, and the Universe throws me into the same 'F***er' energy"* (forgive my French).

My relationship with Mark got better after I sternly told him, *"You are exactly like that husband I just left. I don't have any kids with you, Mark. I won't stick around like I did with him."*

I always gave my boss the respect that any human deserves. I am an intelligent, hard-working woman, and it didn't hurt that I was nice to look at too. But in no way was I going to give away my power to anyone ever again. And with that, we had an understanding, and I believe I gained some respect from the boss man.

I Love My Job
BLOG POST

I love my job. It's in the best location. It has the best atmosphere; people vacationing in total bliss away from it all, so happy to be in Maui.

I remember working weddings. The atmosphere was such a celebration of love. I got that job in the summer of 2005. You know... the *first time* I kicked Scott out. I didn't have to go looking for a job as my dear friend Cindy, a wedding planner, offered me a job upon hearing about my personal status.

At the time, I thought, *"How ironic... working weddings while my own marriage is dissolving."* But I have always been one to roll with the current of life, and this wave took me to a gorgeous sanctuary called Elegant Gardens. I worked 40 weddings in one summer. Obviously, I was not meant to dissolve my own marriage just yet. For you see, by November 2005, I was back together with Scott, living in Texas, reuniting with our firstborn son we lost to adoption.

Well, after **23** years of that marriage, I had finally had enough when I moved to Maui. Once again, I didn't have to go looking far for a job. Kanyon, James, and I were walking back from James' job interview, checking out the harbor before we bussed it back home, when we heard, *"Hey, do you want to go play with the dolphins?"*

I hollered back, *"Oh, indeed we do, but we just moved here, and we are looking for jobs. We have it on the bucket list as one of the first things we will do."*

"Well, hey, I'm looking for a Sunday and Monday girl."

Which again brings me to... *"I love my job."*

Let me just brief you on today. As you may (or may not) know, my Daddy Randy just recently passed away. He died two weeks after I moved to Maui. My first day of work was the day of his funeral. I had yet to shed a tear... until... today... AT WORK...

I had been wondering why I hadn't had any emotion about my father dying. I was carrying on as if some stranger died. I had already grieved my Daddy Randy dying in 2009 when he accidentally overdosed on his prescribed cocktail, and they were able to revive him.

Yeah, I found out weeks later...

When I first received the message, I didn't hear the *"they were able to revive him"* part because after hearing my sister say, *"Did you know that Randy died?"* I fell to my knees, wailing like a Polynesian, shaking and screaming uncontrollably. After a good ten minutes of that, plus my sister screaming through the phone, *"No, Keri. He's alive, he's alive,"* I was so shaken up, I couldn't stop shaking. I was just as pissed that not one single person informed any of his children, ME BEING THE ELDEST!!! I told my sister, *"I have got to go. I'm calling that wife of his while I am still vibrating with shock before TOO much vile sets in!!!"*

Of course, I got the answering machine and was thrilled to leave a raging message. No interruptions while I stated my upset and reminded them, I was his F-ing daughter, goddamnit. Keeping my calm so they could hear my every word with the least amount of swear words for such a situation, especially when you remember I warned his wife about medicating him with pills instead of HIS medicine, marijuana. You can't overdose on marijuana.

So, you see, I just chalked my lack of emotions to, *"I must have already released and processed him dying... Out of sight, out of mind"* (being a Mother of Loss in a closed adoption, I am a pro at this one). I was away from all the family planning, which was a very good thing. I was a big enough bitch on my own Facebook page. But folks, that is as bad as I got. I carried on happily and joyfully, enjoying every day to the fullest with no tears as if my daddy was free.

People were hearing of my loss slowly, and, for example, Jessie (the girl in the booth on my right), who is very gifted and can even read minds, came up and said, *"Oh my gosh, you are handling this so well. I am so sorry. My condolences. I had no idea... you have carried yourself so beautifully."*

I explained, *"I already processed his death the first time it almost happened. You just can't recreate that, genuinely."*

My job requires that I sit in my "office" (an open booth as you would see at a fair or rodeo). It is located right where the tourist buses unload and it's a common event for Asians to take pictures with me. I love pictures, and they must sense our commonality. Not only do I jump in to take a pic of them, but my booth is also right where they first enter the harbor, so many take their first pictures right at my office. Kanyon teasingly said, "*Watch, you will go visit Korea one day and find your picture in their books and on their walls.*" And with our laughter, I added what a beautiful sweet 20ish Korean girl yelled to me as she walked away, "*Your heart rocks!*" I have the best office location at slip **#8**.

The number **8** has been a magical number for me since we got here. First, I bought a car with the license plate, MMT **188**. We named her Magical Moments, Magi for short. My first day on the job was the day of my Daddy Randy's funeral, **8-8**-2012, in slip **#8**.

Today, I was excited to work towards some rent money, Sunday being the biggest day for booking.

I have enjoyed my days interacting with the people. I am meeting more and more locals. The first person to pay me a visit this morning was Tim. Tim is an author who teaches while he writes. Tim had approached me yesterday, putting on an act of being a successful author/lawyer/actor, asking about making a private booking on our sailboat, The Island Star. This was a total blessing in disguise. I hadn't been trained yet on all the details of booking private parties. But come to find out, he was using it as an excuse to invite me to Mr. Longhi's celebration of life party.

Mr. Longhi is a celebrity-like fellow that owns restaurants on the island, and this Tim fellow asked me to attend the celebration with him. I declined and said, "*I don't go anywhere without my boys.*"

He said, "*Well, bring them along.*" Still politely declining, he then said, "*Owen Wilson most likely will be there.*" Well, that didn't change my mind. So, when I never showed up for the party, he decided to come by this morning to ask what happened, informing me that I missed out on a great time. "*Owen didn't show up, but Mick Fleetwood gave everyone a show on the drums.*"

Wow, I cannot wait to be an established local. I have already barely missed Owen Wilson twice now.

As I continued my morning, greeting everyone that walked by, I saw an older gentleman hauling a tripod. I had seen a man on the pier with his easel painting and asked, "*Are you that guy that I have seen painting?*"

He doesn't hesitate to stop and have a lovely conversation with me. "*No, this is a tripod. I photograph and film the local monk seals. Here, let me give you one of my DVDs.*" Dr. Leisure (aka George) took the time to stand and chit-chat, educating me about the monk seals that are residents here in the harbor. He continued to tell me about some amazing interactions he had had with these animals. He explained the seals, knowing them personally, and shared how they recognize and know him, showing off for the camera when they see him. What a lovely man.

Well, I had a lot of interaction with customers, and I am always entertained so well by watching all the different boats pull in. My kind of reality show... Lindsey, the girl in the booth on my left, hopped out of her office and said, "*I eat so well working here. I am going to go get some fresh sushi.*" Every day, there is fresh fish fileting galore going on from around noon-2:00.

Near the end of my day, I started thinking, "*I have enjoyed my day thoroughly. I love singing out 'Aloha' and greeting everyone. But that is not going to pay the bills. I need to work on maybe getting a part-time job until whale season starts.*" I was working for a commission, and I didn't get credit if the people I greeted took my card after the spiel and called back to book. I only got credit if I booked them at the booth. I didn't book anything that day. Right when I started pondering about money, a gentleman approached my office; his father died a year ago, and his father's wish was for his family to all go to Maui and spread his ashes in the ocean in Lahaina. His father had owned a restaurant on Front Street.

I gave my condolences and offered, "*My father just died as well. His funeral was just a few days ago.*" He then shared how hard it had been, and I explained how I thought I was still in shock because I hadn't really teared up yet.

He sympathized, sharing, "*It can take a while for it to set in. It's been a year, and I still have a hard time accepting it.*"

While I was booking him a private raft for his family, he asked my name and said, "*My sister is named Keri,*" and he proceeded to spell my name correctly.

I celebrated and said, "*I was watching to see how you spelled it, and yes, that is exactly how I spell my name too.*"

I then shared, "*I didn't know they could do this, but my family arranged for a Harley Davidson Hearse with bikers to escort my father to his final burial spot.*" With that said, it was like a button was pushed. The tears started welling up, catching me by surprise. I laughed, apologizing, saying, "*I am so sorry. I don't know where that came from. So sorry. I guess I had some feelings stuffed in there after all.*"

Douglas, loving my shared emotion, beamed and said so tenderly, "*Obviously, ones that needed to be expressed.*"

We both laughed softly together, connecting on a level of sincere condolences for one another, and I thanked him for providing the safe soft energy to welcome the flow.

I was able to book something before the day was over, and with it being a private party, it was a great booking for me to help with the bills.

I couldn't help but notice the subtle yet obvious connection with this man that my Daddy Randy must have orchestrated. I have often questioned whether he even bothers coming and hanging out with me. I tell everyone to come and haunt me if they die before me. I don't think I can count this as a haunting, but I cannot deny my father's presence on some level. And on the way home, Kanyon saw someone had carved "RANDY" on the rock wall along the road. I knew Grandpa Randy sent that gentleman to me to trigger some tears that he most likely had been waiting for me to acknowledge from the other side. And he gifted me a great booking for my commission.

After talking to Kanyon and acknowledging all the eights in the space, I pulled out my Doreen Virtue *Angel Numbers 101* book.

First, I looked up my new house number, 209. "*You've been praying about your Divine life purpose, and the answer is: Walk confidently in faith, in the direction of your intuition and spiritual passions. Trust that you are fully supported upon this path*". WOW

Then I looked up my car license plate number, 1**88**. "*Well done! All of your meditating and visualizing have opened the floodgates to increased financial flow*". DOUBLE WOW

I looked up **8** in the number book. "*The number eight signifies abundance and prosperity. The endless loops in this number signify an infinite flow* *of money, time, ideas, or whatever else you require (especially for your life purpose)."* Do I even have to say it? WOW, WOW, WOW.

Being on a roll, reading the Universe, I proceeded to look up cats. Three outdoor stray cats came with the house. I have never been much of a cat person. I LOVE dogs. But as Lenny, the landlord had said, *"Those cats earn their keep. You have no rats."*

I got my *Animal Speaks* book by Ted Andrews. Cats... *"Mystery, Magic, and Independence."*

Well, it doesn't get better than that! Especially when you realize what we named our car... Magical Moments.

Spiders in the Space

Did I mention the spiders that were EVERYWHERE? I guess July-August is the time for spiders. All the spiders that we had encounters with were harmless garden spiders. I still did not like them any better. It was interesting watching the boys capture the spiders and observe them for short periods.

The worst spider encounter we had was at Jim's place in the jungle in Nahiku. The bathroom was an outhouse out in the jungle. You know, an outhouse with open windows and curtains instead of the coffin boxed-in type we Utahns are used to. I could no longer hold my urine. I trotted on back to the outhouse, opened the curtain, and startled a cane spider, which STARTLED me. I calmly analyzed the situation. I knew where this spider was... *it had flopped like an octopus (loudly) to the back corner of the small quarters housing the toilet.* But I didn't know where the huge spiders that *are* as big as my hand were hiding. I calmly and quickly slid inside, pulled the curtain shut, swooped my pants down, and peed as fast as I could. I swiftly finished up and got out of there without ever taking my eye off the monstrous creature.

Spiders (a few translations from the *Animal Speak* book): the weaver of illusion. To the Native Americans, the spider is the grandmother, the link to the past and the future. Grandmother Spider kept and taught the mysteries of the past and how they affected the future. Spider teaches you that everything you do now is weaving what you will encounter in the future. Spiders remind us that the world is woven around us. We are the keepers and the writers of our own destiny, weaving it like a web with our thoughts, feelings, and actions. Spider has long been associated with death and rebirth. Part of this may have to do with the fact that some female spiders will kill and eat the male spider after mating. Because it is constantly building and weaving new webs, it has also been a lunar symbol with ties to the waxing and waning of the moon. The spider can teach us how to use written language with power and creativity so that your words weave a web around those who read them.

Tyler Moves Out

Shortly after we arrived to Maui and moved in, Tyler's girlfriend from the mainland came for a visit. We were just getting our feet on the ground... surviving. I didn't think it was a good time to host a girlfriend from the mainland who was coming for a vacation.

Tyler was the first to get a job. He was an excellent example to James and I. Tyler rode the bus to interviews all over the island. He even went to Lahaina to look for jobs, and arrived back home to let us know he could see us working there and that we should go check it out.

Tyler accepted a job at Costco in Kahului and had a few weeks free before he had to attend training. He flew his girlfriend out, and that visit was the beginning of the end of Tyler on Maui.

To sum it up in a nutshell, I felt Tyler lost focus of the, *"We are in this together. We are one"* concept. Instead of the four of us hanging and getting to know our new home, it was the three of us. While the two of them raced around like tourists, spending money like tourists, we were living within our means... eating as frugally as possible, living off green smoothies, and fresh salsa and chips.

Tyler also started to allow fear into his space. He started worrying about the choices I was making. I knew we needed a car. Tyler said we could get by with the buses. I had just left a husband that always had the final say because of his talent for making money. I had to be strong with my truth and trust my choices... even if it meant buying a car. I felt Tyler was not ready to throw in his all and surrender to the journey.

The final straw that sent Tyler flying back to Utah???... him and Kanyon got into a very heated argument... and Tyler is no wrestler... so glad I wasn't home for it.

Tyler called his mom and got a ticket home the night before his girlfriend was heading back to Utah. It's almost as if it were subconsciously planned.

Kandi Moves In

I don't recall the date Tyler left, but he was gone by the time Kandi moved in. Kandi is Scott's sister, the children's aunt. Kandi has three little ones, (Sativa (5), Bubba (4), Christian (1)) and is raising them by herself. Kandi is a strong woman who was taught well in many ways by her mother. By the time Scott's mother was parenting Kandi, she was a much different mother than when she had parented Scott. After getting to know Kandi, I was able to appreciate their mother, Lorna, on a whole new level. I loved hearing about the children's grandmother in a whole new light.

Ever since Kandi has had kids, I have had Kandi and the kids over. In fact, Kandi lived with us for a short while before and after she gave birth to her first child, Sativa. I watched my baby niece many times from the beginning.

After the last time I held my first-born baby in my arms, I became very selective about which babies I would hold. It was a strange taboo I felt with new babies... a fear, a reservation only for special ones that I allowed to fill the space, very aware that no baby could really fill the void. The only babies I allowed into that intimate space with me were Tyler, Kanyon, Kylie, Liah, Jeremy, Sativa, and Christian.

I didn't know Kandi that well when she was young. When I married Scott, she was six. Their mother, Lorna, and Kandi's father divorced when Kandi was one and she was at her Tongan father's house a lot of the time. I really didn't get to know Kandi until we lived in Texas. We instantly had a connection and were able to relate on many levels. She and I both have children from a man we love. Men that could not get over their addictions and face their inner child wounds while they were with us.

Rewind to Texas 2005... Scott had gotten that offer we couldn't refuse. When Scott first called his mother to tell her that we were moving to Houston, she informed him that Kandi had just gotten a job transfer to the same area. Even though they were both out there, they lived kind of far away from one another (Houston is huge). Hurricane Rita hit, and once the evacuation notice was sent out, it was a huge blessing that Kandi had Scott there. After waiting to sell our home in Utah, the children and I joined Scott in Texas, and Kandi became a huge part of my life. I had always been blessed with Scott making good money, which allowed me to be a stay-at-home mom for most of my children's lives. From the beginning of our marriage, starting with Scott's younger sisters, I nurtured and loved whoever needed it, inviting everyone to my home. Kandi was **23**, a certified welder living on her own making big bucks, AND in love with a certified welding inspector guy.

Kandi became a single mother of three over the years, and I have loved getting to know each of her children very well. I also LOVE that Kandi was one of the few to have witnessed the reunion with our son, her nephew, who is four years younger than her. You know they would have been more like siblings if things had been different.

When things started getting bad with Scott, I told Kandi, *"No matter what, I will always be here for you. Even though I am leaving your brother, you are always welcome at my house, even in Maui."*

Around the same time, I was making plans to separate from Scott, Kandi decided she wanted to live near her babies' daddy to have him help her parent their three children. I had only been in Maui for a few weeks when she called me in tears, asking if my invitation was sincere. The babies' daddy had some addictions. So sad, it happens to the best of 'em.

Kandi sold her car to get the plane tickets she needed to get to Maui for her and the kids. We were running out of money, but James got a job at Ululani's Hawaiian Shave Ice (notorious for being number one worldwide), and I got a job working at the harbor for Hawaii Ocean Rafting. My job was commission only, but I had the roof over our heads, a car to get us around, and food stamps.

Kandi was very resourceful in getting assistance from the state. But they lost her paperwork like three times, and getting that assistance took a little too long. I was using all my money to float for the four of us. When Tyler went home, Kandi called, saying, *"Are you sure? I have no money and am bringing four mouths to feed,"* it only seemed right to chant, *"Together we're stronger."*

It was great having Kandi and the kids in Maui. They brought a huge sense of HOME to our home. It was so good to have more family there. Children are always great vibration boosters, and that was exactly what we needed.

Plus, Kandi's amazing skills... She spread our healthy menu even further. And boy, did Kandi have an eye for fruit. I had heard people say, *"You'd have to be stupid to starve on Maui."* Well, I would have been one of those stupid ones and would have starved without Kandi. Kandi had an eye for fruit on trees, just like a zoologist could spot horned goats on a rocky mountainside. Kandi opened my eyes towards the sky, bringing my awareness to just how plentiful the fruit is on this island.

Dawn Arrives to Maui

It wasn't long before Dawn was in Maui, making sure her sisters were getting settled. It was great to have her arrive so soon after Kandi.

Dawn played such an important role for both of us. She provided a temporary home, assisted us with her great computer skills, and found us the best deals on flights. Dawn was quite the traveler herself and was a pro when it came to planning for a trip. Having Dawn was like having a personal travel agent/assistant, seeing us off to our destination that she believed to be the path. It only made complete sense that she would be the first to visit our new home of Maui.

Cousin Kimber Arrives to Maui

My cousin, Kimber, arrived at the tail end of Dawn's stay. It felt so good to have an abundance of family around. My dear cousin was originally going to come to Maui with her new husband, but there was a change of plans, so her friend joined her for her honeymoon trip instead. Kimber and her friend got into quite a feud and parted ways before the honeymoon stay had ended. I was grateful for their parting ways. Kimber's friend kept my cousin too busy to see me, lol.

One thing I have noticed about Maui... it amplifies what you hold in your heart. I have seen the energy of *"Maui will receive you or repel you."* There is no fooling "Mother Maui." It has been interesting to witness it at play.

I was so grateful for Maui's magnifying magic on my cousin's true inner self. I was on the receiving end of her generosity. My cousin's arrival could not have been at a better time. Dawn and Keith were leaving, and my nest egg of funds from selling my Mustang was depleted. Money was tight, and food stamps were almost gone because Kandi's benefits hadn't kicked in yet. I was worried about getting some laundry, soap and food, when along came my unannounced cousin, whose vacation had turned into a disastrous vacation for her, but a blessing and gift to us. God bless my cousin... she took us grocery shopping and even cooked eggs benedict for us in the morning. My dear cousin Kimber... a master at packing tons in small spaces, which totally reflects the love she emulates from her own small packaging.

September 2012

A Text from Kai

KAI: (*translated from Spanish*) You treat me so cruelly. I love you as a mother, but you never accepted me as a child, no matter how I behaved with you. You always reject me and my love, and now, you even reject your granddaughter! How horrible it is to treat her the way you do! You're lying when you say you love me. I wish I had died at birth to make your life easier.

Maybe then I would be remembered with affection instead of hatred. If you kill me today, it does not matter because I'm dead to your mind and in your heart.

Rather than having someone who treats me with such hatred and cruelty, to only have love to give to everyone else. You can be a mother to all but your firstborn. That I might have even the tiniest part of your love. But no, you kill me with your words, as they are knives that cut me, burn me, kill me. And I'm dead, and you're not to mourn for me.

Learn if you do not understand, woman. Spanish is a language of love, maybe one day you'll hear it.

KERI: First of all, everything is a reflection... a mirroring of what is wrong with our own behavior.

You say, I never accepted you as a child, no matter how you behaved with me. I always rejected you and your love." Well, yes, now that you complain about it. Yes, that is how I feel your behavior has been. Crazy that when I start acting like you have role modeled our relation to be, you get all upset about the mirrored behavior.

You say I'm lying when I say I love you, and you wish you had died at birth to make my life easier. Wow, yes, I have felt like you lie when you say you love me, and actually, to me, it was as if you had died at birth, and it did not make my life easier, that is for sure. But as a reflected statement, you are saying you wish you had died at birth to make your life easier.

I'm sorry to hear that adoption has made your life difficult. I also have grown to realize that adoption is so wrong. If you can't keep your baby, then yes, abortion is better than adoption. Not that I would have chosen abortion. I would have "chosen" to keep my child.

People say to me all the time, "*But you chose it,*" and yes, I did, didn't I? I had looked toward the adults in my life, trusting in their "expertise." I didn't feel like there was a choice. It had felt as if adoption was the only option. The only way I would have avoided the placement was if I had been acknowledged as a mother and given the confidence that I could do it. OR how about this... what if... What if adoption was not an option? What if adoption was just for the dogs? What if everyone had the mentality to Love One Another and '*Adopt*' the Mother? Utilize the village you live in to help raise this child and all children, no matter how young or old the mother is? Obviously, I chose adoption so that I could learn such a mentality and teach it to others.

Honestly, looking back, knowing who I am, who I was... I know I would have been a great mother at sixteen. My heck, I have been babysitting since I was twelve. If only I had realized *Little House on the Prairie* was a show reflecting true history. Girls were married shortly after they came into their womanhood (when they started their periods) and became mothers and wives at a very young age.

Maybe teenagers aren't the model parents that people are striving for or judging to be. But I, for one, have met a lot of amazing adults that are products of a teen mother. Sure, they have had a rough road, but with the help of a village, and by traveling the road they have traveled, they have evolved into such strong, amazing adults.

Sure, the upbringing of some of those amazing adults may have been what others would judge as unconventional, but it has made them who they are. And most importantly, they KNOW who they are and are solid with who they are, with quite the wisdom to go along with it. Granted, they all had some sort of village, or a mentor involved with their upbringing, AND they all love their mothers no matter the conditions or dysfunction. That testifies to me the importance of reaching out and helping mothers in need for the highest good of children everywhere. Because to not accept and love one's biological parents/heritage/culture is to not accept and love a huge part of them.

Bottom line, God sent this precious gift to the woman as a baby in her womb. I have met plenty of young mothers that were sent an unplanned gift from God, and that gift changed their lives for the better, my sister Tabi being one of them. Having a baby *changes* you, even when you don't keep it.

Sweet Messengers in Maui
BLOG POST

I haven't written for a while. I had the most amazing few days! It started on Sunday, September 2nd. I work Sundays, they are better days for selling. Plus, this Sunday I liked the distraction from my personal life. I walked to the bus stop, and standing there, already waiting for the bus, was a woman with a bag of snorkel gear. Always on the lookout for someone I can turn to the "best time on Maui" (i.e. rafting with the DOLPHINS), I asked if she was visiting and started a conversation with Annette.

Annette was here from Germany, vacationing solo. I admired how independent this twenty-nine-year-old married woman was, vacationing SOLO. Our conversation flowed so beautifully that by the time Annette was to get off at Maalaea, she decided to continue with me to Lahaina, where I sell raft rides.

Here's the spiel: "*We cruise the rugged coastline, stopping frequently at our favorite snorkel sights. Many dolphins live around Lanai, cruising the coastline. We are frequently surrounded by spinner dolphins riding our bow or just playing around our boat.*"

I continued, telling her that the dolphins are protected, so we were not allowed to jump in the water if we saw them. If we are already in the water and the dolphins choose to swim with the humans, then that is a very nice bonus indeed. Although the whole two months I have worked here, it hasn't happened. It happens, but it is not a common occurrence. And with that said, I suggested that she summon the dolphins telepathically when she is on her way to the harbor to create the experience she desires.

I booked Annette for a trip and looked forward to seeing her upon her return to hear about her experience.

Monday around noon, the boat and guests drifted back into the harbor, and I asked, "*How was the trip?*"

The first guest to come off the boat said, "*We swam with the dolphins!*"

Wow! I could not wait to speak to Annette!

Annette made her way off the raft, and I exclaimed, "*You powerful woman you! You summoned the dolphins to come swim with the humans!*" We hugged, and she shared how amazing it was. We exchanged info... gotta love Facebook. We are going to be forever friends. Before we said our goodbyes, she asked if there was any way I would be able to take tomorrow off. She lucked out with her rental car. She had reserved an economy car for $30 a day, but they were out of economy cars. The only car they had left was a brand-new white Camaro, and she was looking forward to driving around to check out more of the island. I sadly declined because I had to be responsible since I had a job now. We hugged goodbye, and she set off to get a hamburger before she rode the bus back to where she was staying.

Two hours later work was incredibly slow, so I decided to check out and head home. I was standing in line for the bus when I heard a familiar sweet "*Hello.*" It was Annette! She had just finished her hamburger and was heading back to the hostel where she was staying. We agreed to check out each other's places and for her to meet the fam.

I got home and sensed my son's need to speak with me about his day, so I shortened the visit with Annette. After briefly meeting my son, she gave me the most beautiful message... words that I needed to hear. Obviously, she was sensitive and in touch with her gift. What a blessing to run into her. Annette and I headed over to her hostel. Hostels are a great way to travel. They're homey and cheap. The rooms have bunk beds, basically, you rent a bunk, and there is a communal kitchen and living room. We took pictures with the beautiful white Camaro and said our goodbyes.

I arrived home the second time and listened to my son's upset about what that other son of mine's opinion was about me, him, us, etc. I shared with Kanyon what that amazing new friend of mine shared with me. Hearing her crucial message to focus on the heart chakra helped him as much as it had helped me.

Shortly thereafter, our buddy Jim showed up to say Hi. He was thinking of hitching back home to Hana. I told him about my new friend Annette with her new Camaro, who wanted to go for a drive somewhere and see more of the island. The boys got excited, and after walking down to the hostel to holler up to Annette, they planned to meet up the following morning.

The next morning, instead of taking the road to Hana, they decided to take the Camaro up to the crater and longboard down. I loved it. My new friend from Germany was taking my boys on a field trip and sharing a beautiful ride with them. Boys love nice cars, and that Camaro was a pretty one.

Well, needless to say, my boy went into a *"speed tuck going 20 miles per hour to take a hairpin curve."* He survived and has received a lot of attention, and... it makes for a GREAT story.

I loved hearing the boys tell the story of their day with my new friend and her cute German accent. Evidently, Annette dropped the camera and did not catch Kanyon biting it. It is funny hearing them explain how she freaked out like all of us women tend to do upon seeing an accident about to happen.

Before flying out of Maui to head back to Germany, Annette stopped by to say one last goodbye. She once again gave me a very powerful message that Kanyon and I both needed to hear. It was spooky-crazy how comfortable I felt with someone I had just met who had come from so far away. It was sad to see her go. And alarmingly, every time I think of her, I am filled with so much emotion. Who knows what our connection was, in the whole picture of all-knowing? Whatever it was, it had a strong pull.

Every day on Maui is an amazing one. I love all the people I meet. Whether they are visiting or residents, everyone here in Maui takes such great care of me and my family. Every day is magical with the Universe, Source, Spirit, God, etc., sending messengers at such divine moments.

Just a little more detail to the story with Annette... She was here vacationing solo with the intention of healing. Annette was having fertility problems. Her desire to swim with the dolphins was a desire to have a chance to heal. I loved how she explained to me how she could feel the dolphin's sonar on her body. Annette messaged me on Facebook a few months after her visit to report she was pregnant.

What Did We Do in September?

A whole lot of nothing happened in September with all day to do it. While living in Maui, I loved having Kandi and the kids around on my days off. To see Kandi in her jungle element, spotting all the desirable fruits that this mainland haole is oblivious to, was a joy to embrace.

Jim and Darrin were always swinging by, gifting us samples from ALL their garden harvests. Together, we explored many beaches and hikes. But best of all, we relished just hanging together as a family unit.

October 2012

Homeless in Olowalu

The month started with Kanyon's birthday. We spent the day at the beach with Kanyon catching waves on a boogie board and little Bubba running around on the shore. I loved how close little Bubba and Kanyon were. Kanyon wanted everyone to look their best for his birthday, dining at Da Kitchen. We ended the fabulous day with Kanyon and his birthday cheesecake.

Not long after, money ran out. Interestingly and oddly enough, I was $123.45 short of October's rent. My landlord jumped at the opportunity to evict us from the house. He had been complaining that my company (Kandi and the kids) had overstayed their welcome.

It was a lifesaver having Kandi, especially during that time. I was seriously in shock, thinking, *"No, my mother has been a landlady for many years, and this would never fly. No judge will execute two single mothers with only $123.45 short of rent and kick them out on the street."*

Well, Lenny McClusky must know people in high places because he did just that.

We found a place in Lahaina, but it would not be available until October 24th. We tried to work it out with the landlord, but he wanted us out ASAP (he had other tenants move in the very next day). Lenny McClusky got a piece of paper called an execution, which gives the landlord permission to have a sheriff or constable move you out and put your things in storage. Forcing us to leave within 24 hours, or the cops would come.

Kandi took charge (her benefits had kicked in after they finally found her paperwork). She found Lenny McClusky's old tent from the 70s in the attic, bought a tent from Walmart, and directed us to a storage unit.

Thank God for my job. I wasn't making any money (truly *"volunteering for the dolphins"*), but one of my first dearest friends on Maui was Jessie, who worked in slip 9. Jessie lived at Olowalu. Olowalu is a neighborhood of tents on the beach. I knew exactly where to go and already had a sistah there.

Now looking back, Olowalu wasn't all that bad. I'm just a little spoiled and have always hated tenting. It is very dirty, you cannot escape the weather, there are lots of bugs, and the bathrooms are not the best. I already have trouble in the kitchen when there is a kitchen, and the worst part of all, the sun bakes you in the tent, not allowing any sleeping-in to make the day end faster.

Kandi and the boys loved it. Kids always make the best of things. I personally think little Christian was enjoying this campout about as much as I was... NOT!

Thank God Lahaina had a free outdoor swimming pool to hang at. Anytime we could leave the dirt, we did. I made sure of it. I took the week off to be homeless and watched the kids with Kanyon while Kandi and James continued to go to work.

Infested Home

I survived tenting it, folks! Kandi set the alarm for 6:30 am the morning our new house became available, and announced, *"It's time to get Keri and the kids the f*** out of here."* It was a very joyous moment. Until we were greeted by the rat and cockroach infestation. After auntie Keri had a bit of a breakdown, little Bubba was comforting saying on a happy note, *"Well, at least we aren't living in the dirt no more."*

I looked at him and smiled at his beautiful face, and agreed, *"Kid, you are absolutely correct. We are moving on up."* God bless Kandi for sharing her little ones with me. Children are gifts straight from Heaven.

It was a good thing we were houseless in Olowalu for a week so I could appreciate having a roof over my head and the luxuries of having a warm shower and a kitchen at my fingertips. I would have focused too much on the infestation of cockroaches, mice, and termites had I not been so extremely grateful for those things. I had enough appreciation in me that it fueled me just enough, with the help of Kandi, to fight the worst infestation, and clean up the house.

> *Beetle/Cockroach* (I couldn't find "cockroach," so I looked up beetle instead): As with many insects, the beetle goes through a tremendous metamorphosis from the grub stage to the winged. Because of this, it is associated with resurrection and change. In its winged stage, the front set of wings is thickened into hard covers which fold and protect the soft underside. For those with this totem, it may indicate a need to be more protective or possibly that you are too closed off. If the beetle has shown up in your life, examine the need for metamorphosis. Are you in the process? If so, what stage? Do you need a change? Are you needing new sunshine? Is it time to resurrect some aspect of your life? Is it time to leave the past behind? The beetle can show you how to do this with the greatest success.

Did I mention that my boss owns the old Baywatch boat, the "Scarab?" That yellow speed boat they used for the show.

Scarab: a large dung beetle of the eastern Mediterranean area, regarded as sacred in ancient Egypt.

Centipede: Balance, coordination, ability to survive stress, beauty of movement, psychic movement, connecting with spirit, psychic protection. May suggest that you are letting your fears and doubts hinder you from making progress and achieving your goals.

Termite: End of a phase for you. Termite teaches us how fast we need to complete a job and the dedication we must show in order to do that work. They show us how fast and quickly we must complete a task and they guide us on how to work in a group. Even though they have negative totems due to their destructive behavior, the way they perform will seem impressive and exhausting. They all work together as a team and enjoy their victory. The nesting behavior of termites gives us the wish to build a house for ourselves and our family with immense hard work and strong potential. Stay away from people with negative thoughts. They will destroy you and make you empty-minded.

Gecko: Subtlety of perception. Gecko is one of the reptiles that have a voice. They can stimulate lucid dreaming. Are you being too sensitive or not sensitive enough? Are you being too picky, or are you missing the obvious? It can also reflect that the kundalini or life force is active and flowing strongly, which will heighten all sensitivities – physical, emotional, mental, psychic, and spiritual. The lizard helps us awaken our ability of objective detachment so that detaching can occur with the least amount of difficulty. Lizards can show up to help us break from the past.

Mouse: When the mouse shows up, it is either time to pay attention to details or an indication that you cannot see the forest for the trees. You may be getting so locked into details that you forget the big picture.

Boy is that the truth! I kept saying, *"I cannot see the light at the end of this tunnel."*

By the time Halloween arrived, I was totally ghouled out. I screamed solid for almost a week, startled by huge cockroaches or mice. We walked down Front Street, went trick or treating in our neighborhood with the kids, singing loudly together, "*Trick or Treat!*" and working on our thank you manners and wishing everyone a "*Happy Halloween*" like good little witches. I enjoy children so much. They make life silly again. I enjoy being silly.

November 2012

Facebook Messages with Kai

Kai bombarded me with text and Facebook messages filled with his findings of marijuana facts, reporting the horrible things about the medicine. Finally, I sent him the following:

November 4

KERI: Enough! I am sick of arguing with you. I am glad you were rescued from such a horrible person as myself. Have that perfect life that you have expected to find since your birth to the likes of me. I'm so happy to be able to say for once in my life, "It doesn't matter that he isn't mine, doesn't matter that he is who he is, none of it really matters anymore." Because right now, today, in the Now, it doesn't matter that you reject me the way you do. No matter who I became for you, it ultimately would never be enough because we HAVE lost everything that could ever be. It IS what it is, and I am finally fine with having an estranged son because I have a son and daughter that love everything about me and think I am the greatest. Not to mention all my nieces and nephews that have loved having Aunt Keri, who has been, and always will be, there for them unconditionally. I have a 5-year-old, a 4-year-old, and a 15-month-old that adore and love me as much as I do them (that I get to see every day) So it really does not matter to me or sadden me that that estranged son of mine and that daughter of his that has my face that he gets to look at every day reminding him that she has an amazing grandmother that most likely she will never meet because I won't overindulge on ice-cream and drink the Kool-Aid.

By now, I had made some kind of pact with the Universe, if you will. I was so confused by my pull to smother Kai with the strong mother instinct that I could not balance with him. Gray is so hard for me... it's either black or white, off or on. It became so confusing for me to know when to reach out and say hi and when to chill and wait for him to reach out. I had decided to only reach out when I felt there were obvious signs from the Universe to reach out and say hello.

November 16

KERI: hmmm... I have no idea how to play my cards with you. I accept that it is what it is... I finally am at peace that it is what it is, or so I thought. So why do things keep happening such as... I'm on a bike ride with Kanyon, and he's on his longboard. We travel up this concrete bridge, and he stops somewhere in the middle of the bridge to wait for traffic to clear so he can do some major carving and get some speed down the hill. We wait until there's a break in traffic, and I look down at the handlebars to go, and no joke, your name is carved in the concrete as big as my fist right next to my hand.

To you, it may seem like nothing. After all, I do live in Maui, and Kai means ocean, and I work at the harbor, but others don't run into that name as much as I tend to.

So, when such a thing happens, as it did last night on the bike, I feel I must reach out to you, no matter what my insecurities are about you or how silly you think I am.

So here I am, reaching out as if today is a new day and all the yesterdays never happened.

I look forward to the day when you feel that I am someone you can trust to share your worries and your success with, someone that you desire to be close to, someone whom you want to be around. Until then, know that I am here, and know that I have a pile of mail that is going unsent until I receive a mailing address. I pray for your success and well-being daily/nightly. I love you and think of you always, even when I am unhappy about the situation. I'm just thankful we both speak English, we are both living to have the opportunity to know one another, and we have met.

I'm always here for you.
Love, your mother

November 20

KERI: Had a busy day. I got a lot of things done and enjoyed every minute of it. In fact, it is 1:30a.m. here, and I am barely going to bed. I have been painting the house. I love painting; adding color makes such a difference! The place is looking so much better every day. So glad I have Kandi with me for this journey... together we are stronger.

There is no way I could have cleaned up this place and dealt with the infestation without another woman to help fight the battle.

Today, Kanyon and I were picking up Sativa from school when suddenly, a kid dashed in front of us, and his parent yelled, *"Kai!"*

I looked at Kanyon and said, *"Did you hear that?"*

Kanyon chuckled and acknowledged that he did.

It gets me thinking.... Maybe the whole Kai haunts are reminders/promises that you will be a huge part of my life one day? Who knows what the attraction/Universal message, whatever the heck it may be, is, but it definitely comes in stronger when I try to just forget about you.

Anyway, enjoy the snow. I am enjoying the sun. Have a great day feasting with loved ones. I don't plan on writing unless I get blasted with your name again. I am just taking it as a Universal message to say hello... so, hello... and with that, goodbye. Always lots of love

November 20

KAI: Just happened to check Facebook... thanks for the messages. They were very kind and tender. I am also very grateful that we have been able to meet and have a part in one another's lives.

Mother's Update Letter from Utah

Dear Keri, I am just following up to make sure you got my text regarding Kylie. She is now back with Scott. He says she was lying-blah blah blah, responding to being disciplined. He claims he is still working from 4:30am-1:30pm and cannot get Kylie out of bed any sooner. I can forward all his texts to you if you want - I was up till midnight discussing this. He won't send Kylie to Hawaii because of your pot usage. He claims he won't send money because it will go to drugs. He claims Kylie gets everything she wants and can Skype you every evening. Basically, I told him to go to family counseling, that Kylie is depressed and misses her mother! I also quoted Dr. Phil that a daughter needs her mother, and a son needs his father more at this time in their lives. I reminded him that even though he was *"not responsible for you"* (his words, not mine) anymore, he has two children that he needs to co-parent with you. I kept telling him to call you and open a line of communication.

Nothing short of you coming back to Utah and getting custody legally or physically of Kylie will get her to Hawaii. Scott is talking about sending you $1000 a month, $700 for 1/3 of rent and utilities, and $300 for Kanyon's clothes and essentials.

I hope you two can come to terms with your divorce and civilly co-parent your children. May God be with you. Love Mom

p.s. he just texted and said he's shipping all your stuff to you. I told him to call you.

(Reality check... Scott is addicted to heroin. I haven't received any financial support from him.)

Thanksgiving and Kylie's Arrival

For Thanksgiving Day, we invited some guests over to make for a bigger family crowd. The meal turned out alright. My most favorite part... Christian learning how to jump and playing Farkle with Sativa and Bubba. Kids make the holidays! Again, I am so thankful to have Kandi and the kids in the space.

Things were getting unsafe for Kylie back in Utah. She had moved out of my sister's house and moved in with her father. Scott was doing heroin more and more. Julie had also moved in, and according to Kylie, was also doing heroin. Kylie was starting to not be happy. The final straw was when Scott took Kylie on a drug run with him... totally not cool.

I begged and pleaded for my family to help me get my daughter to Maui, and no one would budge. Scott was threatening kidnapping charges if anyone got involved. Kandi was the first to step up, also feeling the need for her niece to be here. Kandi called her brother and convinced him to lend her money to let her purchase a one-way ticket to Maui for Kylie because that was all she could afford. When Scott "got paid," he could buy her return ticket to Utah.

Kylie was worried Scott would not get her on the plane on time. Scott had promised, then pretended that he got Kylie a phone she could have for traveling. It was the day before takeoff, and Scott was not coming through with any of his promises. Kylie claimed her dad was acting very strange, unpacking her clothes, hiding her birth certificate, and he was high on heroin most of the time. Kylie suggested I call my niece Hilary (a young confident, extremely loving mother herself), who did not fear Scott and his tactics and is genuinely great at "kill you with kindness." Hilary immediately agreed to pick Kylie up the eve before her departure.

When Scott got home later that night and found Kylie gone, he went a little crazy, but Hilary calmed him down, promising Scott that she was just the backup plan. If he arrives before 9:00a.m, Kylie will be ready so he can take her to the airport. But if he isn't at her house by nine, then she will take Kylie to the airport. Hilary was the hugest help and support. She used her own money to get my daughter a phone for travel, making sure she had $40.00 for food on the plane.

When Scott never showed up in the morning, the airlines had to delay Kylie's departure once they realized Kylie was a minor. Hilary even paid the extra $100.00 it cost to rearrange her flight and have an escort to take her through the airport and make sure she got on the flight.

Hilary called me immediately to inform me of the situation. Hilary had to be at her daughter's performance at noon, so we had to find another escort for Kylie. Kandi and I called all the aunts. Between Scott and Kandi's sister, Eva and her daughter Alice, someone would be there within the hour.

Shortly thereafter (like, 10:00ish), I got a hold of Scott and was able to inform him about the situation and suggested he take this opportunity to be his daughter's escort. Scott headed to the airport straight away. I was very glad when Scott arrived to sit with Kylie until her take-off. A girl needs her daddy's love.

I could not wait to see Kylie. It had been four months since I had hugged my baby girl. I waited anxiously at the gate for Kylie to arrive. I hardly recognized my growing teen. She looked so grown up. Kylie landed in Maui on November 29, 2012, the same day our Stoney dog was born.

December 2012

Casper, Wyoming Makes the Maui News

A little inside information... Kai was attending college in Casper, Wyoming when our reunion took place. I had been to the little town multiple times while he was in attendance there, with the majority of our visits being at the college itself. I became very familiar with the theater department as he was an aspiring actor. On a few occasions, I joined him in his other classes. I had even gone with him to his science classroom to study the names of all the little parts in these physical bodies of ours that he had to learn. I enjoyed sharing the methods I like to use when I study and need to remember things for tests. He seemed genuinely interested in my silly ways, and they did help him remember the few things that were not sticking. Anyway, with this groundbreaking news in the space, how could I not reach out and write to that boy of mine who was attending Casper College? Oh, and by the way, it soon became a regular morning ritual for Sharyn, the Reef Dancer booth babe, to bring me the morning paper from that day forward.

December 2

KERI: Oh, alright... I will write. So yesterday, Sharyn (from the harbor) brought me the Maui News. The Maui News consists of like seven pages, including the sports section. Sharyn doesn't bring me the paper regularly but was inspired to ask if I would like some reading material? It had been extremely slow at the dock, and I was thankful for the reading material. The front page caught my attention with a tiger shark attack on a tourist paddle boarding. That story took me to page A4. On A5, there happened to be a story about Casper College in Wyoming. Some crazy person stabbed someone in a nearby neighborhood, then went to the science building and stabbed the professor in front of the class, and then continued to take his own life for class that day. Wow... quite a story, but how strange that a story from Wyoming/Casper College would make it to the Maui News, being a newspaper of little news. WEIRD... but whatever.

The fam picked me up after work, and we headed straight to the grocery store. Leaving the store, Kanyon grabbed hold of that same Maui newspaper that had made it into my hands. I asked Kanyon, *"Interesting... Why are you reaching for the paper today?"*

He said, *"Oh, I don't know. Why? What's up?"*

I calmly smiled and said, *"Oh, it's an interesting read today. That paper made it into my space as well. Check it out."*

He checked it out, and the paper took him to A4, which had him see the story on A5. *"Oh, my heck. Mom, it's time to say hello to Kai. You need to write him."*

"Yeah, I guess."

So, today I came to work. It's slow, and I'm painting my nails when Fisheye comes walking up. I haven't seen him in a while. *"How you doing Fish? What's up? What's new?"*

Fish is this old Japanese guy that hangs at the harbor, born and raised here in Lahaina. I love talking with this wise one. He sports a straw hat and little shaded eyeglasses and walks around with his wooden crutches for added support... great accessories!!! After answering, *"S.O.S. Same Old Shit,"* accompanied by his sharp Japanese laugh, he then asks me, *"How is that son of yours? Have you made contact lately?"*

Confused for a moment, thinking he must be mistaken because I see my son every day, but since I just got Kylie, I answer with my clarification, *"Oh, you must mean my daughter. Yes, she has landed, and she is here!"*

Fish promptly says, *"No, your older one, in his 20's."*

"Interesting you should ask Fish. I don't speak to him much these days."

I then got a beautiful speech from this elderly wise man with a Japanese accent saying, *"Blood is strong. It means more."*

"Interesting that you should come up and volunteer such beautiful words,

confirming my truth, but after all, we are all one, and it really doesn't matter anyway."

After a wise pause, he states, *"Yes and no, but it does matter."*

So here I am, explaining why I am writing to you to say hello. Why do I need an excuse to feel ok about contacting you? I don't know. Obviously, I feel unwanted and need justification for why I am invading your space...???

Well, for all that it is worth, I love you. I think of you always. It's impossible to permanently not. In fact, it hurts most of the time, so I use a lot of energy pretending it doesn't matter. There isn't anything I can do about it anyways.

Hope things are well. Hope things are great. Hope things are everything you wish them to be.

Kai's Birthday Month

December 4

KAI: Keri, I had a very beautiful dream about you last night. It was very sweet and tender, and I must admit that it was sooo nice spending time with you there. It was like all the past was mended, and you were healed of any and all pain the past caused you. You were just you... sweet, tender, loving, kind. There was no anger, no resentment... just you and I spending a wonderful time together.

KERI: Dreams are wonderful. Nice to hear you think of me. I wrote to you a few days ago via FB (Facebook). Dreams are predictions... sounds good. I am doing well. I love my job. I'm selling more books than trips. Too bad I only make, like, $4 a book. Bringing awareness is my passion which is how I know what my purpose is. And yes, I'm able to bring awareness without anger, and as long as I have people that heal and learn from the God-awful path I have traveled, it helps with the regrets. I will always dislike adoption and have nothing good to say about it as people do with slavery, but as with that, we have to live it to understand it, to change it, and get rid of it... the same as ending slavery. Love One Another, *'Adopt'* The Mother... helping others without having ownership and keeping mother and child together best we can. It is what it is, we are who we are... yep, I'm the same, and it's just that Hawaii gets it... it's called *hanai*.

December 23

KERI: Happy bday. I still need your zip code. I'm at a loss for words... have a good day honoring yourself on this day. Love to you.

KERI: U good? Today a monk seal has been hanging out right at my office. I'll try to get some pics with this phone for you. Not a great camera/phone, but I thought how crazy that the first time ever for me to see a monk seal was today (on your birthday) in front of my neighboring boat, Kai Akua, all morning.

KAI: *Pretty.*

KERI: Don't know about pretty, but she had a very sweet disposition. She startled everyone when she bobbed up, eying the catch for the day, showing her teeth, reminding us she is a wild thing.

KAI: Missed you last night. Sharon, Tabi, Mai, Daisy, and I stayed up late talking. They told me wonderful stories about you.

KERI: Hmmm... wonder what the stories were?

KAI: Just about when you were younger.

KERI: Oh, Chip and Dale stories, aye?

KAI: Haha, what? No, just about how sweet you always were before years of Scott crapping on you... the hostess with the mostest, and the bell of the ball.

KERI: Well, that's nice to hear that I am being remembered in a better light.

KAI: Yup. It would have been great to be able to meet you back then, before all those bad things happened to you.

KERI: Hmmm... that confuses me. I am the same as I have always been. Before all the bad things happened to me... losing my firstborn to adoption was the worst thing I have ever been through. So yep, it would have been nice to have never been apart so you could know me. I am the same person I was since my childhood.

KAI: With a lot more anger. And I really don't mind that you wanted to put me up for adoption. You don't need to act like it was this awful thing that someone else did to you. I know very well from all the sources that you were pissed about being pregnant and wanted nothing more than to get that baby out of your life. Seriously I don't judge you at all for that. I would have felt the same way if I were in that situation. So, stop with the victim thing. You chose to give me up. Oh well, life goes on, and I still love you. And I don't feel any resentment towards you for it, so quit beating yourself up over it. You have had many more hurtful things happen to you, I think.

KERI: I don't beat myself up about it. I just hate our relationship.

KAI: Keri, don't pretend like you wanted to keep me. I get enough lies from Scott. I don't need them from anyone else. Everyone else that was there told me you couldn't wait for it to be over and go back to your life. Yeah, well, let's be more honest, and maybe it would be better. You didn't want me. That's understandable. You were super young and practically a virgin, and Scott would end up treating you like a scumbag anyway, so... I wouldn't want that for myself either. If you really ever want a relationship, you are going to have to let the past go, whether it's anger towards others or whether it is guilt for giving me up.

KERI: I can't have this convo right now, especially via text. I'm at work fixin' to be on the raft in twenty.

KAI: Have fun, be safe, say hello to some whales for me, and try to forgive whoever it is you need to forgive for us to get along. 26 years for heaven's sake! It's about time to let the past go and move on. 26 years ago... stop going back there. Forgive, heal, and live for today.

KERI: 26 years ago, got us to this moment, and it gives issues to everyone involved in the situation, even if you can't see it. And, you were raised by people that don't share my same beliefs, so now you have the characteristics that I don't enjoy being around. So, I am living for today and helping mothers in need make sure they know what they're doing before they give away their child. So, when YOU can get over it, and I can enjoy your company, then talk to me.

This sounds so mean, I know. I was so sick of walking on eggshells for so many people. I was not going to sell out anymore, and I could care less what anyone else thought. I'm sick of family members judging how I handle things; I just have to be real now. I just can't pretend anymore, being nice to spare everyone's feelings. For once in my life, I am honoring my feelings. I'm the one that lost my firstborn son, not them. What do they know about what my thoughts were, what my loss is, what grief I feel on a daily basis? Who is anyone to think they know how I feel or have felt?

Monk Seal

And, of course, I read into this strong message from the Universe. But what did it mean? Firstly, let's just state the facts. The first time I saw a monk seal ever in my life was on Kai's birthday... bobbing around the back of Kai Akua's boat in slip **9**, with a kickback chill, sad puppy dog sort of demeanor. Then when the fishermen were unloading the large fish from that boat's catch, the monk seal got more alert and wild looking, swimming into my slip **8**, using my slip as her own personal area, and welcoming the snorkel trip back.

Let's go look up "Seal" in the *Animal Speak* book:

Seals: Although they will spend more time on land, the seal is more at home in the water. If a seal has shown up as a totem, it is time to do some questioning. Are you getting out of balance? Has the imaginative faculty opened so much that you are not staying grounded? Are you listening to the inner voice? Pay attention to your dreams. Much of what you are dreaming and imagining may have a strong basis in reality – no matter how far-fetched. Seals keep us grounded so that we don't get lost or caught up too strongly within the imagination. The archetypal force of the seals helps those with them as totems learn to balance the inner imagination with the outer realities – making both aspects more colorful and beneficial.

Reflecting back on this time in my life, I recall my being *"too much in the Cosmos."* Well, that is what a gifted Hawaiian healer told me. I had called her looking for healing help for me and my daughter. My daughter Kylie was not adjusting to Hawaii and us very well, and we were having a hard time with her not being on the same vibration as us. The healer lady explained that I needed to do some heavy grounding to bridge the gap between Kylie and me. She even guided me through a meditation over the phone while at work at the harbor.

Kylie and Kai are very similar. In fact, I have often been very grateful for having Kylie. She gives me a front-row view of how it would have been to raise Kai. If you become a parent, you too will realize the different relationships you have with each one of your children. It's not having favorites; it's not loving one more than the other. It's just a unique, different relationship because we are all unique individuals, and I don't think you can have an identical relationship with any two. Kylie and Kai have a lot of the same interests and personality traits. All three children are great combinations of Scott's and my gene pool. But energetically, mothering those two takes more from me. Kanyon has always been so obedient and has always been one to direct me, even at a very young age. I have been told by more than one sensitive that Kai and Kylie are Scott's karmic debt, and I was gifted Kanyon to help keep me grounded so that I can stay on the path of what I am here to do. After being told that and studying how energy cycles out and clears the old vibration and how the cosmic clocks work... it made perfect sense to me, and I could let go of the guilt I had that I did not do a better job with Kai and Kylie.

But let's go back to what this message of the monk seal coming for a visit in slip **9** under Kai's name could mean.

9: Get to work, lightworker – now! The number 9 means that you've completed all of the prerequisites to achieve your life purpose. Stop procrastinating, as it's time to start taking action steps. Even baby steps are useful.

Well, I have always imagined and dreamed that I would feel whole with all of my children close to me. I have Kylie back, but I don't have that older one. I am supposed to be grateful that he was saved from me or something... I hate the whole thinking surrounding adoption. But that dream of Kai being a member of my family, honoring his place as a son of mine, never went away when I signed my rights away in 1986. And that dream has been harder to ignore since our reunion in 2005. I have obviously been successful in raising my vibration to more of a one-love vibration, helping me to love everyone and forget about the boundaries of who to love.

Let me also fill you in on Kanyon's advice to me during this time. "*It's time. You need to be writing that fourth book, Mom.*" But I honestly did not feel I had anything positive or interesting to say. I was not completely happy with my life. I do not enjoy being broke. I was not enjoying living like a hobo away from family and friends, even though those family and friends thought I had lost my marbles.

You could take this message from the monk seal in many ways, one of them being, I need to hold faith that Kai will shed his skin and become that son I imagine him to be. I need to stay grounded. It's time to write my book.

In due time, Kai will be in my space, alert and present in the relationship mirroring the energy of the monk seal and the number **8**.

8: Abundance and prosperity. The endless loops in this number signify an infinite flow of money, time, ideas, or whatever else you require (especially for your life purpose).

I have become a firm believer in reading the Universe, like inside messages telling me which path to take or having the confirmation I need that I am on the right path. I have a lot of people, Kai and Kylie for two, that think I am crazy with my trust and ease with the Universe speaking to me. Everything is energy, and this world is a world that attracts. You know... the Law of Attraction... energy is energy, whether it is in the form of a seal or the energy I hold in my space. I challenge you all to start reading your surroundings and receiving these beautiful messages through nature and numbers. I honestly don't think I could have traveled my path as gracefully as I have without the Universe speaking directly to me. Not only is it a fun game, but it also brings peace of mind. It doesn't harm anyone, so why cut yourself off from the divine messages from this omnipresence that is at our fingertips to grasp.

Santa Sent Sapna

Things were getting hard financially. My paychecks were still pretty much nonexistent. Christmas was around the corner. Thank God I have food stamps and the money from watching Kandi's kids. It basically paid for my room and board. I had no extra money and was very grateful that my kids were old enough to handle getting nothing for Christmas.

Being one that is always in communication with God/Source, I had been praying for some kind of magical Christmas in Maui.

Auntie Dawn had planned a Christmas visit to Maui with her dear friend from London. We were sorely disappointed upon finding out about a change in plans. Dawn's father, whom she had recently met, was in his last stages of life. Dawn chose to stay by her father's bedside, but her friend from London still wanted to keep her plans of spending Christmas in Maui. We were delighted with the news and excited to meet this long-time friend of Dawn's.

I loved getting to know Sapna. We are close to the same age, and she is also from a divorced home. Both of her parents remarried and had children, giving her two younger, half-blooded bonus sisters for her to love and enjoy. Sapna totally gets one-love living and was an excellent example for us all. She was so giving and graceful, loving us so unconditionally with no judgment about our choice of medicine, even though she does not partake.

I about fell over in shock when I found out what Sapna did for a living. She is some sort of peace officer in London. She has a uniform that has a cop-like vibe. I forget what exactly she does, but she does not carry a gun. She goes in before the guns come out, talking sense into people, helping them make better choices, and then carrying on their way. I love the sounds of how London runs things... not quick to ticket, but quick to watch over and protect in a way I have always thought officers of the law should do.

Sapna was the best gift I think Santa has ever brought me. She couldn't have come at a better time. The honeymoon with Kylie was over, and it was nice to have Kylie hang out with Sapna and listen to the wisdom I have been trying to communicate to her. Daughters always hear messages better from others besides their mothers.

Sapna was helping ground our home that was picking up on chaos.

She joined our family beautifully, sharing much needed love for the holidays... reading to the little kids, sharing wisdom with the older ones, and spoiling everyone with gifts and daily shaved ice.

I loved witnessing Sapna overcome her fear of the water and the creatures that are in it. When she first arrived, I turned her on to a whale watch. It was the first of the season, and I was personally a little disappointed with such little action. I apologized that it wasn't more of a thrill. I had such high expectations, but it was one of my first whale watches as well. She then shared her fear of the water and the creatures that are in it. She reassured me that we were close enough to the whale for her. *"It was a great time! Don't apologize."* She loved it!

Sapna spoiled us for Christmas. She was concerned about Kandi, sensing the tension between her and Kylie. Sapna was continually on the lookout for how she could give service and love to every single one of us in this family unit. When Sapna was leaving, she took us out for dinner at Kimo's. After hugging her goodbye and dropping her off at the airport, she gave Kandi and me her last American dollars.

Christmas Eve Whale Watch

Sure beats Chinese food! It has been a long-time tradition for me and my family to go out for Chinese food every Christmas Eve. In Utah, wintertime can be such a hibernation time. Utahns spend a lot of their time watching TV, going to movies, dining out, and gathering with family, especially during the winter months. What a blessing it has been to spend Christmas Eve with my sister Kandi, watching whales.

It was the best whale watch I had all season, with whales breaching everywhere, whales checking us out, and even going under our boat. It's called a mugging when the whales get close. We went out for the morning watch, but we did not really do anything special in honor of it being Christmas Eve. My kids are grown. I was extremely grateful when Scott's packages arrived for the kids on this very Christmas Eve day. Looks like they will have something to unwrap on Christmas after all.

Holidays can be real bummers when you don't have any excess to celebrate them. There are always some kinds of expectations we create that revolve around holidays. Not being able to afford the distraction of Christmas (thank God I live in Maui with year-round summer, to be able to focus on other things such as nature and whales instead) made me realize what those Jehovah's Witnesses have been trying to explain. *"You don't need a holiday to give to and acknowledge loved ones."* Traveling this path with only enough funds to live within my surviving needs, I have come to this joy of the Jehovah's Witnesses. Not only is there less stress of a have-to checklist, but I have also noticed an even pace of unconditional love just by being in the moment and not allowing the distractions that holidays tend to distract us with.

Christmas

I had signed us up for the Sub for Santa thing with the Salvation Army prior to sending for Kylie. Scott had been raised on Sub for Santa Christmases, and we have heard over and over how disappointing it always was for him that nobody ever got what they really desired or asked for. That fueled his drive to spoil our kids rotten with EVERYTHING they desired and asked for. We were delighted with the gift from the Salvation Army... a fishing pole. Something I have never thought to give my son, amazingly enough.

I was so glad my kids were old enough that I didn't feel the need to stress myself out struggling to get them tons of gifts like they have been accustomed to receiving. I was even more glad when Scott's gifts for the children arrived on Christmas Eve. Scott had sent a tablet for Kylie, and indoor basketball shoes and a keyboard for Kanyon. That, along with Sapna and Kandi being so giving, and gifting us all so well, our family had a very magical Christmas.

I was so thankful to have Kylie home for Christmas. I couldn't imagine Christmas without her. It's hard to be away from family and loved ones during holidays. And once again, I was very grateful for those three beautiful children of Kandi's in the space for the holidays. When serving her, I am always honored to be involved with her kids.

Christmas Text to Kai
KERI: Sending Merry Christmas wishes from Hawaii... thinking of you ever and always... looking forward to the day when we can stand each other. I will be sending your packages soon. Enjoy the season, and let's have a better year. Sending love to you.

January 2013

New Years, Hawaiian Style

Bringing in the New Year felt like celebrating the 4th of July. The neighbors strung firecrackers on a long rope and hung it up for a loud popping fire dance. I thoroughly love having summer weather year-round! I never realized how much Utahans are forced to hibernate indoors because of the winter months. I am a skier, but the cost to go skiing has skyrocketed. Snow skiing is now a hobby that only the rich can indulge in. I love how going to the beach is free. You don't even have to pay to park.

Kai Announces New Arrival

January 5

KAI: You probably don't care, but just FYI you are having another grandbaby in August.

KERI: I'm glad Daisy will have a full-blooded sibling. I loved having Tabi. And the FYI is nice. It's not that I "don't care," it's just that I strive hard every day with acceptance. It is what it is. I threw my role as your mother and grandmother of your kids away. Legally I'm no one to any of you. I tried to play the illegal way, honoring the DNA connection, but the rejection in that is too hurtful. I'm done being unhappy, and the whole scenario around you brings such unhappiness to me. As cold-hearted as this may sound, I have to accept you are nothing to me and believe that whole degrading program that I was just a vessel to get you here, and according to the adoption world, my part with you is over.

January 12

KERI: How's your knee? Kanyon had a basketball clinic today. It was a great one and for free. They flew some sports trainer guy in from Washington. If it's not enough to see your name everywhere, today I heard it all day. This 4-yr. old girl (that was playing with my little 4 yr. old, Bubba) was named Kai, and a rowdy little thing she was.

KAI: It's doing better. I'm walking on it. Turns out fractured kneecaps really hurt! Anyway, the doctor said no activity for at least a month, but I'm in three city leagues with Braden, so I'm pushing for recovery in two weeks. Here's to hoping.

KERI: Well, energetically when one hurts themselves, it is from the energy in our space being weak in that area to get our attention to deal. i.e., When your feet give you trouble like mine were, it actually means *"fear of moving forward."* The knee represents pride and ego, inability to bend, wanting your own way, resenting authority. Just like when Kylie had warts... warts are explosions of hate and judgment. As soon as Kylie cleared her anger and quit judging, her warts finally went away. You most likely think I'm crazy silly, as you always do, but it is that simple to heal ourselves. Analyze and use the info as you wish. I hate being down, but lots of time for reading, and I love to read.

KAI: Ummm, either that or they just play a lot of sports and have an accident. Although I like your explanation of my injury, I do feel a lack of support from family in moving forward in the things I hold most dear. However, I have the constant support of Heavenly Father in my life. So again, injuries happen, and one did to me not much more to it than that.

Not everything has to be analyzed and understood by man. In fact, the sweetest things in life are those that we simply don't fully comprehend, and we humbly acknowledge that we lack understanding and just have faith in the Lord and his judgment and goodness.

KERI: Yeah, when I was your age and life was simple and sweet, I had the same belief. But when shit hit the fan in a huge way, I needed further knowledge of *"WTF, why me?"* when I was being such a good little daughter of God, serving in his church to the depths that I was before 2005. Glad to hear you are so content and happy with your life.

KAI: I have a simple sweet life because I choose to smile at everything the Lord has dealt me. Your attitude of *"why me"* is you failing the test that was given to you. Just because you are serving in the church does not make you exempt from trials and hardships. Rather, it strengthens us to be able to bear the burdens joyfully, and it fills us with love that we can have patience in our afflictions until the Lord sees fit for the tempest to pass.

If we just live our lives acting like victims, what will we learn? How to complain? I would rather live my life to the fullest, grateful for the good times AND the bad. I know those hard times can be blessings if I have the wisdom to see and accept them as such. When we live our lives not as victims but rather with grateful hearts, always following Job's example when he said, *"The Lord gives and the Lord taketh away. BLESSED be the name of the Lord!"* When we live with this attitude, we have joy in life, not because its void of trials and hardships, but because, come what may, we have it ingrained in ourselves to love love love each day given us, love love love each trial we are blessed to endure, and yes, love love love the sweet blessings that come from patiently enduring and serving in God's kingdom.

KERI: Ok... this is one of the reasons I have a hard time having a relationship with you... you are so closed-minded; it's your way or the highway. I understand your annoying characteristic in this because I was the same annoying way at your age, saying the same exact, *"The Lord brings to you, and it is what you make it."* I have prayed to God to make obvious signs appear to let me know I need to reach out to you, and living here with your name EVERYWHERE, I have requested the signs be louder, so I don't have to talk to you every day, and crazily, it has. I don't enjoy interacting with you and pray someday I will. I can't ignore reaching out when things such as meeting the Casper theater dudes and having the little four-year-old's name yelled continually in my ear. I will continue to be obedient to my Lord and reach out to you when it is an obvious sign. Soften up, get real, and let's try to like one another.

KAI: Hahaha, me close-minded, my way or the highway!? Hahahahaha, wow, that is priceless. That's coming from the woman who cuts off anyone who doesn't agree with or bows to her ways! You try to cut me down and make me feel ignorant because I don't conform to your ways. I've lived your way, Keri. I was a victim. I saw those who lived in the church as judgmental & vindictive, that the world was against me, and that we should all just live freely without judgment and without responsibility. I felt that religion was society's evil way of making us conform and restricting us from being who we are. I lived that way, Keri, so don't you dare try and condescendingly tell me I am close-minded. Why do you think I changed? I changed because I met the Savior of the world who forgives sins and heals the brokenhearted. He taught me how to live, how to have joy, how to forgive and be forgiven. I live in His true path. I don't try to live by His law because I love His law. His law frees me and is the reason I have joy and happiness. How foolish and unkind of you to constantly try and trample such a gift I have been given instead of encouraging me to stand strong in the convictions I have been given by God. No, no, you couldn't encourage or be proud because that would require humility, something that is extremely lacking in yourself.

You want to talk about real? Real is family, real is love, real is living now and enjoying what we have been given, not cutting all ties with our loved ones because they scolded or judged us, which by the way, only comes from love and concern. You talk of love, and I laugh at you to scorn who are you, who cuts me down. You never try to build me up. Who rejects the angel Daisy who happens to be your blood? Who are you to speak of love? If getting "real" is becoming cold and pessimistic like you, then no, Keri, I will never get "real." I guess I'll just live happily in my "fantasy" world.

KERI: I remember you before religion... so hurt inside with rejection and abandonment issues, f-ing any girl you could get. I was unclear in a lot of ways back then too, but I've grown so much emotionally and spiritually, found happiness from within, along with Kanyon, and we got closer to God than ever. It took a man treating me like shit, smoking heroin in a daze, feeling rejected by him with him having to numb himself... Kanyon and I loved him unconditionally with him in our space, watching him go through withdrawals. Where you don't even allow anybody in your space unless they praise you like Mai. So, when you visit us, you just feel like a normal person because we see greatness in everyone who has love in their heart. We left religion after our spirituality grew out of it, when it began to contradict.

KAI: And really, Daisy and I both have wonderful women in our lives that love us for who we are and don't cut us down for how we live or what we believe. It's soo funny that you see the church as this awful judgmental entity when you are the one that judges us and hates and reviles against us. We don't need your anger and judgment. We have already adopted Tabi as the birth grandmother/mother of Daisy and she fills the role graciously and lovingly, so you don't need to try to interact unless you want the way we live in your space. We certainly don't need the way you live in ours.

KANYON: This is Kanyon - You obviously don't even know the start of what the f***'s gone on here. We were watching heroin destroy my father's soul. We had to go within ourselves to find happiness and then leave everything to get away and live in Maui, choosing to be houseless and happy over a mansion with unhappiness and fakeness. My mother is the most selfless person I've met in this dense world of ego, taking in any child of God that needs motherly love no matter the age. Where you won't even take time out to talk to your brother, JC, to send love even with his loving soul. So, stay up on that high horse, looking down on everyone, 'cause God knows. I know our mission is to heal others through love, not covering up emotions by numbing them with pills. Your ignorance brings us frustration, so lose our number till your ego subsides and we can stand even talking to you through text. I've lived your Mormon ways, which is a great spiritual foundation, but we have expanded our knowledge through talking to enlightened, wise people who get life.

The way we live our lives? See the judgmental ways. What way do we live our lives? Lovingly and in the present? Cause I'm happier than I've ever been and closer to God than I've ever been... meditating and connecting to Source. So, keep judging us as those "drug addicts." If only you could see what really goes on in this house. God knows we're all happier when you're out of our space because you just disappoint us... so lose our number 'til you can come forward with love. I love you Kai. I just don't let you judge my beliefs that have been proven to be true.

KAI: I never once said anything about drugs. I could care less what you do with your lives. I'm referring to you all living like victims because you do. You parade around boo-hooing about what life has done to you instead of moving forward. So quit acting like a little turd who's just pissed off at life and must bring others down with him. JC has nothing to do with it. I don't speak to a lot of old friends cause I'm grown up and have a family of my own and responsibilities that take up most of my time, but that's something you know nothing about, so why waste my breath. You have chosen to end up with a 5th grade education, never work and "just be" ... Boy, so much responsibility. Must be tough. No wonder you have soo much time to get down on everyone else. Don't worry, I haven't had your number saved in my phone ever. Keri just texts me from time to time to let me know how ignorant I am. I agree with you kid. Let's just pretend that we've never met. We had good times back when I really was an ignorant selfish prick, but ever since I've changed, it's been nothing but cruelty and rejection from you bunch.

KANYON: Done throwing pearls to the swine... keep your beliefs in life, and I'll keep mine. You don't know us or what we're capable of. I've learned more through mentors with experience than I ever have in school. School doesn't give me the information I require for this mission. So yeah, society only programmed me 'til ninth grade when I broke away, found myself, my mission, and the mentors to teach me the wisdom I need. I don't boo-hoo about what life's done to me. I rejoice about where it's gotten me and what I've learned from it. It's gotten me to where I am now, and I love where I am. I'm so in the present and high off life and Source. So, keep loving, relating to, and healing. Talk to you when you can understand and love unconditionally...

KAI: Sounds good. We never met, deal?

Letter from Mother

Dear Keri, Aloha from the mainland! I haven't been able to reach you by phone, so I thought I would write the old-fashioned way. We get so used to instant connection that letters become obsolete. I tried to ask Scott about your phone, but I couldn't even understand what he said. He was mumbling so badly. I, of course, am very concerned about his constant drug use. He said something about sending you a phone, but that is what he said a month ago, so I don't know if that will happen.

It is sooooo cold here. We got another snowstorm yesterday...12" added to our 12." We are covered in it. The skiing should be good though. At times like these, I dream I am in Maui with you where the sky is clear, and the air is warm. I'll just have to endure here till spring!

Your dad has been really sick. He got what I had, but he has been running a fever of 102 (just coughed a lung up and couldn't breathe). His fever has broken, so he is going to go out and plow snow! Can't keep that good man down! We have the worst air in the nation, or haven't you heard? Our respiratory illnesses have outnumbered the nation. They are calling it the "Brigham Lung Disease" Haha, get it? Instead of Brigham Young... Oh well, so much for my Salt Lake humor. We are making up for all you healthy people in Hawaii. It's put me back on daytime oxygen and resorting to watching TV or reading all day. I have cabin fever BAD! But I am going grocery shopping today. John usually does all the shopping, but he needs his energy for blowing snow.

The Quinn's (my mother's side of the family) will be marching in the St. Patrick's Day Parade on March 16th. We are having a float and matching T-shirts. I'm going to decorate my Jazzy up. We walk down three blocks to Gateway Mall, and then there will be food and entertainment. When Kelly called me and informed me, I kind of had an anxiety attack about it. Good thing Tabi and Shanae were there and talked me through it and said how fun it would be and that their whole family would want to participate. If you were here, I know you would want to do the march decked all out in green. It should be fun.

How is the whaling business going for you? Are you booking lots of tours? How is Kylie's schooling going? Has she rebelled yet? What about Kanyon? Is he able to play on the basketball team? I talked a little bit to James last week, and he sounds good. Seems he's planning on coming in for a visit between March and April. It will be good to see him all bushy headed and all. Are you guys coming in for a visit too?

Well, I'll close for now and leave you all with my love and prayers. Be happy and at peace. I know you are loving all those who need loving. May God's blessings and healings pour down upon you and your family. Please let me know your phone number. I put my cell number back to a landline, but John and I are sharing the Verizon cell, so I can still receive texts and Verizon to Verizon free. Love always, Mom

Kandi Moves Out

There were so many dynamics at play that got totally amplified when Kylie arrived. Kandi was processing the loss of not having her babies' daddy in the space and had just gotten fired from her job. Understanding the process of such, I was overcompensating for Kandi's distracted thoughts, cleaning up after her and the children more and more. I was getting very tired, praying to God, reminding Him that I am too old and tired to be working this hard for free and then coming home to a house in such chaos, to then have to clean the house and make dinner just in time to go to bed. And it's too bad that money has so much power to get in the way of things. Kandi was getting funds from the state to pay me to watch the children as long as she was working or volunteering. This was a huge part of my income to be able to pay for my share of the rent. When Kylie moved in and demanded that she get paid, it just became a nightmare for Kandi... who to pay? Kanyon and I felt like we were fired.

Kylie and Kandi were bringing the worst out in each other, acting like junior high sisters. I saw fault with both of their behaviors and stayed neutral, allowing it to play out as need be.

It wasn't pretty, and Kandi left, stripping the house of many things, and moved in with a boyfriend.

Kanyon and I missed the kids, but I think we all needed a break from each other.

February 2013

Whale Season at Its Peak

Whew, the whales finally came, and so did the paychecks. I was able to pay the difference in expenses after Kandi moved out. I was looking forward to spending the extra money on nice things, such as maybe a new outfit or maybe a night out to eat with the family, instead of more rent. I was finally able to save and accumulate enough extra money to get a few things to send to Kai and family in the name of his birthday and Christmas.

Humpback Whale (not in the *Animal Speak* book, but what about the humpbacks? Does the encyclopedia definition stick out?): In the winter months, the humpbacks fast and live off of their fat reserves.

Well, it is winter, and I am hoping that this is as slim as it gets as far as fasting and living off of my fat reserves.

Letter from Mai

MAI: Hey Keri, So, just wanted to send a big THANK YOU for the package that we received. It was so kind of you to include all of us, and the gifts were so great. I LOVE the dress.

A little update on us... I'm not sure what you do or don't know, so I'll just be open about what is going on.

I know Kai told you we are having a baby, but we found out that the little tyke is a boy, so that is very exciting. He's due in mid-July, so Daisy and he will be very close.

Daisy is growing like a weed. She's got her two bottom teeth in and is perfecting the art of crawling. She definitely keeps me on my toes.

Kai is finding new interest in real estate. He wants to buy property and rent it for additional income. He's been pretty focused on finding and buying his first investment home, but it probably won't happen until after we get home from selling. Speaking of which, we will be selling in Miami, Florida. Everyone's pretty excited, especially to get out of the Texas market. Which also means that we're going to have a Florida baby boy.

As far as how I'm doing, my belly continues to grow daily. I feel as though I'm becoming a pro at being pregnant, being as it wasn't that long ago that I was pregnant with Daisy. I feel as though I'm handling this pregnancy a lot better though. I have a lot more energy and can do a lot more. Thank goodness too, because I've got a little one to take care of.

Well, that is about it with us. Definitely feel free to respond with how you all are doing, but of course, you shouldn't feel obligated to do so. Thanks again for the great gifts! Mai, Kai and Daisy

KERI: Mai, so good to hear from you. Thanks for the update. Tabi and I are 14 months apart. My mother says she wanted to get diaper duty done and over with all at once. But being that she was a teen mom, I doubt she did it on purpose. I, for one, am thankful for having a younger sibling so close in age; she has been like having a twin. I'm happy to hear you liked the package. I wish I could have sent more, but it is a sacrifice to live here... very expensive just to eat. I love living here and am so happy this is where I ended up.

Glad to hear all is well. Things are getting better and better. In fact, I was just interrupted by Payton, a little girl I befriended that went on the Kai Akua fishing trip yesterday. The cute 3rd grader is going out on the glass bottom boat today and ran up to say hi. I just found out where she is from...CASPER, WYOMING... go figure, of course, she is. When Kai energy hits, Kai energy hits.

Anyway, I hope to have financial abundance soon so that we can schedule a visit to Utah. Sounds like skiing is going to be great this year. I don't miss the snow, but glad to hear Utah has been pounded.

I would be happy about Florida as well. I like Texas, but I would love the opportunity to check out as many places on the map as possible in my lifetime. I need to get on it, lol.

Well, thanks for reaching out and saying hello. It helps with the feeling of having some kind of connection to y'all. Take care, Lots of love.

Stoney McStonerface Stone

When Kandi and the kids moved out, Kanyon strongly felt the need to have a dog. I was very grateful for whale season. I was able to shell out a few hundred to get Kanyon his dog.

Kanyon researched all the puppies in the area. After looking at one female Catahoula pup in Kula, we paid the Humane Society a visit and found an Australian cattle dog mix. Even though Kanyon was hoping for a female, we took this playful male home with us. It was a match made in heaven. Not only does he have markings of hearts all over, but he also has a marking the shape of Maui, AND he was born November 29th, the very day that Kylie landed on this island... both babies landing on Maui the same day!!!

Kanyon and I had been told by Crystal back in 2008 that Kanyon has a contract with a dog. And this might be the dog she had seen along with her knowing that my home is by the ocean. This dog has been the best dog ever. You just tell him something once, and he gets it. Having a dog is perfect for getting you out of bed regularly. Dogs like routine and walks every morning and night... love it.

On one of the first outings we took Stoney on, we ran into a dog that looked just like the dog Kanyon had to leave behind in Utah, Zeus. It was like Zeus's blessing of approval in a symbolic kind of way.

Sharks at Work

It's always a treat when the sharks come to work. What kind of message could they represent? My *Animal Speak* book doesn't have 'shark.' So instead, what we do is analyze what sharks do... their job is to clean the sea. I looked it up on the internet. *Protection is offered; if there is a situation in your life that you need to "scare away," you will be given the power and confidence to fend off negative elements or get rid of them completely.* Well, guess what, folks?

Scott Gets Arrested

When Kandi moved out, we took a break from talking to each other. Well, you could say I was taking a break from talking. That cold-as-ice behavior tends to kick in when I don't feel safe in a relationship.

I remember Kandi had called me on a Monday morning asking if I had heard from Lorna, their mother. I hadn't. Kandi then proceeded to tell me that she had given her mother until that day to inform me what was up with Scott. For some reason their mother wanted to keep it a secret from me. I had already been wondering why Scott wasn't answering my calls or calling me back.

I guess Scott had broken into a few houses in the middle of the night with a loaded gun like a crazed maniac strung out on heroin. When they finally caught up with him, they charged him with 10 counts of crazy insane behavior.

Unbelievable... I knew things were getting unsafe for Kylie, but I did not see this coming. I feared that she would wake up to something to the effect of having to call 911 to help revive her father. I guess this is actually a better scenario. At least Scott will get the rehabilitation he needs.

It's crazy how expensive rehab outside of jail is. I remember researching how I could get Scott into a State of Utah rehabilitation center and was told there weren't any available beds. If you ask me, there is something wrong with that picture. Why wait until some kind of havoc and destruction comes to provide a free rehabilitation program called jail???

I was soooooo very glad I had my daughter at this time.

I was happy Scott was safe and getting detox treatment. They transferred him to the hospital area of the jail. His usage had escalated from smoking heroin to shooting it up.

Rumor had it that the judge wanted to throw the book at Scott and give him 40 years in prison. WOW, that is just overkill silliness if you ask me. But I guess if a person is going to be a threat to society, then lock them up for 40 years because we wouldn't want any old geezers taking us down. Maybe the judge will feel it's safe for Scott to be back on the streets before he reaches 84 years of age. Wouldn't that suck? Dying in prison/jail?

Truth Be Told

I have a strong truth in *"time heals,"* and I, for one, was thankful for this quiet time for healing. Our house had escalated to such chaos. I welcomed the peaceful quiet without worries about how I would make the rent for the next month since Kandi was leaving the household.

My income from babysitting was no longer coming in, my food stamps had decreased in half (the state felt I was making too much money. $700 for babysitting, and with the whales here I was making $1000 a month. I am still confused about that... I have come to the conclusion that the state wants to keep you struggling), and with Kandi moving out, that left an extra $500 for me to come up with to pay the rent. This was making quite a financial change in my monthly living expenses toward the negative. Good thing the whales are here for another month. Like I told the state, *"I don't understand your fear of my supposed abundance? I was barely able to afford blow-up mattresses for me and the kids... just when I thought we would be able to get a step closer to comfortable living, I felt like a chair had been kicked out from under me."*

March 2013

Rachel Comes and Goes

Before I could even worry about finding a roomie, James came home to announce that Rachel, a friend of his that I adore, needed a place for a month until she headed to Peru. We welcomed Rachel into our home with open arms. It was awesome having Rachel here. I love having roommates. There is always something they teach me.

Rachel was a true blessing in so many ways. She moved in with a coffee maker and other household items Kandi had taken with her. Rachel brought with her all kinds of good healthy food makings. Kanyon was ecstatic; he wanted to step up his organic living, desiring to use things like flax seed. Rachel was a great example, making healthy organic meals simple.

Rachel didn't stay long. That month came and went in a blink of an eye.

RACHEL: Keri, Kylie, Kanyon, and James: And so, the journey continues... or begins. I can't even begin to thank you all enough for hosting me and being the most AWESOME, loving, caring, wonderful, amazing stoners and family a gal could ask for. Keep manifesting and sending good vibrations. The world is at our fingertips. I love you all dearly. I am very excited to share my stories and be a part of yours. Love, Rachel

It was while getting to know Rachel that I discovered an interesting pattern; **June 26** is a total soul mate connection for me. My only full-blooded sister, Tabi, was born on **June 26**, providing a companion (i.e. roommate) for me until I married. Tabi then had a son on her birthday, delivering to me my beloved nephew, Tyler (who, remember, was our escort and first roommate in Maui). And then Tyler moved back to Utah, and Kandi moved in... Her birthday??? You guessed it. **June 26th**. Do I even need to tell you when Rachel's birthday is??? **June 26th**. Upon realizing the strong pattern with my roomies, I read into it some more, looking it up in Kanyon's *Zodiac Bible*, and found that **June 26th** is a soul mates' birthday for my birthday of

April 29th. People born on this day are gifts to me from the Universe, giving me the added love and support needed to continue on this path. (Kanyon has brought our attention to the perfect feng shui of it... with me being Taurus, Kanyon being Libra, James being Aires, and having a Cancer in the mix completes it, creating total balance for the elemental signs; earth, air, water, fire.)

This got me thinking... What does it mean that Kai's wife was born on **June 27th** and delivered my first-born granddaughter on her birthday? If you read into it via Numerology, 26 (2+6) equals **8**, that magical infinite number that is strongly in my space. According to Doreen Virtue's *Angel Number 101* book, the number **8** signifies abundance and prosperity. The endless loops in this number signify the infinite flow of money, time, ideas, or whatever else you require (especially for your life purpose). **27** (2+7) equals **9**, which means completion. Doreen's definition:

> *9:* Get to work, Lightworker - now! The number 9 means that you've completed all of the prerequisites to achieve your life purpose. Stop procrastinating, as it's time to start taking action steps. Even baby steps are useful.

Everything in perspective and translation, right? I see the message here.

Jr. Pays Us a Visit

Jr. was part of my army that the Universe had delivered. After my nephews moved in, Jr. was one of their friends that lived in my house before I fled to Maui.

JR.: MOTHER KERI!!! So, good news... life has been stressful here in the city, so my father and I spoke, and I wanna come visit everyone. I miss the motherly love you gave us. I miss how Kanyon and I used to say, "*Yeah buddy!*" every second, and his little sister who reminds me of my little sister, and last but not least, James. You guys look so happy, and I feel as if I need a couple weeks or even a couple days in Hawaii to forget SLC for a little. What are your thoughts on it? I don't know the area well, so if I were to come, I would like you guys to show me around and for us to just enjoy each other's presence. I miss you all. Message me back as soon as you have time. Thank you, and I hope I can see you guys soon. p.s. I talked to my boss about how long I can have off work, and he said two weeks. So, what do you think? One Love, Jr.

KERI: I can't tell you how happy your message made me!!! I gathered the family around and read your beautiful words aloud. We were celebrating with every word, doing cartwheels in our hearts, leaping for joy. WE CAN NOT WAIT!!! Just let me know when. We will receive you with open arms. Come soon because now is the peak of the season for whale watching. You gotta go on our raft and see the whales, sonny boy!

JR.: See! I miss that love, ohh so much! Just confirmed with my father, and it's settled. Tomorrow I will look for tickets and soon fly out to Lahaina, Hawaii. Once tickets are purchased, I'll immediately send you the exact date of departure and arrival. I'm excited to see my second family! I love you all, and I'll be sure to keep you guys updated, Mother Keri. Kisses and hugs. Speak to you guys really soon. I'm so happy right now!!! Jr.

arrived in early March. It was perfect timing. Kanyon and I had been feeling rejected by Kai not embracing who we are, and then the Universe sends son/brother energy to us through a different source named Jr. LOVE IT!

Jr.'s stay came and went quickly. He left with a desire to return to Maui for good within a few months. It is always such a good feeling having a little bit of Utah come for a visit, bringing that familiar family feel.

Word from Scott

Keri, Kanyon, and Kylie, how are you guys? I hope all is well. As you know, I have been in jail a month, and it looks like I have another four months. While I am here. I am in alcohol and drug rehab, and I am also studying lots of computer programs and learning how to build a website. I want to use my time wisely and learn and grow as much as I can while I am here. I am also clearing my Chakras 3-5 times a day and am learning to meditate.

So how is Hawaii? Kanyon, I hear you made a deal with the school and are learning to blow glass. That is awesome. I hope you are being careful on your long board and have been playing ball. Your talent and grace are rare ones, and you should always use your talents to better your life. You are an amazing son, and I love you so much.

Kylie, I hear you are in school but want to come home. I will be out in August, so you can come live with me if you want and if it is fine with your mom. You don't like Maui? What don't you like about it? I am so proud of the young woman you have become. You are smart and beautiful. I hope you are making good choices and behaving for your mom. I love you tons, and I am excited to see you.

Keri, sorry about this, but I have some stuff starting soon, so I will have my employee send you some money. I also have to make a change on your taxes and submit those. I got a few of them back this year, so luckily yours hadn't gone in yet. I will get someone to finalize those and submit them this week. I'll let you know when I have the revised return and the expected date you will get that. How are you other than that? Hope you are still loving Hawaii, and all is well. If you and/or the kids have time to write, that would be awesome. Love, Scott/Dad

Cardinals Everywhere

Kylie is so unhappy here. She and Kanyon are getting into raging fights... they cannot live under the same roof. I could barely afford to take Kylie out to eat for her birthday. We went out to Leilani's on the beach in Kaanapali. I had saved and gifted Kylie $200 for her birthday. We spent the day at Whalers Village at Sephora for Kylie's birthday. We saw cardinals all around that day.

Let's look up what cardinal means in the *Animal Speak* book.

Cardinal: Renewed vitality through recognizing self-importance. The male cardinal makes a good parent and often shares with the female the task of egg incubation. The male will always feed the female while she is in the nest, as well as the baby cardinals.

Well, that is good enough for me. I have been digesting the idea that Kylie needs to be in Utah near her father.

JC Inquires

JC: Hey, Ms. Keri, How things going?

KERI: Things are crazy. The only thing I know for sure is that I am at peace... all I can control is myself. I get a little sad that I cannot relish in grandma hood, but I'm sure if I was still in Utah, the head games would still be going on, and I wouldn't be relishing in grandma hood anyways. I love living in Maui, I love my new friends, and I love my new life, even if I am still sleeping on a blowup mattress. We are looking forward to your visit. Let me know when you will be able to make it. Food is pricey here. $7 for a gal of milk, so save up. We are completely living within our means and are still struggling financially. I know God is blessing me and continues to bless me. It's not easy being the provider. Glad I am a hippie's daughter. Kanyon and I can live in rags and be happy, but Kylie, on the other hand, is having a harder time. She says, *"I'd rather be crying in a mansion than be this poor and 'happy.'"* Obviously, she hadn't been as unhappy as Kanyon and I in the mansion. Can't wait to show you our new home in Maui. Love you!

Now if you haven't read Book One in this series, you most likely do not know who JC is. JC is my *Golden Boy*; a nickname Scott and the boys had given him. In 2006, when we were united as a family in Texas with Kai, JC had been one of Kai's first good friends that he brought home (they were both on the college basketball team). JC quickly "adopted" our family and has been a part of it ever since.

Laundry Gets Lifted

I have come to the conclusion that *Life Happens*, and the best way to deal with it is to live it one moment at a time. It's good to have dreams and goals... they help keep us focused on what we do want because on this journey... well, so far, we have experienced what we **don't** want.

I had dreams and goals of having this perfect little family and becoming this perfect little grandma, relaxing and enjoying my later years in life. I have worked hard at reaching that goal, only to find that wasn't my path.

Having my dreams and goals crumble right before my eyes was a hard realization to face. In that moment, and for many moments after, I felt like all my dedication, my service, my sacrifice was for no reason. And to feel like my life was all for no reason makes it pretty hard to have any reason to move forward... because where in the hell is life going to lead me? And how will I live the *perfect little life* I have always dreamed about? If my path, my blueprint, obviously doesn't have the *perfect little family* program (that I have been taught is everyone's goal) as the end of my journey in this life, then what is the destination?

I was getting impatient for the destination and not enjoying the journey. It was really scary charting into unknown waters with only my 15-year-old son and my nephews. In a matter of months, I had left my husband, my house, my daughter, my eldest son, my first granddaughter, all my family, the dog... I had left everything and said goodbye with an act of faith that my 15-year-old would help guide me.

It had been an amazing journey thus far, healing at the harbor... which was by far my most favorite part of my 43-year journey. But I was starting to question the destination that was not coming quickly enough for me.

Kanyon had been telling me that it was time I started writing the 4th book, but honestly, I didn't feel motivated to tell anyone the story. In my eyes, there still wasn't much to be *that* grateful for. After all, I was getting sick of living like a hobo away from my family and close friends. The sacrifice didn't match the reward by any means. I was tempted to throw in the towel and succumb to moving back to Utah, giving in to all those mind games, willing to sacrifice my passion and reason for living (bringing awareness) ... After all, my life was lived, my choices had been made, nothing could change my past. Maybe it was time to just accept that life stinks and give in to aging like an old folk, keeping my wisdom within me and becoming that quiet reserved person that I never thought I would become.

And then, to top it off... the family's laundry got lifted off the clothesline.

Kylie called me from home, scared to leave her room because she had spotted a homeless-looking couple out back getting ready to take clothes off the line. After arriving home and analyzing the situation with our dear neighbor William, we came to the conclusion that the homeless-looking couple Kylie had spotted (who had left our hose on, flooding out the backyard after being interrupted taking their outdoor shower) must also have taken William's clothing that kept coming up missing, along with Jr.'s, Rachel's, and now ours. All lifted off the inner clothing line that was not exposed to the back window.

This violation was the cherry on top of how I was feeling around this time. It wasn't necessarily the missing items that was the upset (obviously, we had enough of an abundance of clothing that we didn't even know exactly which items were missing from the few clothes remaining on the line), as much as it was about the feeling of being kicked while you were down.

After arriving to work the following day, Povi and Capt. Tiff were the listening ears I dumped the, *"Can you believe the nerve of some people!"* speech on. I wasn't looking for any handouts or sympathy. I'm just someone who expresses my life's upsets and joys to those who will listen. And what a blessing it was to have Povi and Tiff be those listening ears... Within 24 hours, those two had collected 18 bags of donated clothing, along with a card from Povi with extra cash to help this single mother in need.

I have never been so moved in my life. The compassion and quick response... I was so impressed with the outpouring of love from this harbor family of mine! This act of love was just the motivation I needed to start writing my story.

Along with the donations came a new roommate... a huge moth we would see periodically.

> *Moth*: The cocoon is only spun by the moth. Symbolically, this means more shielded protection. Represents transmutation and the dance of joy. They remind us not to take things quite so seriously in our lives. They awaken a sense of lightness and joy. They remind us that life is a dance, and that dance, though powerful, is also a great pleasure.

I can never hear that message enough. Kanyon was always reminding me to enjoy the journey.

Messaging Mai about Kylie

March 28

KERI: Hey Mai, Kylie has demanded to go back to Utah. She refuses to go to school here. She hates the beach, the weather, and the "*boring*" people. (She's not into bliss yet... she's still young, wanting more excitement than Maui has to offer) Well also, we aren't living in the conditions she is used to. We all sleep on blowup mattresses, which is way better than the ground... she just didn't experience the homeless part or sleeping on the ground part of our journey to be grateful for the roof over our heads and the blowup mattresses. I really can't blame her. Anyway, she has insisted on moving back and living with Julie if she must. I told her that Julie was not an option. I told her that the only options were Tabi or you guys. Tabi is hesitant, but Kylie will be asking her. I'm asking you because you are the mom of the house, and it will mostly affect you if she were to move in with you guys. Talk with Kai... feel free to say no. Let me know your feelings on this so Kylie can get a move on with her life. Talk to you soon. Lots of love

March 29

KERI: Hey, got the message back from my mother. I didn't think it would be a go, but I wanted Kylie to see me advocating for her. I didn't think the reason would be Sanderson related but whatever. I know the only reason she wants to go back is because of her friends. It's a hard age to leave friends and make new ones. I have to admit I am glad to hear everyone reject the idea of taking Kylie. And I love that my mother was willing to do so if needed. Kylie rejected the grandma idea, so obviously, she was leaving for the wrong reasons. Only time will tell, but thanks for digesting the idea. I realized through all this, there will most likely never be a relationship between us or any of your kids. Adoption is final - lose kin for life... totally my bad. Aloha

MAI: Keri, I had every intention of getting back to you on this. I wanted to talk to Kai first, but my brother Eric just got home from his mission last night, so it's been pretty busy. I wanted to tell you that we would love to have Kylie. The only issue is that we are leaving for Florida at the end of the month and wouldn't return until October, so obviously we wouldn't be able to have her until after that. I'm sorry I didn't get back to you sooner, and you believed that we were rejecting her. Not at all the case... I'm not sure I understand when you say the reason was Sanderson related. So, is she deciding to stay? I don't want you to think that there can't be a relationship between us. We want one to be. I think I may be missing a piece of information that has been communicated through your mother. I'm not sure. Anyway, let me know... talk to ya later.

KERI: It's no big deal. It's just my mother said that Kai said the Sanderson's are very involved with your life, and it would be fuel on the fire... so whatever. Kai probably knows best. I had forgotten how in the beginning those Sanderson's were wishing they could take away my other children too. I had forgotten, but yep, he is right. They most likely would get possessive of my daughter too.

Honestly, folks, Kylie hates it here. She has refused to wear anything else besides long pants and sweatshirts. Her complaint... "*It should not be warm in the winter.*"

I told her, "*I don't plan on ever being cold in winter again unless I visit.*"

I understand her desire to be with friends. I remember when I was her age. I also remember Pat's words that Kylie is not part of the Hawaii journey. I understand that now that Scott is where he is supposed to be, Kylie is to be back in Utah. I don't fully know why, but I can see how Kylie being near her father and having face-to-face visits is exactly what both of them need. They need each other.

Kylie first came to me, demanding to live with Julie. I am over my annoyance with her. She can have Scott all to herself now. And to be honest, I am ever so grateful she is there for Scott, loving him, taking care of Kanyon's dog, cleaning up after that husband of mine, and taking care of all the family belongings as well as she has. Honestly, I think it would have been harder for me to accept letting go of Scott if there wasn't someone there to love him.

I never thought I would come to that conclusion. But I honestly feel for the girl. I can only imagine her issues from her loss. Losing her 1st born son, Scott's 2nd born son, to her parents. The version of the story I have is one of those late discovery adoptee liar-liar pants on fire stories ... poor dear. But one of the side effects of losing your child is collecting other children and aiding mothers in need. So, when Kylie was asking about living with Julie, it gave me a moment to feel total forgiveness for the woman and accept her as the bonus mom.

As much as I did not want my daughter living with that woman, I just had to surrender and trust whatever will be, will be. I told Kylie the same, and when Kylie told Julie... my mother got a phone call.

Julie contacted my mother, telling her that she didn't think Kylie moving in with her would be such a great idea after all. I guess Julie was playing good cop, thinking I would play bad cop and say no. When I didn't say no, Julie informed my mother that the judge had ordered no contact between Scott and Julie because, I guess, come to find out... Julie was with Scott the night of his arrest, and it was Julie's car they were driving.

Whew, so glad that didn't work out! But how grateful I was for my nonchalant demeanor and ability to forgive and *let go and let God*.

I feel I had done the same with Kai's parents, the Sanderson's, over and over like groundhog day... forgiving and starting again, striving for their acceptance of me as a mother to Kai, an added member of their family possibly... only to constantly be reminded, *"Oh yeah, let's not blend."* It's hard for me to act as anything other than family. After all, they did adopt my son.

Kylie Hates It Here

I talked to my mother today. We finally figured it out... Kylie is going to go back to Utah and live with Grandma. Kylie hated Maui so bad, she was determined to live with whoever would receive her. My mother always jumps in for the rescue, and she has great skills from working as a state assistance specialist. She knows how to rehabilitate, and Kylie needed some rehabilitation.

It was quite challenging to have Kylie in the mix. She didn't go through the first half of our journey with us, surviving as one... And to tell you the truth, I don't think she could have survived it. We needed all the positive thinking we could muster to climb the upward curve to get back to a desirable place that only existed in our hearts.

I had warned Kylie about our living conditions, and she had heard about the infestation. By the time Kylie arrived on November 29, the infestation was under control for the most part. We live in Maui, and you are going to have bugs. It was quite comical to see Kylie's reaction to just one bug here or there. She had no sympathy from any of us. We had lived through a Halloween horror show with all those bugs and rodents until our abs were rock hard from all the screams we shrieked before October was over.

At first, Kylie loved being here with Kandi's kids. Kylie is a strong nurturer, and she tends to take charge, thinking she is the only one watching the kids. When in all reality, that is just her way of enjoying interacting with her cousins. She didn't realize we were getting along just fine before she came.

Kanyon and I were so excited to show Maui to Kylie. Kylie did not even wait for a sunburn before saying, *"I hate the beach. It's sandy, and the sun hurts my skin."* More and more, Kylie hibernated at home with her electronic gadgets.

I felt bad that I couldn't give Kylie more quality time and attention. Kanyon and Kylie did NOT get along. Kanyon could not understand her need to have me all to herself at times, even though he was privy to getting me all to himself for so long. Everything the other one said was *"stupid."* Their hate for one another grew so intense that I just could not referee the two of them any longer. I chose to ignore both of them instead of continuing to try harder to juggle my time to teach them how to understand one another and get along.

It was good to have James here for Kylie to hug, love, and hang on to, but he worked most of the time. Kylie would only hang out with us when James was home. I just couldn't give Kylie the attention she needed. All my energy was going toward surviving, being the sole provider for my family. I needed an extra parent or family member to help. I was very grateful that my mother understood, saying, *"Each and every one of your children has needed to be an only child. Each one of them requires a lot of individual attention."* With that, my mother volunteered for the job, paying for Kylie to fly back home to Utah so she could be the apple in Grandma and Grandpa's eyes, getting oodles of attention along with guided direction and scheduled counseling sessions, plus a program my mother developed called ESTEEM.

April 2013

Letters with Scott

April 9

SCOTT: Hey guys, I got your letters on Thursday then I got my letter back last night that I mailed a month ago. Crazy slow mail.

Everything is good here. I'm in a program called CATS that is like rehab in jail. It is good. It keeps me busy, so time flies. I will be out sometime mid-July. The first three weeks in here sucked cause I boohooed and felt like I didn't deserve to be in here, but once I accepted it would be a minute, and just started doing my time, reading a lot, got a bunch of educational books and studying those, got a book on building websites and new computer programs, started working out every day... then time started flying. So even though I am locked up, the food sucks, and my bed is hard, I am better than I have been in a while. I am reading like 3000 pages of books a week, studying a couple hours a day, reading scriptures, praying daily, and just being grateful to be alive. I have lost close to 45 lbs. since I've been in here, and I am getting my muscles back. My mind is clear, and it is getting sharp and quick again.

Kylie, I hear you will be back on the 19th. That's good. Then you can come see me on Sunday the 21st. I'm excited to see you so we can visit and I can see how beautiful you are becoming. Are you all super tan?

Kanyon, I'm glad you love blowing glass. That's awesome. I hope you are being careful on your longboard. I hope you are staying in shape and using your mind, studying, and learning many things. You are an amazing young man, and you can do whatever you choose to do. Use your talents to better yourself, your family, and mankind in general.

Keri, thank you for your letter. It came at just the right time with a message that I needed to hear. It helped me break through some hurdles that I was having trouble getting over.

Jail sucks, but these six months have been invaluable and are helping me progress so quickly. This whole experience has been a blessing. I have had amazing cellmates that have shared their wisdom, and now my celly is a kid Kai and Braden's age who works out relentlessly every day. That motivates me to work out and get back into great shape. He is a really nice boy, and we have a lot of fun. All and all, the whole experience after the first three weeks has been ok. I'm reading and studying so much. I forgot the brain is a muscle, and the more you use it, the stronger it becomes. At first, I could barely read 200 pages a week, but now I am reading a 400-600 page book a day, plus studying social studies, math, science, language, and learning how to build websites and about various computer programs. Also, I go to AA, CA, LDSA (LDS substance abuse program) every week, and Bible study and Mormon church, so the influences are great.

Well, I love you all and can't wait to see you guys. Kylie, I will see you in a few weeks. Love, Scott, Dad

April 13

KERI: Scott, it was so good to get your letter and hear how well you are doing. I love that we are still friends after all that went down. You are an amazing, powerful soul, and I am excited for you to step into your power and love yourself to the fullest capacity... you deserve it.

Tax returns, or any money for that matter, would be great. I am extremely nervous about how I will be paying for rent and other things. The whales are gone, and my boss has already loaned me $1000 and has told me no more money until thou is paid back. Even in the good months, I never made more than $2000, which only handicapped me more because the state lowered my food stamps amount, and now I am back to making nothing. I will have to go in and meet with those welfare people that make you feel like a LOSER wanting free handouts. If I didn't mind tenting it, I would not even consider going in, but I do not want to do THAT again.

So, Kylie is heading back to Utah. It has been hard to have both her and Kanyon in the same house without having another parent to give one attention while I'm with the other. The competition... not so much from Kanyon, but with Kylie, is too much. Kanyon doesn't understand her demands to exclude him. Kanyon has always been one for unity and *"all together now."* But I can understand Kylie's upset. I just can't be the referee for it all anymore. I am so glad Pat warned me that Kylie would not be part of the Hawaii journey... and boy is she not. She hates everything about it here. Which, again, I can understand. The poor dear lost her family, her dad, her house, her room, her belongings, her state, AND her friends... all in such a short time. It will be good for her to be there near her daddy.

Plus, remember what I was told... children are karmic debt to help refine and clear our energy. Kai and Kylie are your karmic debt. And because of the mission I am to do, I was gifted Kanyon to ground me and get me where I need to be.

Kanyon loves and adores you. He cannot wait for you to join him on his path but also knows that this is perfect for the NOW to help heal for what is to come.

Kandi and I are on speaking terms. Everything happens for a reason... you may not understand at the moment but allow yourself to flow with the current of life without resistance, pretty much saying *"Yes"* to everything... *"I will go where you want me to go dear Lord."* And when you flow toward the direction that brings peace and happiness in your heart instead of thinking your way through it, you will be guided to where you need to be. Even if, at this moment, you are sleeping on a hard bed in jail (or on the ground homeless in Olowalu), it is all just a step to a better place. You figure you have been prolonging the step because of fear. My fears used to be being alone and having to financially provide for myself.

2012/2013 is all about facing our fears. There will not be any fear-based thinking allowed on the New Earth. The speed of manifesting power is going to be so instant... Fear will manifest and create horrible things that would destroy our planet.

I am so happy to hear you are reading so much. Choose wisely what you fill your thoughts with. Only read what you would want to create in your world. No more *Sopranos*, *CSI* stuff. Make it more along the lines of *Bewitched*... make your world magical, happy, and full of bliss, peace, and love for everyone. Lots of love Darling, Friends Forever, Love Keri

Boss Almost Pays Me Salary

I was able to afford the rent for February and March, but by April, my paychecks had become less and less. I had to spend a good portion of my check on food. It was pretty close to the $600 they had taken from my food stamp allowance.

When it was time to pay rent, my boss comforted me saying, "*We will work it out. I like you.*" I informed my boss of my predicament, letting him know I was going to have to find a job that paid a base because this commission business was not working out. I gave him the opportunity to pay me a salary to keep me working there for him. I felt like I had shown him my value as an employee during the past six months, serving his company over and beyond, not worried about what I was getting paid. My mentality is that of an employer, and I had treated the job as such, putting the company in my best interest. I let my boss know that I needed $2000 a month to be able to live on. I was glad he *liked* me because I really did love working the booth at slip #8.

I gave my boss until Monday to decide what he could do for me because, on Monday, I was going to meet with Steve at West Maui Parasail. Steve paid hourly plus a bit of commission. Mark was so sweet trying to figure out a way to keep me as his employee. He even offered for me to move into his Front Street house that he used as his boat yard rent-free to help compensate for my earnings. Mark always rented out the rooms individually and he was clearing out the tenants, or so he thought. I was willing to go wherever the Universe would provide. I have learned life falls into place if you just ride the current, saying, "*So it is,*" or "*Yes*" to everything, just like in the movie *Yes Man* with Jim Carey.

Everyone thought I was nuts to accept the offer, but always staying open to possibilities hasn't failed me yet. And it didn't fail me this time, either. Obviously, living in the Front Street house was not in the Universal cards for me. Mark could not clear out all of his tenants and said he would have to take back his offer. I thanked him graciously and told him, "*No worries. Whatever is meant to be, is meant to be, and obviously this is not to be.*"

On April 1st, Easter Sunday morning, Mark delivered a rose and a check for $1000 to help me pay my rent. I was very grateful for the loan and had no choice but to pay a visit to Steve at West Maui Parasail. My visit with Steve went well. For a whole hour and a half, Steve took the time to get to know me and decided he would keep me in mind, ending the interview with, *"Call me on the First of May."*

Easter Sunday

Once again, the holiday was spent in a very untraditional way. Normally Easter is another big money holiday. In the past, I would buy each child a Sunday outfit, a summer outfit, an Easter basket full of sugar and silly toys, along with a family gift of some sort like a ping pong table. This was the best Easter yet for me. I don't know if the kids would agree, but I loved not having to rush around worrying about spending money on a holiday in order to honor a life-size bunny that is supposed to resemble Jesus somehow??? I never understood how the bunny got involved with Passover.

I loved that I had to work, so I didn't even have to worry about *what* we would do on this Easter Sunday morning. I loved it even more when the boss man asked if I could crew for the 1:00 whale watch. Hell yeah! Best Easter EVER.

It was a great whale watch. A mother humpback whale was slapping her peduncle (tail) at us, telling us to back away from her and her calf, so we sought other whales to watch.

> *Humpback Whale*: The whale teaches us to hear our inner voice, to be in touch with our personal truth, thus knowing wisdom and feeling the heartbeat of the Universe. You will be shown how to go deep within yourself to stir your inner creativity and imagination. You will also be taught to not become too lost in your imagination but to live in the "real world," everyday waking reality.

Personal Reference Letters for Scott

Scott's attorney asked that we gather as many letters as possible regarding Scott... to disclose Scott's potential by sharing Scott's personal past.

KERI: I am Keri Stone, Scott Stone's wife since 1988. Unfortunately, in 2012, I had to leave because of Scott Stone's poor choices. I fled to Maui with my kids to get out of the situation. Prior to 2011, Scott was a great provider to many households besides our own, having been self-employed for 20+ years, providing many jobs for many Utah families. Scott has a good heart and was always the first to volunteer when someone was in need. Scott always helped out in church.

I believe that intense counseling to work on his inner wounds from being so neglected/abused as a child is the only way for Scott's sobriety.

I was asked to write a letter... I honestly don't know what would be best for Scott. He has done healing sessions in the past, rehab programs, church... Scott always returns to numbing the pain. It's easier than facing his pain. Who knows what will help him take ownership of his unhappiness and choose to change.

I have three children with Scott. We lost the eldest to adoption and reunited with him in 2006, which, in my opinion, was the trigger that started the downhill spiral for the both of us. All the children and I wish Scott the best. Scott's recovery is everyone's wish. I don't know if jail is the answer, but I feel Scott needs a very supervised program. Sincerely, Keri Stone

KANYON: This is Kanyon Stone, Scott Stone's son. I wanted to share my perception of the situation since I have known him for 16 years.

My dad is a sensitive soul and has been hurt since he was a little boy, which has hardened his exterior persona. He began drinking for his sorrows and then popping pills to numb his issues of the past. His son, my older brother, was stolen from him; he was coerced into signing relinquishment papers. His other son (my half-brother) was taken as well... just to mention some of the hardships taunting him from the past, making it harder and harder to move on. So hard that it eventually led to heroin, which made him so numb I didn't recognize my own father.

His past has stolen his power, and he has sabotaged his happiness. It's time to heal the deep issues left behind before we talk about him being sober... which we did for a month by doing just that; giving him love, having a ceremony, acknowledging his past. I saw the extremely strong warrior I had almost forgotten. I've seen this extraordinary genius do so much more, so I have no doubt he can overcome this addiction through unconditional love.

"Change your thoughts, change your life." - Dr. Wayne Dyer

Can a psychiatrist get down to the root of the problems?

I pray every day that he'll be free soon so that I can cure my dad. I've grown so much and have discovered reiki and the wonders and miracles behind it. I thank you for clarifying my father's mind so that he can be in the physical world, grounded in himself, sitting in his issues. From this point forward, it could be either divine or fatal, depending on the choices made. He has so much love in him that I know will come out if he can let go of the cords. Reiki would be extremely helpful... with meditation, music, anything to connect with Source and Mother Earth. All he wants is love. I ask you to give him love for me until he's able to be comfortable with himself, accepting himself, so he can manifest his dreams.

I've seen him with a clear mind, bettering society. Clearing his past through acceptance will manifest the man that every day I strive to be like. I saw the loving, intelligent, spiritual, enlightened, funny, and striving to be Christ-like, going to church. The hardest worker I've ever seen, diving into projects accomplishing faster than most. My father provided for my mom so that she didn't have to work. Providing through his million-dollar companies, he would build on manias, manifesting the life of a king. Then not facing the past or healing his chakras and his soul, he would manifest bankruptcy, repeating this cycle multiple times.

I'm currently learning the art of glass blowing. I'd teach him to keep his mind, body, and spirit alive and growing constantly. My goal is to grow all my fruit and vegetables with Maui's powerful sun. Along with hikes, jumping off waterfalls, swimming in the ocean, working out, meditation, yoga, writing music, singing, dancing, talking and learning all the time, all day, gathering around, giving love and good vibes.

Thank you for taking the time to get to know my father before deciding on his fate. Much Aloha from Maui.
Kanyon Stone

JOHN: I served as a Bishop in the Church of Jesus Christ of Latter-day Saints from 2004-2011. During this time, Scott, Keri and their family lived in our neighborhood in Sandy, Utah. I got to know Scott well during the time that they lived here. He is a good man and supported his family. While he lived in our community, Scott attended church regularly with us. Scott volunteered to serve in our scouting program and attended scout camp for a full week along with his son. I also got to spend a lot of time with him and his family at youth basketball games. Both of our sons for a time played on the same teams. In sports, he also was very encouraging in his support of his son, as well as other young men. He often took time to visit with them personally about their development and was always available to offer encouragement.

Scott has been through some difficult times in his life but has always strived to work hard and support his family who needs him. Please call me if you would like to visit further about Scott Stone.

Sincerely,
John Martin

Dan Moves In

Dan moved in at the beginning of April. Dan worked in slip 9. With me working in slip 8, Dan and I had gotten to know each other well, seeing each other every day at work. I enjoyed our conversations. Dan had been living in my boss' Front Street house along with other roommates. After boss' bike went missing, Dan was kicked out. I witnessed Dan scurrying to figure out what he was going to do. Dan was so miserable and sad during this time. After hearing about a couch falling through, I offered mine.

It has been interesting getting to know the people that enter my space via slip 9. First, Jessie, my dear sistah friend that lives at Olowalu. I don't know if I ever told her this, but she reminded me so much of my dear twin cousin Jessica. Jessie wasn't in slip 9 for very long. It's hard living off of what these booth positions pay; most days it costs you money to go to work. That tells you how much people love it at the harbor if they are working it... me especially. To be working it as long as I have been, with the little bit of income it provides... let's just say, I have been very blessed to have the forewarning that I would be volunteering with the dolphins. If I hadn't, I could have easily focused on the lack of pay, which just brings misery, but instead, I was able to focus on the free healing it provided, sitting in solace, with the ocean at my back.

I have loved all the people I have had the opportunity to get to know. Each character has brought a little bit of home to me, filling a family void after having just left all of mine.

Dan was the next character to move into slip 9 after Jessie left. Dan is from Orem, Utah... just down the street from where Kai's wife's family grew up. Dan works for the slip that runs the fishing boat Kai Akua... I'm always connecting dots.

I have loved getting to know Dan. He is an adoptee raised in the LDS religion. A Native American, taken in (along with his older brother) by a typical all-white large LDS family. Dan is a returned missionary and college graduate who was married in the temple and has had two children: a son and then, a daughter. After eight years of living the program and going to church every weekend, this family did not remain *"Together Forever."* Dan had informed me that he was a recovering addict, but not to worry, he would *"never touch the stuff again because detox is a horrible one."* He and his wife had divorced. His wife remarried, and it had been eight years since he had seen his children. Basically, Dan was someone that I could understand, and he was someone that could understand me.

It was nice to have Dan in the space. His area was in the TV room, open for anyone to enter. Dan blended in really well and felt right at home. We enjoyed his humor, his wisdom, and his stories. I felt safe with Dan in the space. I felt we could trust him in the space with the kids. We welcomed Dan into our family 100%. He was very helpful on multiple occasions. I took Dan in without expectations, just serving and loving another brother, just as Christ would do. I felt it was the right thing to do. I believe it was meant to be. Everything is about lessons and fine-tuning ourselves, clearing karma. But then, slip 9 had its laptop stolen. Dan was off on an errand, and someone lifted the laptop as if they knew when he'd be away from the booth.

Slip 9 had no choice but to tell Dan, *"Somehow return the computer, pay the $500 for a new one, or don't come back."*

Crazy thing... I was talking with a potential customer when I sensed the energy of theft. I looked over, saw that the booth had people there to watch over things, and then turned back toward the person I was chatting with. Come to find out, it was at that exact moment that someone had reached over in front of everyone and just grabbed the laptop and walked off.

Definite note to self... pay better attention and trust that feeling next time I feel that.

Dan came home seeming genuinely remorseful for what had happened. He appeared down on life. I tried to explain my understanding of how things work in my new way of thinking... explaining my truth that our life is our creation. We are the ones attracting everything in this illusion we call our life. If he wanted to change his life and start attracting a better life for himself, then he needed to look inward and do some inner healing.

Dan was very receptive to my hoodoo voodoo lessons. Over the days, Dan seemed to be getting cheerier about life. Again, I must say, we enjoyed having him around. Must I also again mention I collect children... I tend to mother adoptees even when they are my own age. I understand so much about why they do the things they do... why they are chameleons. And boy, are they such great actors, being who you want them to be, not wanting to displease anyone. Adoptees often have strong tendencies to lie and help themselves to your belongings. I hadn't held fear about Dan being a liar or a thief... But when things started missing at the house when good ole Dan was home, it created SUSPICION.

I hate suspicion. I hate having to even think about the thoughts of accusations towards others. The only time I have thieved was before I was eighteen, and it was from the mall. Never did I steal from anyone or any other place, other than those department stores, during my adolescent years. I have a hard time understanding why someone would just help themselves to your possessions. But obviously, I had some karmic debt to repay from those early years.

I had no choice; I had to ask Dan to leave. I acknowledged his value and let him know he is loveable, but he violated the trust, and I ended it with, *"I'm so sorry, Dan. I hate that it has come to this. I still love you dearly, Dan."*

And with that, Dan quietly packed up his belongings and exited without even a goodbye. God bless Dan.

Marie Checks In

Marie is another child I have collected... you know, that side effect from losing your own.

I met Marie through my dear JC. Marie is JC's *"pretty friend"* that lives in Utah. JC had met Marie a few years back while visiting us in Utah. Marie continued to visit our home, even after JC was back in Texas.

MARIE: Hey how r u?

KERI: I'm hangin' in there. How r u doin'?

MARIE: I'm tryna save to come out n visit u!

KERI: No hurries, I don't plan on living anywhere else.

MARIE: Ha ha ha I don't blame u... I'm thinkin' it's about time to get out of Utah... FOREVER!!! What happened to ur dog Zeus?

KERI: Actually, the Julie, Scott's ex from 1986... she finally got her man AND Kanyon's dog. At first, we were trying to get him to live with someone else when Scott got thrown into jail, but gave up on that. As long as the dog was being taken care of was all that we really cared about. Now that Kylie wants to go live at Grandma's and move back to Utah, she is saying that SHE should be able to have Zeus... which I really like the idea of, but my life has been out of my hands for a long time. I have learned to just roll with the currents and 'I will go where you want me to go dear Lord' right...

MARIE: I totally understand that... and that all makes sense! Just let it roll... that's what I've been doin'. There's a few things goin' on rite now that at times I want to rush to a conclusion on how to fix it, but then I just fall back and try to relax n try to remember to go by how I feel day by day instead of how I think I will feel tomorrow... if that makes sense.

KERI: Makes complete sense. Good to hear that is how you are rolling. The more you can stay in the NOW and handle everything with your full consciousness and focus, you will be more present with your entire decision making on how you handle every situation. Remember to stand in your truth, speak your truth and let your voice be heard. Now is a time of facing our fears. Face it head on to get it out of the space. My fears: being alone and having to support myself. Here I am. It has been scary, but I have finally reached a comfort level with living within my means and not worrying about tomorrow. Today, I have everything I need, and yes, you are absolutely correct; you have got to just make your choices on how you feel, not what you think... that explains why I am basically volunteering for my boss, being the best employee he has ever had. He has been loaning me money to survive, and who knows, maybe that is the best way so I can still get food stamps, lol. Lots of love, I love that you are finally Facebooking me... it's the only way for me to communicate these days.

MARIE: Yea I'm happy I actually have time to message u from fb, and oh boy Ms. Keri... That is the truth; I hit a storm the other day... whenever I get sidetracked on what happened in the past, or I try to think or try to analyze what's going to happen in the future, I've been tryin' to bring myself to the Now n how I feel in the Now! It's hard sometimes... especially trying not to be hurt from past experiences...

KERI: Meditation dear sistah... dedicate 20 minutes to meditate. That's all it takes to help clear that old energy and raise our vibration... so exciting when you allow yourself to *let go and let God*.

MARIE: Ur right Ms. Keri, I don't know how many times u have to tell me that. Hopefully, this is the last time. :) So, I assume by a comment u made earlier that u don't have any handsome friends! Or do you?... LOL oh my goodness I wish u were still here or in TX since I seem to travel there quite a bit now... I miss our talks.

KERI: I miss our gab sessions as well... and you guessed it!!! I do not have any handsome friends that I am spending time with. I just barely have been opening up to the idea of it. I am so damn picky, believe it or not. My criteria has only gotten worse since leaving Scott. My bar is so high, they have got to be pretty near Jesus status, looks and all. I am fine being alone. Being married to Scott was kind of like being alone... it was like being alone with benefits, haha.

MARIE: I've been thinkin' that I may never get married with all the stupid stories of people who are getting separated cuz they like someone else. u just feel like marriage isn't even respected anymore. makes me scared to get married.

KERI: I think you are wise to think, never to marry. I honestly think that thing called marriage is a thing of the past, old ways. New Age ways... every moment is a choice to be in a relationship with anyone. I don't plan on ever marrying again. In my opinion, it is just a way to get society/the man in your business and keep records of your whereabouts. But most importantly, the man in my life from here forward is going to be of choice every day... not a contract, or a promise of anything... promises are made to be broken... **YOU WISE WISE WOMAN**... good girl, lol

James' Birthday

What an eventful day. April 18th is my nephew's birthday, AND Kylie was flying out of here. I had the day off but headed to the harbor anyway... Nicky was giving me a beach cruiser bicycle. I took the dog and walked down to the harbor. I got to the booth at five minutes to 10:00 to find my work needed crew for the 10:00a.m. whale watch. Hank watched the dog, and I jumped on with Captain Justine. Prior to leaving, Justine and I were chatting about my daughter leaving today. *"What plans do you have to see her off?"* Justine asked.

"Well, she hates the sun and the beach, and I don't have any money to take her out for a meal even, but maybe I'll just take her to the grocery store and have her pick out something for me to cook for her. I have food stamps."

We went on our whale watch with Justine guiding me on how I could assist her with the trip. Justine, being the great teacher she was, suggested, *"You can start with mingling with the guests."*

I'm great at mingling. We had a great group... a three-generation family from the cruise ship. It was a great whale watch. We got back to the dock, and before running off, I asked Captain Justine, *"Is there anything more you need from me?"*

"Girl, you need to count tips before you leave."

Folks, what a blessing that was! I thanked Justine, *"Thank you so much! I now have money to take my daughter out to eat before she leaves!"* My daughter's flight had been postponed until 1:00am. I deep cleaned my house, did laundry, got dolled up, and then the fam headed to Bubba Gump's. James was at work and had already eaten, so I told him he had a rain check on me.

We had a great time at Bubba Gump's and got home with like an hour to spare before we had to think of heading to the airport. I had the boys load up the car with Kylie's bags, and we enjoyed our last moments at home. Kylie was so excited to get back home. She would get her bedroom back, her things back, most of her family back, her friends back, and she would be close to her daddy so she could visit him in jail.

I will miss the luxury of reaching out and hugging my daughter.

But honestly, shortly after she arrived, she did not want any hugs or kisses. She quickly settled into your typical teenager mode, wanting to be left alone. Before Kylie arrived, we were on the phone all day every day, like best friends. A lot of the time, she would call just to sit and listen in as if she were here.

I am looking forward to being her best bud again. It was perfect for her to be here when she was... but honestly, it's like my mother said, *"Each and every one of your kids have needed to be an only child so they can get all the attention needed."* And boy, is she on the mark with that. Having her and Kanyon under the same roof was tearing me apart. If it were possible for me to create another me, I would have loved the challenge, but with only one of me, the challenge was too great.

It just happened to work out that on the very next day after Kylie's take-off, Kandi and the kids moved back in.

I didn't feel like this was a backward move. During our separation (that truly needed to happen), lessons were learned. I told my dear sister, *"Things happened for a reason. Lessons have been learned, and it's time to get back on track."*

I can see the divinity of it all. The timing is perfect for Kandi and the kids to be back. She needed help with those beautiful children, and I needed help with mine. Plus, I wouldn't need to worry about the rent as much now that she was back to contribute.

Let's Break It Down:
Kylie Goes Home/Kandi Moves Back In

Yeah, all that happened within 24 hours. I felt like my life was on fast-forward, and I was glad. I thought back to what Pat (the healer from Mapleton, Utah) had said, *"You are late... the Universe has granted you more time."* It's been a journey. It's been a ride.

I'm so thankful for the knowledge I have gained. This road I've traveled has had some bumps and curves, but that is how I KNOW. I love that I have a large, extended, natural, and *"adopted"* family.

I Facebook messaged my other gifted light worker mentor, Kim Page, on February 20, 2013. I was stressed about my financial lack-of. I had been a diligent hard worker, serving others for free for a good majority of my life, and it was starting to get to me that no one was willing to pay me. Not my boss, the state food stamp office, the former husband, my family... NO ONE. When Kim responded to my plea for confirmation of good fortune, I did not like the answer. She said, **"Remember... It's HOW we do what we do, not WHAT, that breaks us through."**

I have finally realized the truth to Kim's message. When pondering Kim's message, I noticed a slight feeling of desperate energy I had in my space (something my gifted angel reader and homeopathic doctor friend, Crystal Doty Anderson, told me to work on clearing back in 2010). I've always known my words would be read, that my story would be told. But being in a bit of a rush to get to where I wanted to be, I blocked some things that needed to happen.

It dawned on me this very day, five days before my 43rd birthday, how ideally the Kylie story all played out. I tell everyone that Kylie is a fine tuner; she amplifies the situation and is quick to point out faults, mirroring huge projections of others LOUDLY. Kylie came into the space, and rocked our world, shook her aunt Kandi and Kanyon up, and left on her way just as sweetly as she had arrived.

This surrender I speak of ... Before, I was still steering my life, making choices, trying to push in the direction I wanted to go with my mind, trying to figure out what to do next to speed up this process to get to the best part of the ride that is *"My Life."* I have finally washed away the need to rush around through it, trying to force it to happen. I have mastered accepting every possibility of the path with positive gratefulness and a no-worries attitude.

This last little episode of Kylie hating Hawaii has been very eye-opening in many ways. First, she insisted that she go live at Julie's house. I was a little annoyed that I would have to hear her name again, let alone have my daughter be parented by this woman I felt had stalked me for **23** years. But I just breathed deep breaths and heard Kylie out. Kylie made sense. She was saying, *"Mom, what better person to take care of me? She is a stalker for real... she calls me round the clock checkin' in to see what and where I am."*

And with that, I thought, you never know where the correct path truly is. Maybe this path would end cycles that needed to be finished. And who am I to know which ones are Kylie's to end? And, realizing that a side effect of losing your child up for adoption is collecting children and realizing that Julie is also a Mother of Loss as well... Kylie knows best where she is to be. If she is to be living with Julie, her dad's number one fan, then so it is. Whatever is meant to be will be. And with that, I was grateful to the Universe and for Julie being there to clean up after my husband, take care of the dog, and help take care of my daughter. I told Kylie, *"You're right. Ok, whatever will be will be."*

I loved the healing process of letting go of trying to dictate what will and will not be. As soon as I surrendered and accepted it, Julie panicked, telling my mother that she couldn't have Kylie. Remember, Julie was with Scott the night he broke into family homes, and he was driving her car. The judge ordered Julie to stay away from Scott.

Not long after, my mother volunteered to love and adore my daughter and give Kylie all the attention she needed. I was grateful for my mother's quick response to help get Kylie back to Utah. My mother has been dealing with Kylie perfectly. She respects me as Kylie's mother, and all in all, I do have the final say.

Shortly after Kylie arrived in Utah, there was a small family get-together at my sister's house. After I heard about my two children,

Kylie and Kai, going to a family get-together at my sister's house with my mother and father, I realized how grateful I was that my sister could step in my place and play the role she was playing. A role I wish I could have been always playing. A role I used to get ferociously defensive of... Only because, of course, my motherhood was stripped away from me with that first one.

Seeing how my mother was taking care of my youngest child Kylie, and hooking up with that oldest-born child of mine, Kai... I couldn't help but connect the dots of how it has come full circle bringing healing energy to my mother's space for sure. You figure I was a single mother in need, even though I was almost 43, I was a mother that needed a village to help me raise my child... *no different than when I was 16*. It made me really understand and see the full circle; becoming a single mother at 16 with a mother who was unable to co-parent, now being given a chance to do just that. I loved seeing what that "would of/should of/could of" looked like with that first grandchild of hers. God bless my mother.

And God bless that bonus father of mine who adopted me when my daddy left. He was giving Kylie all the father energy and love a girl could ever ask for. Kylie had been screaming for that energy since the day she was born, and my dad has always given it to her, kissing her on the nose with his loud kisses.

Going to Grandma's was a blessing ready to unfold. Kylie needed that father energy ever since she was born, and Grandpa could give it to her. Kylie was doing great! My mother raised me and mastered some skills to know just how to deal with Keri Jr., who has her father's flare. Knowing and loving Kylie's parents, as well as my mother does, qualified her as the most capable woman on this planet to take care of my daughter, Kylie Dawn.

Which got me thinking... Shame on that adoption agency for misinforming my mother and judging and telling my young mother that she married too old of a husband to qualify to help any mother in need, including her own daughter. I realized for the first time that my mother should be the angry one! I was glad I was able to witness my mother helping me with my child like she should have done starting with that first baby of mine. It doesn't matter how young/old I was/am, IT TAKES A VILLAGE TO RAISE A CHILD, people. Quit judging and thinking, you all know what is best for a mother's child. The highest good of any child is the love and support of their mother. No one can replace your mother. It is what it is, we are who we are. We were born into the situations that we were in order to heal and end cycles that have been going around in circles from the beginning of time and helping us evolve into better human beings by understanding the cycles of life. To know up, one must know down. And who are we to take away the journey/ride of any other and impose our beliefs/judgments on any other? I appreciate people sharing and bringing awareness... which was not what those social wreckers were doing back in 1986.

I had finally arrived at a space of, "*I don't care if anyone hears my story anymore.*" One of my gifted teachers in the past told me something to the effect of, "*The unspoken story gets more and more desirable,*" with the message being, "*Don't be too quick to tell and give it all away. Save it for the book.*" And you know what? I think I finally really get what she meant.

Today at work, I had a few groups of travelers that got on the "asking questions wagon," wanting to know what brought me here, what was my story... and you know what, for the first time, I really didn't care to tell it. I just politely answered, "*Life Happened.*" In fact, one of those travelers was a solo traveler who I sensed would benefit from hearing my story, as most do. She lingered around my desk, but for some reason, I did not give it to her. After pondering what was up with me and why I didn't share my story, I realized that if people wanted/needed to hear it, then dear Lord/Universe you were going to have to deliver a literary agent to me, because I am finally at a place in my life where I believe if it is meant to be it will be. I am exhausted *shouting* awareness for all to hear. I figured I had traveled the road and had gained wisdom, and that wretched part of my journey was over. I have found healing, and if I am meant to share how I arrived at this healing place, then it will be. But until then, I will be writing this 4th book and realizing that I am just fine being a harbor rat if that is all I am to be. Nothing wrong with it. I love my harbor family. I just wanted more for myself, like a pillow top mattress in a nice home with no bugs and a nice view. I also wanted to be a grandmother to all my children, but I can accept being a grandmother to all children, even if mine won't have me.

Lizards Thick in the Space

It seems everywhere I went, there were lizards. I looked it up in the *Animal Speak* book.

Lizard: Lizards are sensitive to vibrations in the ground. Their eyes are sharp with the ability to detect the slightest movement around them. They also have acute hearing. All of these characteristics give it a symbolism associated with the psychic and the intuitive. The **ability to perceive subtle movement** - physical and ethereal, waking or sleeping – is what lizard medicine teaches.

Individuals with a lizard totem should listen to their own intuition over anyone else's. One of the most significant characteristics of some lizards, and their claim to fame, is the ability of the tail to come off. A predator may grab for it, its paw landing upon the tail, only to be surprised as the tail breaks off and the lizard scampers to freedom. The lizard then begins the process of growing another in its place.

This detachment is also part of what the lizard can teach. They can help us to become more detached in life to survive. Sometimes it is necessary to separate ourselves, or part of ourselves, from others to be able to do the things we desire to do. The lizard helps us to awaken that ability for objective detachment so that it can occur with the least amount of difficulty. The lizard can show up to help us break from the past. It may even indicate a need to explore new realms and follow your own impulses before you get swallowed up in what is not beneficial for you.

I saw the great message for me during that time. Celebrating my 43rd birthday, I realized that I had envisioned myself as retired and loving my grandkids, living comfortably, and helping out. I had envisioned myself cruising with the family, with me being very involved with my grandkids and us traveling everywhere together. It was getting to me that I was far from my visions. Good thing I was seeing lizards!

My 43rd Birthday

All in all, I had a great birthday. Had a great phone call with Alex, one of my nephews in Utah, that happened to call to get Kylie's new number. I then had a fun call with Kylie sharing about our day and our convo with Alex. Kanyon and I hung out on the kite beach all day. Kandi treated us to the best lunch ever at the Whole Foods Deli (I found a lemon tart pie!). My birthday ended with a hike with the kids to a beautiful viewpoint overlooking Lahaina. We topped off the night by eating my lemon birthday cake. So glad to have Kandi and the kids, along with James and Kanyon, here for the ride and to share my birthday with me.

May 2013

The End of Whale Season

Whales were migrating home, and the paychecks became obsolete as well. I had a great journey *"volunteering"* for the dolphins and was thankful for the paychecks that the whales brought. I didn't know what tomorrow would bring or which direction to go for sure... I felt like I should start researching it. I pursued other options, searching the web, diligently looking for jobs that pay. It was very discouraging to not be recognized as a value to anyone.

I continued to chant... *"Abundance- the ability to do what you need to do when you need to do it,"* along with faithfully honking the horn melodically through the Pali tunnel while singing the tune, *"Abundance rushes freely to me. Abundance is here."*

I needed to continue to see everything for what it was... if I had extra money, a dependable car, or even a great-paying job, I would have been off playing instead of writing. I also saw the blessing in the car breaking down, not only creating the perfect workout for me, but also creating the perfect opportunity for my job to serve as a great obedience school for Stoney. Walking to the harbor from above the Cannery Mall was the perfect walk for Stoney who was rewarded with love-filled greetings from visitors and harbor regulars.

I woke up in the morning needing some kind of comfort that I was almost there. I was so done working as hard as I was without the comforts I had left behind. I came with only a suitcase of clothes and my old laptop, and the only new items I purchased were a toaster, blender, Kanyon's laptop, a blow-up mattress, and a pair of durable flip-flops. The reality that that was the hardest I had diligently worked for the lengthy duration of almost a year with little to show for, was quite bleak. The future did not look bright.

I was able to turn my frown upside down with the help of my dear sister Kandi, who believed in me and supported me in the writing of this book. She was a great help for me to see working for Mark as the true blessing that it was. *"Think of your booth as your office space to write your book. What a perfect spot, next to the ocean and with this dead time, not many interruptions."*

I was very grateful to have Kandi back in the space. She saw the value in me. That morning, I was so down on myself... rent was due, and I had worked all month and would be lucky if I got $300.00 for the many hours I had put in. I was grateful for the paychecks that were coming with the whales but had to put it all towards the rent and food during the time Kandi had moved out, so needless to say, I never got ahead in any way, and I ended up being grateful for my clothesline being targeted...through that, not only did it motivate me to write, but it also blessed me with some new (old) clothes.

But you know what, as blessed as I was, it could get discouraging when you were doing everything in your power to change the situation... serving and loving others over and beyond, to not be "rewarded" if you will, in some luxurious way such as a paycheck.

It is crazy how many people love my serving, helpful qualities when they don't have to pay for them. It's a shame what curse money puts on things. It's a hard reality that money has had its power for so long that people cannot fathom serving and loving others when they see a need. It can be disappointing on many levels for me when I don't feel others are following the Golden Rule, "*Treat others how you would want others to treat you.*" Especially when I felt I had followed that Golden Rule so well for the majority of my life.

The message from the *Humpback Whale*: During the winter, humpbacks fast and live off of their fat reserves, migrating thousands of miles in the name of posterity... breeding, birthing, and weaning. The Humpbacks are known for their song.

I see this message as living within our means (our reserves) during winter. After all, my passion is in the name of posterity, bringing awareness for better generations... my song.

Scott Writes His Kanyon Boy

Kanyon boy, how are you doing? How is life in Maui? I heard about your wallet coming up missing with $300 in it. That sucks, but what do you do? You need to keep your money hidden when you live with so many people. I love you so much, and I miss you tons. I can't wait to see you. I am excited to come to Maui and hang out with you. How is the glass blowing coming? Are you getting good? What kind of things can you (have you) made? So, you are babysitting for Kandi? How is that going? How is Stoney Stone? It's funny that is his name because most of the people here in jail call me Stoney, and the rest call me Stone. Funny huh?

So, I saw Kylie Dawn a week ago Sunday. That was nice. She looked amazing. She is getting so grown up and beautiful. I am getting really buff again. When I get out, I shouldn't have much, if any, body fat, and I will be in great shape. I will be ready to hit the gym hard and get buff like I was in Houston again.

I am excited to get out and start making some money and getting on with life. Today is Wednesday, May 8th. My celly's name is JD. I have been with him for 43 days. It sucks though, because he is leaving on Saturday. I'm not looking forward to getting a new celly. We work out together, and we both like our cell hecka clean. We play a lot of cards, and we both have times when we like quiet so we can read. Oh, and we both like to go back to sleep after breakfast until lunch, hehe. I know, lazy boy. I read about 400 pages a day of fictional novels, then I am studying math and social studies, and I have a bunch of computer books, my scriptures, some self-help stuff my mom sent me, and my LDS addiction recovery book, so lots of reading, studying and contemplating changes to make in my past behavior. My head seems a lot calmer. I think it makes my handwriting neater.

I'm not too good at meditating, but I am working on it, and seems to be getting better. Are you taking care of your mother and being respectful even when you don't get your way? You need to be because your mother needs you now more than ever. She is an amazing mom and woman and deserves your respect. If you ever have any complaints, think about what kind of mom you could have gotten and be grateful for how wonderful your mom is. Also, always live in the Now. You can't worry about the past or the future. You can only be the best man you can be Now. Always be a good example to those around you and be proud to be a son of God.

So, I have the pic of you with blue hair in your fighting stance hanging by my bed in my cell. Also, one of Kylie in black and white, about age 4, and one of you and Kylie in aprons with Kylie holding a big pan of pasta. Then a few others. It is nice to have them with me. You should send me some current ones. I can get four 4"x6" max size per letter.

So, do you do any fishing out there in Hawaii? Have you found a group to play ball with? I'll bet there are a lot of them that play at the church. If you are interested, you should check that out. That should be fun for you, plus get you some more buddies to hang out with.

So, I had $14.00 left on my calling card to call you with, but I talked to Mom once, and that was $9.00. She answered another time, and that was $4.00, so I am just waiting on another calling card so I can call you. I love you tons and can't wait to see you. Love dad

Keri, I'm out of money on my card, but I am working on getting more on the account, and then I will call on the weekend. That 2nd call you answered was still $4.00 even though we hung up quickly, so that answers that. I'll talk to you soon. Love Scott

Mother's/Victory Day

Let me tell you about Mother's Day... I have always hated the day, too many expectations, too many disappointments. I think most mothers feel this way. Imagine the perspective I have had; every Mother's Day was a reminder of what I was not from 1987 on.

I loved sharing emails with Mai while she was on her LDS mission in Russia in 2010. I learned a lot about Russian culture; one of my favorites... "*Victory Day.*" I believe I even blogged about it and added it to Book 2. Anyway, Victory Day landed on the same day as USA's Mother's Day. For Russians, that day was the day Russia conquered the Germans. Russia doesn't celebrate Mother's Day or Father's Day. They honor women on "Woman Day," and men on "Men Day."

2010 was a horrible Mother's Day, as always, and especially since the reunion with my son in 2006. It just angered me that when Kai was on his mission, he was only allowed one phone call... wow. Good thing Kai was not one to completely obey the rules. However, I quickly adopted this Victory Day concept instead of our Mother's Day. I vowed to a friend that I would never celebrate that wretched holiday ever again. But I will willingly acknowledge my victory of living through and enduring three children, yes count that as three... It was especially hard living through the loss of that first one. I am a Mother of Loss.

Anyway, that Mother's/Victory Day was, I think, my most favored one of all. It was treated as a regular day. I love how all my days run together as one. I love how Hawaii still runs businesses on Sundays. But I never would have guessed that I would be seeing my skin doctor on a Sunday, Mother's Day Sunday. I loved the idea of getting shit done on this retarded holiday. Better yet, his office was right on Kaanapali Beach with patient beach parking.

Kylie was the first to text that day, wishing me a great Mother's Day. With her living in Utah, she was up at the crack of dawn our time, even on Sundays. I had great convos with Kylie. We were back to being great phone pals.

Kandi had to work, so Kanyon, the kids, the dog, and I went to my doctor's appointment early. I got the fam situated and then headed back to the office to let them know I was an hour early and tell them which car was my car, so they wouldn't tow it. As I walked back to the fam, I passed a familiar bald man, Dr. Wayne Dyer... O.M.Heck, I feel like I know the man. I automatically turned and acknowledged his name as a question, "*Wayne?*"

I noticed he was dripping wet after exiting the pool. I loved how genuinely his eyes met mine as he took his time being in the NOW and allowed time for my introduction. Feeling for him, thinking he most likely would rather chit-chat later, I kept it simple with, "*I recognize that face. I'm Keri Stone. So very nice to meet you.*" I told him that I lived in the area and I most likely would see him around.

After asking my name again, shifting his handshake to a more gentlemanly form for a lady, he released with a wave goodbye and bid me a good day, "*Enjoy this Mother's Day.*"

I didn't need more of that beautiful man's time. I felt honored that of all the days I could have met him, it happened on Mother's Day. Especially when you know how much I dreaded the holiday because of who I am. If any of you are not aware, Dr. Wayne Dyer totally gets it because he grew up in an orphanage and in the foster care system.

I then moseyed on back to the kids and watched the two pups (Stoney and little Christian) while Kanyon took the older kids to sneak in the pools. After hanging out at the beach for an hour with the family, I walked to my doctor's appointment and had my two moles cut off: one from my left forehead, and one from my right back. I'm adding these details because it has got to mean something, and I plan on looking it up later.

After my appointment, I rounded up the kids and we drove home. I called my mother and wished her a Happy Mother's Day and told her the exciting news about who I had met. Of course, my mother corrected me, saying, "*Wayne?? You mean Dr. Wayne Dyer. Not just Wayne.*" My mother wasn't as excited as I had thought she would be. She is more into Dr. Phil, and even mentioned once that she had submitted my story for his show and never got a response.

I informed her, "*That's because my story is too big for Dr. Phil.*" She chuckled and said she wondered if they had thought she was making my story up because it was a crazy one.

Well, after not getting the response I wanted from my mom about my excitement about meeting Wayne, I updated my Facebook status.

> *I had a great day. My daughter was the first to wish me a happy day. I hung out in Kaanapali with Kanyon, the dog, and the kids. Went to my Dr. apt... I know... on Mother's Day?! But that Dr.'s apt was on the beach with parking, and as a reward, I personally met Dr. Wayne Dyer. He had just hopped out of the swimming pool, and we were crossing paths. Dr. apt went well, cut some moles off for Mother's Day. It has been a Mother's Day that I will never forget because of the strange untraditional way I spent my day. I used to live for holidays, but now I just live.*

Much better, I had cousins, my brother, sistahs, and friends that understood my excitement.

After posting that post, I received a text from my oldest son, sending his love and wishing me a good day. It had to have been late in Florida, but I thanked him for the text and sent love back. I carried on about my day being a normal day, often forgetting that it was Mother's Day. But when the thought came in and my mind drifted to Kai, I quickly shut it off because it didn't matter anyway. This horrible day was an obligation day. I would rather have the sweet calls when a person really wanted to talk rather than felt like they had to. And I was just as guilty at this *have to* obligation on Father's Day. I had two dads. It was tricky.

But what did today mean? When I have strange days, I can't help but to read into them.

> *Skin*: Protects our individuality, unresolved feelings of irritation, criticism.
>
> *Mole*: Growths of skin. As the years pass, moles change.
>
> *Growth*: Nursing old hurts...

hmm... Okay, well, let's look up right and left.

Right: male, *Left*: female.

Well, the forehead mole was rough and bumpy and old, and was on the left... Kylie ... and the one on my back was flat and just changing color, and on my right... Kai. ... Reading into removing my moles, I could see a message of how my actions are removing the rough and bumpy old unresolved feelings of irritation and criticism. I'm done nursing the old hurts. Time for fine-tuning and change.

After being rewarded with my interaction with Dr. Wayne Dyer and him bidding me a good Mother's Day just shortly before my mole removal appointment, I think it was safe for me to say that I didn't need to worry about either of those two... everything was going to be fine. I was removing all that energy of unresolved feelings out of my space and protecting my individuality.

Family Letters

May 24

SCOTT: Kanyon boy, how are you doing you handsome devil? How is Maui? How is Stoney Stone? How goes glass blowing and babysitting Kandi's rug rats? How is James doing?

I am just doing my time, working out, exercising my body, mind, and spirit. I'm still waiting on them to take me to CATS. I should be going there anytime. My celly JD, that I was roommates with for 47 days, left a week ago last Saturday... So 13 days ago. I got some long-haired rocker dude for three days. I then got a guard that likes me to move one of my buddies, Noah, in with me. That is a lot better. We work out together, and we are a lot alike. He gets a lot of food every Friday on commissary and tries to feed me, which I don't like. I am trying to be all swollen and ripped up when I get out, so I am trying to just eat enough to put on muscle and have energy to work out as hard as possible. I go out in the yard every day and get some sun too (at least an hour), so I am getting tan.

So how often are you watching Kandi's kids? Are you being a good example to them? You are an amazing young man, and I know you know what is ok to teach these precious children of God and what is not ok.

So, I have seen Kylie twice now. She seems to be doing very well with Grandma and Grandpa Poulsen. She seems to like school up there and has been going to church and Young Women's. I think that will be very good for her. She will be going to the Stone reunion also and spending some time hanging out with Kathy and her family. I am hoping that all of those experiences will soften her up and help her to be an amazing loving young woman. Hopefully, she doesn't get overwhelmed by Grandma's rules. I think the rural area and the animals, and such will do her good.

Are you working on your body, soul, and spirituality daily? You are the generation of the future Kanyon, and we need you to be physically, emotionally, and spiritually strong so that we have an army of amazing warriors that can help turn the tide of today's society, and Mother Earth can be treated better and start to heal. You are an amazing spirit, and I love you so much and miss you every day. I am proud of the young man that you have become, and I want you to enjoy your youth. Don't stress about the little things, and don't let insignificant matters create anger in your heart or become an obstacle that creates strife between you and your friends and/or loved ones. Life is too short to hold on to grudges or have anger in your heart. Fill your heart with love and compassion and be the one that everyone loves and admires. Live every day like it is your last and treat every goodbye like it will be a long one. Watch out for your mother and remember how much she does for you and how much you love her. I love you so much, and I miss you every minute. Your, Dad

May 24

SCOTT: Keri, how are you? I hope you are making do. I'm doing everything I can to get out of here ASAP so I can assist you and Kanyon. I know it is hard being on your own, and I am sorry for that. I am glad you have Kandi and James to help you until I can. I hope you are enjoying Hawaii and that it is not all stress and worrying about money.

You are an amazing woman, and I will always love and respect you. I hope you can find peace with the whole Kai thing, and I'm sorry that I wasn't a bigger support to you with that and a lot of other matters. I'm sorry that I failed you as a husband and a supporting parent to our amazing children. Thank you for always taking amazing care of me, and for defending me, and worrying about my physical and mental well-being. I have no complaints about you as a wife, a true friend, and a mother to my children.

I will always look up to you and your amazing example of unconditional love and acceptance of all people. I hope that you have peace and closure with Randy and that you know how much he loved you. I will do all I can for the rest of my life to be a good friend to you, an amazing father and grandfather to our children and grandchildren, and to walk in strength as a recovering addict and alcoholic. I work every day to become physically stronger, emotionally, mentally, and spiritually, free and unbound by mortal bonds. I look forward to coming to visit you guys in Lahaina. Love always, your friend always, Thanks for being you, Scott.

May 31

KANYON: Big Dog. Hey Dad, I love hearing how great you are doing. I'm doing better than ever, got my torch, and I harvested the big AK-47 and Great White Shark marijuana plants I grew. I've been watching *Spirit Science* on TV. It's so enlightening. I love hearing your mind, body, and spirit strengthening... The balance of the trinity is important.

Society is finally thinking with their right brain again and recognizing the spirit aspect. They can actually measure the electromagnetic frequency of any living thing, including plants. I've been learning about sacred geometry, quantum physics, and a lot that goes along with things we learned before, like chakras. James and I are delving deeper into how this Universe works.

Mom is doing amazing. She is looking for a job, but until then, we watch the kids. The kids are great. They're getting huge! Sativa & Bubba went snorkeling with us, but damn, those Tongans hella chow!!! Haha.

That's cool you could pick your cellmate. I'm excited to see how ripped you are. I've been really missing lifting with you and Kai. James doesn't work out with me.

Yeah, those kids are going to be the coolest kids. They already are so intelligent and skilled. I took Bub to go bombing hills with me on his knees. He charges the hills as fast as me!! Then he slams his shoes on the ground for breaks.

Kylie is going to get the big picture finally, I think, but it might have to be a slap to the face if she can't see the less obvious signs. She just needs to find her passion, fine-tune her frequency and manifest her destiny. It can be hard to believe we control our fate because sometimes we are not clear on what we want, or if your frequency matches something like a car wreck then so it is. The more you take back your vibration and tune into intuition, the more the choice in your highest good rings true.

I'm so grateful your left and right brain are so balanced. This new generation of children... indigo, crystal, and rainbow, that have been coming since the 80s have been coming more and more. I'm so grateful to come from two indigo parents because if I would've had two left-brain linear-thinking parents like Kai did, I don't think my frequency could have handled this dense world.

The balance of the minds is spreading with the polar shift happening. Sirius, the brightest star (aka the Big Dog Star), is orbiting closer and closer. Life on Sirius has the highest frequency and electromagnetic frequency, and electromagnetic frequencies affect others around us. So, they are raising our vibration. It has happened many times in history. Bronze to Iron, to Silver, to Golden Age. It used to not happen so frequently, but time is speeding up and we're learning lessons faster, so now it's every 13,000 years. Dogon, Egyptians, Mayans (Lumerians and Naacals) in Atlantis, Sumerians, and Buddhist monks (Native Americans) all knew about the consciousness levels. This is the peak of peaks. It's going to be like nothing we've seen before; Mother Earth is going to be in a beautiful state of harmonic unity and One Love.

I love you so much, dad. Your soul is full of so much love, and you, not like a lot of people, see the big picture. I'm so grateful for your touch of genius and the amazing environment you gave me as a kid, manifesting what I was to become. Environments really affect what you subconsciously manifest within you.

I love you so much. Soon we'll be on our land together here in Maui. Your son, Kanyon boy

P.S. Maui looks like a swimming man. We arrived on his heart chakra in Wailuku, and now we're on his third eye in Lahaina.

Here are the meanings of the Chakras, for those of you who are unfamiliar:

1st Chakra: Root (ovaries)

2nd Chakra: Sacral (adrenal glands)

3rd Chakra: Solar plexus (pancreas)

4th Chakra: Heart (thymus)

5th Chakra: Throat (thyroid gland)

6th Chakra: Third eye (pituitary gland)

7th Chakra: Crown (pineal gland)

Speaking of chakras, let us talk about the age when they are developing, the demons that come out when there has been trauma during those years causing an energy leak, and the outcome when healed.

1st Chakra: 0-5 years; Pride - A sense of belonging

2nd Chakra: 5-10 years; Lust - Control over emotions

3rd Chakra: 10-15 years; Envy - Self confidence

4th Chakra: 15-20 years; Anger - Unconditional love

5th Chakra: 25-30 years; Coveting - Live within your means

6th Chakra: 30-35 years; Gluttony - Serve others

7th Chakra: 35-40 years; Slothfulness - Heal others

May 31

KERI: Dearest Scott, it was so good to hear from you. I loved the artwork on the envelope. Yes, I am enjoying Maui. How could I not? It has been very challenging most of the time. Life is challenging, and it is why we signed up. It's quite the ride, AND boy, has it been a ride. I have, for the most part, enjoyed most of the ride. After all, it's all about one's attitude as to how enjoyable the ride will be.

Anyway, how is jail, honestly? I imagine you are doing well there. I bet you offer a lot of mentorship with the younger hooligans. Everyone needs someone, no matter who you are or what you have done.

Oh my heck, that reminds me... I was reading this magazine that made it to my hands, and there was this article about how a 21-year-old went gorillas on his mother and killed her. He was an honor, and perfect, student. When he was in his last years of high school, his father died in a rescue, being a firefighter and all. The family was a supposed strong-knit family and very RELIGIOUS... ought to worry about what the neighbors think, aye. So anyway, this 20-something-year-old son was a nerdy lookin' feller. He loved computers, and I guess his voice never changed to a deeper tone, and his mother always razzed him about his femininity, trying to toughen him up or whatever it is one does? But anyways, his grandmother, the mother's mother, testified for the boy revealing how it was, with the church they were involved in and the grandma being a member as well, & how the mother was with the boy. I guess the sentence was decreased in half.

Everyone was horrified that the grandmother would choose the boy's side after, in his fit of rage, he bludgeoned her own daughter. She was an amazing woman who stood by her grandson because she could understand his snapping from his mother ridiculing her grandson's feminine behavior. The grandmother's husband left her, saying she left him spiritually, so he is leaving her physically.

I share this because as crazy as the grandson's actions are, it really isn't WHO he is.

I watched a thing on YouTube, *Ask Teal*, and she was describing the hidden positive intention in "bad" actions. For example, when someone kills, they kill because they don't feel a sense of human connection, and when they kill, for a brief moment, they feel a sense of a human connection.

Another example she gave was when someone gets M.S. (Multiple Sclerosis), like my mom has, the positive intention for creating this in her space is to receive help from her husband because she was feeling lonely and overwhelmed with her duties at home. Doesn't that sound like my mother? All the examples were amazing and made complete total sense. I will copy my notes and give you some to read.

Anyhow, religion can be bothersome. Speaking of bothersome, that biggest fan of yours (girlfriend/friend/secretary) or whatever you are calling her these days, Julie. Well, darling, I can no longer deal with that woman. I tried to be nice. I tried to be sensitive. I tried to be understanding... I cannot do it. I will not interact with that woman any longer. At first, I was thinking maybe I would be able to bring her some kind of healing, being a Mother of Loss as well, but she needs another person to offer her that. It's a conflict of interest for me. Isn't that what they call it? If you know the person with attorneys or something???

Anyway dear, what I am saying is I will deal with you directly or through my sister, or my mother, or even through your mother, over dealing with Julie. God bless her, but I have got to remove myself from people that don't serve me in my highest good, and she is far from fitting the bill for that. Thanks for all the love and acknowledgments. I love that we have divided as good friends and united parents. Keep up all the good work.

We love hearing how well you are and can't wait to SEE you with our own eyes. We love how amazing you look and must feel.

Let me know as soon as you do what your sentence for sure will be. Let me know about taxes. Dawn was telling me I could apply and get free money for being a mother in need with no income. If you for real sent in some kind of tax anything, please let me know. Having a grant from the government for being a mom would be great, but I don't know what you have already FOR REAL filed. Talk to you soon. Lots of love, thanks for the lessons, Keri

My Perspective These Days

I have come a long way, as we all do, gaining a new perspective on the reason for life and why we choose to sign up for this experience.

I am grateful for all my traveled paths; they have brought me the knowledge to back up my current beliefs. Being raised Mormon was a great foundation for me, as well as being born from a hippie's DNA with those influences in the mix. The downs in life have definitely shown me what I don't want so that I can envision and pursue what I do want. Because basically, that IS exactly why we are here. Sure, the lessons to KNOW why, when, what, how, where, and all that, but on the path to knowing, we are developing our individuality... Our individual likes and dislikes that create our own uniqueness, separate from Source/God/All. And that right there is the beauty of it. We are not to be like everyone else, just following suit. The ride of life is to find oneself.

Some need to touch the fire to find what they really, really like, and some of us don't. Life is all choices.

So now that I have come to the perspective that life is all about choice and finding oneself, and knowing the individual uniqueness of oneself that is called a personality. Okay, now that I know what I don't want, and I can focus on what I do want, it's as easy as clearing the energy out of the energy centers, that is, our chakras, and enjoying this thing we call Life.

So, in the meantime, while I am waiting for my vibration to catch up and match with the vibration in my vortex escrow energy field... my Life Essence... I am to stay in the NOW, making choices that bring me happiness.

Happiness raises your vibration. Sometimes it is hard to find happiness; sometimes it's hard to feel like there is even a choice for happiness. This is when I really ponder on life, pray, smoke a bowl, meditate, and get to analyzing. *"What is it all for anyway, and what am I supposed to be doing with myself? Especially because no one wants to hire me for money to serve and contribute to society on this planet Earth with the program that is currently running."*

My pondering always leads me to one conclusion that I have not wanted to accept because it sounds too simple to be true. But as my son Kanyon keeps reminding me, *"It's the journey to enjoy, not the destination."* It's true. Life is about the experience of it. If all I do in a day is love and serve others, even if I don't make a dime doing it, I am doing exactly what I am supposed to be doing for my highest good. Being a single mom and trying to provide for my family... this simple concept is hard to trust in and roll with. I have lost all of my material objects, my family, and at times my sanity, but at the end of the day, *"It's me that will always be here for me,"* so I better first and foremost take good care of me.

The best way to take care of me? Just look towards the children... Children are pros at being in the NOW. Children are opening their chakras all day long. They are playing, running, jumping, skipping, laughing, coloring, blowing bubbles, drawing... the list is endless. When I am serving and loving others, especially children, I am reminded, *"Keep it simple."*

I don't even recall when the world started giving the dollar so much power. I am assuming it was just the cycle of things with the fall of the Golden Age cycling through the Galactic Belt to the Iron Age. People working together as a community shifted to people working independently to get their own selves ahead of others. They worried about themselves doing more work than others, thinking they *deserved more*. They created the really rich, and the really poor, and distracted everyone from our focus of why we are here; to enjoy the sensation of this physical realm where we are all individuals with the power to choose to be One Love instead of separate love. Together we are stronger, and we all have our different strengths that make the whole of us stronger.

I have finally come to the conclusion that I don't need to be chasing the dollar to survive in this world by being so independent and full of worry about myself and my children. We are meant to live like the dolphins do, in pods/families working together and providing food and provisions for all. Animals don't have jobs or money, and they live peacefully in nature with an abundance of food and shelter... until we humans disrespect Mother Earth in pursuit of that dollar for bigger and better, and destroy nature, which will slowly destroy us in the end.

A perfect day for me??? Wake up when I want to (which, when given a choice, is surprisingly quite early), take the dog on a morning walk, help Kandi with the kids, read in my beautiful yard, work in my garden, harvest my garden, go on an adventure with Kanyon (even if that just means grocery shopping), art time is always a must... but mostly, just hang with family, working and enjoying life together as one. I cannot wait for my life to be filled with bliss from living from the heart and pursuing activities for pure joy.

I used to feel guilty or bad for eliminating the things that did not bring me joy. Forcing myself on others, for example. I feel like I was using a lot of energy forcing myself on my family, my husband, Kai, and Kylie. My biggest dream was to always be united as one in my own little family unit (after all, isn't that what will bring us happiness and joy?). And when that dream was not meshing out the way I had envisioned it to be, I can now see how I was clinging on to it, *forcing myself, my will, on others*, bringing unhappiness for everyone.

I used to judge others for simply walking away from their family and obligations in pursuit of their happiness. In fact, I hated that Scott walked away from our family and obligations in pursuit of his happiness. But obviously, the things that brought me happiness, and the things that brought Scott happiness, were completely different. Or maybe the things that I thought would bring me happiness were the things that brought me unhappiness (obviously). All in perspective, right?

My happiness meter has definitely improved since leaving Utah. It is now obvious that I was not meant to be there any longer. I felt there was no purpose left there for me. Everyone needs to feel they have a purpose, and everyone needs to feel loved.

It was easier to surrender to life than I thought it would be. I was holding on tight to what I knew, even though there was nothing to make anyone happy about it. I felt exhausted and broken, like a freshly tamed wild Mustang. I took calm big breaths and *let go and let God.*

I quit chasing after relationships, trying to fix them. I

surrendered to anything that came my way, with faith that God and the Universe would work it out. I have surrendered to such a degree that I often feel deserted on a deserted island and am fine having no one to talk to. I have finally found peace and happiness within myself so that I can totally understand the concept that we were all One consciousness before the Big Bang Theory, and there was no individualism like there is now. I love the individual I have become, and I love that I no longer need any other individual to validate how much I am loved. For you see, I love me, and that is all that really matters.

June 2013

Scott Faces Sentencing

June 2

SCOTT: Hello Kanyon bear, how are you? I love you so much, and I miss you so badly it makes my heart hurt. I am so proud of what an amazing, sensitive, caring, and gentle man you are becoming. I am excited to see you bloom into manhood and start your life as an adult. Always remember to love what you do for work, and always be the most informed and the best at what you do. That way you will be valuable and in high demand. Keep your mind clear and strong, work on your emotional state, and if you have demons in your closet, talk about them and get them out. Keep your body clean and strong. Always consider everything you put into it or do with your body, mind, and soul, and make sure you will not have any long-term regrets.

I am working out hardcore, and I am starting to see amazing results. When I first came here, I was wearing a 4X top and bottom uniform. Now I am in 2X of both. But I will be going back to a 3X top cause my arms and shoulders are getting too gigantic. Yeah, that's right, son, I used that word instead of saying big or large. I went clear up to gigantic. Haha.

So, are you being loving and respectful to your momma? Please be sure that you are. Also, remember that you are partially responsible for raising Kandi's kids since you are spending so much time with them. So be responsible and choose carefully the things you put into their minds. Don't teach them at a young age that weed is the path for them. Let them decide for themselves. Remember that society still considers it illegal, and there are health-related side effects from any kind of smoke.

Are you being smart with your money? Have you gotten yourself the things you need to do glass blowing? I hope you don't take my advice as lecturing because that is not my intent. I just want you to be the most amazing man that you can be.

I have my sentencing on the 16th, which is 2 weeks from today. I hope I get out that day and go down to the rehab center in Payson. If the judge signs off on it, then I will go that day. My attorney says there is a good chance that he will. If not, then I would have to do CATS in here. Which isn't my first choice, but it would be ok. This too, shall pass.

Today I have been here 202 days. If I had to do another 120 or so, I would be fine, but that is not what I am praying for or putting my intentions towards. I am excited to get out of here and get back to life and work. I have some great business ideas, and I am excited to get going on them. Also, to get land and build a house. I figure I can have a house here that I build myself and can help you build a house on your land there. That way, I can go back and forth for work until I get the new companies to the point that I can spend most of my time over there.

I watched the movie *50 First Dates* about a month ago. It was hard for me. Between the 80s music on the soundtrack and them being in Hawaii, I ended up teary-eyed in my cell.

So, I had my birthday 8 days ago... 45. Kind of sucked being in jail for that, but at least I am alive, healthy, and clear-headed, so I won't complain. I'm thinking when I get out of here, I will have to get me some 36 waist pants. My legs are thin and getting toned. My upper body is really strong and toned.

Still have a little skin on the bottom of my 8-pack, but the top half shows when sitting or standing, so I'm glad about that. Ab work has been brutal, but it is paying off. I love you son, and I am excited to see you. Love Dad

SCOTT: Keri, how are you? It's been a while since I have been able to call, and I miss your grounding voice. You have always been able to calm me when I am stressed or upset. It is Sunday today, and I have been locked down since Tuesday at four because I gave some old man with back pain some ibuprofen. He has no money to go to the doctor, so he just has to suffer through the pain. It's sad. So yeah, I have had to stay in my cell 24/7. Tuesday from 4:00 p.m., Wed, Thurs, Fri, Sat, Sun, Mon, Tues, Wed... Thursday I can get back out again. I guess it's not 24/7 on Wed, Fri, and Sun, because I can go out into the concrete yard for an hour after lunch. I will be grateful for that time in the sun.

I will call on Thursday. I guess I am calling Kandi's phone. Julie told me about the drama of the phone calls. I was annoyed about the whole thing. I told her that the two calls when we talked were on the card that Kathy got me, so it was really none of her business. After being in here for so long, you learn not to sweat the small things.

I got some colored pencils, as you most likely gathered from the envelope that this letter came in.

How is Kanyon doing? Is he being safe on his longboard? I have been worrying about him. I wish he would wear a helmet. Has he been playing some ball? I told him about the church around the corner. I'm sure they have games going on over there, and I'm sure he could meet some nice boys.

How is James? Hey, do you have any recent pics of the kids? I can receive up to 4 4"x6" pics per letter if you do; maybe one of all of you if you have one.

So, Kylie has been to see me a couple times. She seems to be doing well at your mom's house. She looks amazing. She was going to go hang with Kathy last I heard. Kathy has been cool. She emails me regularly and has sent me food and hygiene items and bought me a phone card and some books I wanted.

Cyndy has been emailing me, also. They bought 18 acres north of Rexburg and have been building a home. It should be done before summer is over. It sounds like it will be a nice home. They are surrounded by horse pastures and stuff. They have a big pond on their property. They have a water trampoline and stocked the pond with fish; perfect set-up for their family.

When I get out of here, I want to come to Hawaii for a couple weeks and spend some time with y'all. I'm thinking, worst case scenario, I will be here until October 15th. I'm still waiting to go to CATS. I cannot believe how long it has taken me to get over there. I'm definitely starting to get antsy.

I have been reading a lot and have a lot of projects, but my mind is so clear and sharp these days that I run out of books a lot. Then I have to beg and borrow until the next library date, which is every two weeks. We can only get six books per order, but I have a few buddies that only order 2-3 books per time, so they order me a few each week. I'm also working on getting a subscription to *Sports Illustrated* and *Time*. Those are the two that are weekly, so that will give me plenty of up-to-date reading to do every week. I am also getting a BYU course catalog that lists all of the required classes for certain degrees. Then I am going to get the textbooks for the courses that you can rent at a place called campus book rentals.com, and I will study the books and do the course work. That should keep my mind sharp and busy and give me an edge on making money when I get out of here. I am going to study construction management and computer technology degrees, work and information.

So, I have some pictures in here that I have set up on my desk where I write and do work. I have five Jesus pics, I have the one of Kylie and I at a daddy-daughter date, I have two temple pics, one with me and Kanyon when he is like one, the one of Kanyon with blue hair in a boxing stance, one with Kanyon and Kylie in aprons with a thing of pasta, Kylie when she is like three, a black and white one with her pony on top of her head where she is wearing a shirt with flowers and a tiger pattern across the middle, one of the Washington DC temple, one of Liah when she is like 1, in yellow holding a watering pail thing, and one of Jason, Braden's son.

If you talk to Kai or text with him, have him send me some pics of him and his family, will ya? Tell him I can receive four 4x6 per letter, but unlimited letters. Also, can you get his address? If you receive this before I call Kanyon/Kandi on Thursday, they can have that info for me. Thank you, darling.

It's funny cause I get lots of time to layout when I'm not on lockdown, and I am getting pretty dark. I will get out, and everyone will be, "*I thought you were locked up for 8 months, but you look like you have been in Hawaii.*" I am going to say I have been there in spirit, just not body. Haha, kind of funny, I think.

How is book #4 coming? I am excited to read it.

I have been craving your potato salad, baked beans, potato hash, and just your cooking in general. As well as a lot of other things, but I won't go there.

So, I am getting a journal, and I am going to write down all of my memories and stories from my life. I wrote down all of the states that I have been in, and it is 33. A good chunk of them you have been to with me. I am excited to do a lot of traveling when I get out of here. I want to go to Ireland, London, Paris, all over Italy, and Venice. I definitely want to spend more time in New York, as well as upper New England, and more time in Florida and Texas. I would totally live in a little beach town like Port O'Connor. I miss the ocean and the smells of small-town beach life.

So did you like my envelope? I know I am not an artist, but I thought a little color would make the letter super exciting when it came out of the box. I hope it did that for you guys. After all, life is about joy, and every little bit of joy can be amazing. I miss cold cereal, real meat, and ice cream. Mt. Dew a little, but the longer I am in here, the less I think about that.

I am getting healthier and healthier every week. My body is lean and muscular, and I will have a 6-pack within a few more weeks. They definitely don't give you enough food in here to maintain any excess fluff. By the time I get out, I should be a lean little tank. It feels good after letting my health go so much for a few years. My heart and lungs feel amazing, and my skin and coloring are clear and healthy, and tan. Today is 110 days clean and sober with very little sugar, caffeine, and no soda or carbonation.

I plan on doing construction consulting and estimating when I get out, and I have been studying how to build and design websites in here, so I will do some of that also.

I am excited to get out and stay busy being a daddy and a grandpa. It's crazy that Mai and Bethany are both due in July, huh... Mai with a boy and Bethany with a girl. I haven't heard yet how it is going for them down there in Miami, but I am glad they have each other down there to build their successes together, and the girls and kids have each other for when the boys are at work. Your mom has written to me a few times and is always positive and upbeat, which is nice.

Well, I am going to wrap this up so I can mail it in the morning. I hope all is well. I miss you guys tons.
Love always, Scott

July 2013

Scott Writes

July 1

SCOTT: How are you? How is paradise? Are you doing, ok? I worry about you all the time, and you are always on my mind and in my dreams. I am doing fine. I am using my time wisely. I just finished the *Book of Mormon* and have started reading it again. I am also now reading the *Doctrine and Covenants* (*D&C*) and Spencer W. Kimball's book, *The Miracle of Forgiveness*. It is amazing. I am also reading a twelve-book series called The Left Behind, which is a novel, but it incorporates the scriptural revelations from the New Testament. I am currently on book ten. I am going to start the Work and the Glory series again and get the Porter Rockwell series as well.

One of my friends is also reading a Sylvia Brown book, and he is going to give it to me when he is done. I am just finishing up the last computer book that Kathy sent me. I am going to get the BYU course book that lists all of the classes for their construction management and law degrees with a list of the corresponding textbooks, and I am going to start bringing those in and studying all of that info.

I just finished writing Kai a 22-page letter. It was pretty deep stuff. I felt better after I shared some deep thoughts with him.

So, did you know that when you recite the Lord's Prayer, it brings your chakras into health and balance? It goes like this:

> *Our Father, which art in Heaven*: 3rd Eye, 6th chakra
>
> *Hallowed be thy name*: Crown, 7th chakra
>
> *Thy kingdom come, thy will be done, on earth as it is in Heaven*: Throat, 5th chakra
>
> *Give us this day our daily bread*: Root, 1st chakra
>
> *And forgive us our debts as we forgive our debtors*: Solar Plexus, 3rd chakra

And lead us not into temptation: Sacral, 2nd chakra

But deliver us from evil: Heart, 4th chakra

For thine is the kingdom: Throat, 5th chakra

And the power: Crown, 7th chakra

And the glory forever: 3rd Eye, 6th chakra

So, it works amazingly. I have it on two papers. One, like I just wrote, with the chakra name and color after it. I read that first, and after each line I focus on that chakra until I feel it balanced and I can see the correct color. If I can't get the color, I reread the line and concentrate until I see it. Then I move on. Once they are balanced, all of them, I get my paper which just has the prayer on it without the chakra information, then I read through it twice more, slowly and methodically, to make sure everything is in balance and is humming smoothly. I do this once or twice a day. Then I go through my copies of Doreen Virtue's Angel Michael cards, and I say each of those prayers. I do this, say my morning prayers and read 30-90 minutes of scriptures, before I allow myself to go onto otherworldly activities or books. This really has me feeling the spirit and, in his embrace, always. It also helps me feel in balance.

Thank you for all you have taught me and for the groundwork that you have laid for me to be ready for this time in my life. I love you and always will, and you will always be one of my bestest friends. You are an amazing and powerful woman, and I look up to you. I draw strength from your strength, and you have taught me so much about unconditional love, mercy, charity, and forgiveness. So again, thank you.

So, the Doreen Virtue cards that I have for Archangel Michael... This is an example of one of the prayers. This one is for detaching from a situation. The prayer goes like this, *"Archangel Michael, I ask you to use your flaming sword to cut any attachment to fear or drama so that I may be centered in the knowingness that peace is everywhere within me and this situation."* And I say that with this whole jail and legal issues in mind.

This next one I use with you and the kids in mind. *"Dear God and Archangel Michael, thank you for watching over me and my loved ones, Keri, Kanyon, Kylie, Liah, Kai, Braden, Mai, Bethany, Daisy, Jason, new baby boy Casper, and new baby girl Tawni. Please help me feel secure and at peace and fill me with faith so that I may focus on my priorities and enjoy a healthful happy life."* I have like fifteen of them. They are Oracle cards.

Oh, I like these next three. *"Please help me clearly hear, see, feel, and know the divine guidance that I have asked and prayed for. Allow me to keep my ego out of the way so your wisdom can come streaming through me, for my own benefit, and for those around me."*

And, *"Help me perceive all of the love that surrounds me so that I can feel safe receiving, expressing, and giving love."*

And finally, *"Dear God and angels, thank you for helping me see myself as you see me: through the eyes of love. Thank you for honoring and respecting me. Please guide me to do the same for myself. And grant me the courage to speak up on my own behalf. I ask for your protection in all of my relationships so that I am surrounded by loving and kind people."*

So, I go through all fifteen or so of these daily. Then I have a stack of pictures which include Kanyon, Kylie, Liah, Mai, Kai, Braden, Bethany, Daisy, and Jason, as well as Jesus and some of my favorite temples. I look at these all with love, and it really helps me stay in a great frame of mind. It helps me stay filled with love and peace.

Hey, I called your phone three times today even though there is no money on it. I do that because your voice calms me and helps ground me. I can hear you when you answer, but I guess you can't hear me. So just talk when I do that so I can relax. If that is ok. I know I am not your problem or responsibility anymore because I was a jackass, but if you don't mind, it would really help me this month while I am stressing about my court on July 22nd and my sentencing. I am going to fast on the 22nd for lunch after court, with a prayer and lunch. So yeah, when I call like that, if you can say something that will calm me and allow me to smile! Thank you.

I am anxious to get to rehab, so my days will be busy. I won't have time to stress about what is going on out there or worry about you and the kids. I know I always will, but that's just me. So, we have a job starting in a few weeks that Kelly is doing with me, so money should be coming in by the end of August.

Sorry about the handwriting. I am working out doing sets, then sitting down on my bunk and writing in between sets.

So Kanyon doesn't think my letters are too preachy, does he? I just want the best for him, and I have a lot of father time to make up for with all of the kids!!! Ok, my lady, I'm beat. I did chest and triceps today around noon, and now I just did abs and lower back. I am also adding a fast-paced workout in the mornings that starts tomorrow at 6:30, so I better get some sleep... night. It is 5 to 7:00 p.m. where you are. I wonder what you are doing now. I will write more tomorrow. I hope you are fine with these long letters from me. I just pick up my pencil, and all these things I want to say flow from my hand.

I'm really glad we can be friends and that you don't hate me. I was a horrible husband, person, and father, and I'm glad to be alive, healthy with a second chance to be a good person, an amazing friend, father, and grandfather, and to be a Christ-like person that is humble, loving, compassionate, caring, and generous ... basically be a person like you.

I'm sorry I took your love for granted. I'm sorry that my thinking patterns are all messed up. I'm sorry I let programming from my childhood affect how I treated you, and mostly I'm sorry that I killed your wifely love for me. That was an amazing gift that my Heavenly Father gave to me, and I killed it, and I'm sorry. I know you tried so hard to have an amazing family and to be an amazing wife, and I was so caught up in my BS and my addictions. I'm sorry. I love you, and I'm glad we are still friends, and I can share with you and co-parent with you. When the full brunt of this lesson is over, I want to be a support and an amazing friend to you because you are in my dreams every night, and I am happy when I am sharing my thoughts and life with you.

So, I think I told you I am reading this book about Sylvia Brown called *Adventures of a Psychic*. It is really good. She is amazing. I can't put it down. I got a list from the library of all of the LDS fiction books, and there is an LDS series called the Seventh Seal Trilogy, so I am excited to read that and see how it compares to this other one.

I guess there is a phone that I can get sent to Kanyon where I can call him unlimited times a month for $29. I'm working on getting that to him. That will be nice so I can talk to you both. I hope you are ok with me calling you when I need to talk. When I get scared, anxious, or upset (sad), I remember when I was dope sick after the peyote days, and you had the CDs on the TV from that guy, Wayne Dyer. But then you laid there by me and rubbed my forearm, and I felt such love and peace. I can meditate about that feeling, and it brings that feeling all over my body, so thank you for that.

How is Kanyon doing? I need to get him that phone, so I can talk to him daily. I know he needs his dad right now, and it kills me to not be able to talk to him. So, are you tired of reading my chicken scratch yet? Is it boring and redundant? If so, I'm sorry. I just like sharing with you.

I never got the letter you sent or the pages of your new book. Not sure why.

Thanks for listening,
Love you, Scott

July 20

SCOTT: Hey Kerrr, how are you? I finally got the first pages of your book and your and Kanyon's letters last night. Your book sounds amazing. You are getting so good with your writing. I'm amazed at how well all of your sentences, paragraphs, and pages are flowing with such symmetry these days. All I can think of is when your mom and Tabi used to talk like they were so much smarter than you. I always knew it wasn't true, and it used to upset me when they would treat you like that. I have a good idea for a book, and I want to write it while I am locked up, but it doesn't flow for me like it seems to for you. I need to get it down and put most of my manuscript on paper while I have time on my hands.

So, Tabi came and saw me on Thursday. It was good to see her. She looked amazing. She looked so thin and beautiful. Her face looked like the Tabi from when we first got married. I was glad to see that. She looked so good. We had a good visit. So, Kylie is going to be moving back down to Tabi's and going to Brighton High, so that should make her happy. I signed a guardianship paper so Tabi can handle Kylie's stuff. So, with the ORS (Office of Recovery Services) stuff, I wrote them a letter telling them that you have Kanyon and are supporting him, and our deal is that I am to take care of Kylie financially, so hopefully, they will reverse any costs to you and put it all on me

I was bummed about you having to cut the pics out of the section of the book draft that you sent. Their stupid rules are ridiculous. I was hoping you could send it broken up so each envelope had four pics in it, thinking there was maybe one pic per page, but I didn't know there were like four per page. You would have had to send 1 page per envelope, so the cutout thing worked.

My current celly is a strange guy. He is here for murder and is kind of dirty, gross, and annoying. At first, I was like, *UGH*, as you can imagine. But I thought, what would Keri do? So, I chose to love and accept him as a child of God. That made it tolerable, and I get along with him now and don't get too annoyed with him. So, thanks for that example. It really comes in handy here.

Today is Saturday and I have court on Monday. I'm excited to get that over with and have everything locked in with an end date I can put on my calendar and countdown to.

So, the book I am reading is, *The Lost Symbol,* by Dan Brown. It is about symbology, freemasonry, and Noetic science, which has to do with the law of attraction, ancient and sacred geometry, etc. They talk about how human thoughts have mass and can be weighed and analyzed. It is very intriguing. I am reading the *Book of Mormon* for the 2nd time, and *D&C* for the first time. I didn't realize how much clarification of revelation, heaven, and the afterlife is given in the *D&C*. It is really informative. I am going to start the Bible next week. I think I will read the New Testament first, then the Old. Then I have a couple of novels; a law-type, similar to Grisham, and the 7th book of Harry Potter, which is the last two movies. Between all of those books, doing Sudoku, crossword puzzles, etc., *Sports Illustrated* (I got a subscription that comes out weekly, so that is nice), and writing letters and emails, I stay pretty busy.

Tomorrow, I have church, and I will get a book on church history and maybe a Bible study guide. Those seem to help me understand some of the meanings and stuff. I only allow myself a couple hours of TV a week. I need to learn to use books, conversation, and fun to center and relax instead of TV. That way, I can minimize TV time on the outs.

My workout routine is getting a little boring because I don't have a gym or weights, other than my 2'x18" box I fill with papers and books. So, I had Kathy look up exercises you can do with body weight, and she sent me three big emails full, so that was nice. I am going to mix it up starting with Tuesday's workout. I made a couple new friends here, and when I told them we had a 26-year-old son, they were like yeah, whatever. I was like, what do you mean? They were like, you can't be more than 35. I was like, I am 44. They were shocked. They are in their mid to upper 20s. One said, I hope I am that fit at your age, and the other two were like, we wish we were that fit now. I laughed and was like, well, now's the time. All you have is time, so 30-60 minutes a day, and you will be all yoked up in 60 days. A lot of the younger generation is lazy, though. I have approx. 15 days left, then I will go back to minimum, then I should go to CATS soon after that. I'm excited to get there, hit it hard, apply what I learn, then get on with life. Have my free agency back!!!

So today is Sunday, August 4th. I had court last Monday and pled guilty to a 2nd. I have sentencing on September 16th. My attorney says there is a really good chance that the judge will let me go to a private rehab that I have lined up. If, by chance, he doesn't, then he says I would most likely get 180 more days, which with good time, would be 120, then I would do CATS and be out on January 14th. So, I'm praying for the first option, then if that doesn't come to fruition, then the second option.

I'm ready to be done here and get on with my life already. Have Jasper and Tyler moved out to Maui yet? How is James doing? How is Kanyon boy doing? How are things with Kandi? Is Kanyon still watching her kids while she works?

Jasper Arrives

Jasper was here with us for a short time. It is always nice to have Jasper in the space. It felt good to have our army come together again. It definitely made me think of Zila coming for a visit soon.

Jasper brings great male energy to the space. That father of my children has some intense shoes to fill. It helps fill the void when family fills in. Because after all, it takes a village, and I love the village that has been orchestrated for me to dance and rendezvous with.

August 2013

Girlfriend in the Hood

My dear long-time friend Amy flew in with her family for a visit! It was so good to have a girlfriend to chat with that has known me for most of my life. We had a day of it. We checked out the horses nearby and had an interesting interaction with a horse with some kind of allergy, or maybe my fairies got to tickling his nose.

Horse: Travel, Power, and Freedom. They are symbols that can express the magical side of humans. It has been a symbol of desires-especially sexual. The taming of a stallion would then be the taming of sexuality and dangerous emotions. Are you feeling constricted? Do you need to move on or allow others to move on? Is it time to assert your freedom and your power in new areas? Are you doing your part to assist civilization within your own environment? Are others? Are you honoring what this civilization has given you? The horse brings with it new journeys. It will teach you how to ride in new directions to awaken and discover your own freedom and power.

Thoughts... Feelings

I get to missing Kylie, Kai, and what could be if I were still in Utah. But I don't stay on that disc for long. It's a bummer, and in all reality, I would never want to go back to living in Utah, ever.

My life is on a fine momentum. I have the best job ever working for West Maui Parasail. I love all the interaction with all of the dear people from all over the world visiting Maui. I love my boss. I love everyone I work with. I love still being at the harbor and being with all of my dear friends I call family. I love living on Maui. I love having Kandi and the kids here. I love having my boys here. I love having Kanyon by my side. I love the many friends I have. I love all the men that flatter me with compliments and shower me with love. It is all these things that I focus on to keep my vibration soaring, to keep me in my vortex so I may finally receive all of those wants and desires that I have been unconsciously resistant to in the past. I had unconsciously been holding on to vibrations that did not serve me and unconsciously believed I didn't deserve my wants and desires to manifest or have held onto fear.

Things are falling beautifully into place. I know it is just a matter of time before all of my wants, desires, and dreams come true.

Kanyon and Scott Write One Another

August 4

SCOTT: Kanyon boy, how are you? How is life on the island? I saw on the news that a tropical storm hit the islands. Was that scary? Any damage to your place there or to your garden?

Have you been playing ball? Are you making any friends your age over there? Are you still watching Kandi's kids while she works? When are Jasper and Tyler coming to Maui? I had my court last week, then I will get sentenced on September 16th. I guess it's a good chance that I will get out that day and go to rehab if the judge signs off on it. If he doesn't, then I will have to do CATS and get out on January 14th. So, I'm praying he will sign off on the private rehab. That will give me just 6 more weeks until I am free. I am still working out every day but Sunday and doing abs at least 5 days a week. I am super tan and super skinny.

I should be going back to minimum tomorrow, so that will be nice. Then I will be out of my cell for more hours. So, 26 hours locked down, then it repeats itself. So back to all of that freedom will be nice. More time outside every day, and it is easier to have a routine when on the same schedule. Well, I'm going to mail this off, so... I love you tons. I miss you. I will see you soon. Love Dad

August 25

KANYON: Dear Dad, I haven't got any calls, and I just miss talking to you. Jasper's been living with us. We all were talking about how much we miss and love you. We are planning our visit to SLC around when you get out. I want to stay with you till you figure out any fines and whatnot. Then we can bounce to paradise and be high off life together. Me and Jasper were talking about how grateful we are for all of the amazing wisdom you've gifted to us. I'm so lucky I got an Indigo child with a high frequency as my dad. I love you. I just got my glass blowing set up put together. I've been blowing glass all night. Glassblowing is such my passion. Ray and Charley helped me out so much with getting into it. Life on the island is amazing, as usual. The first time Jasper went boogie boarding, is when the tropical storm rolled in. There was lightning going off everywhere. Me and Jasper are so excited to see how ripped you are. We don't want to look too small next to you, so we have been doing yoga. I also got some dumbbells and have been hella pumping iron.

My lyrics are coming together so perfectly. I have a message that I've never heard any song come close to so far. I'm getting a free recording program on the computer with a mic so I can start making my own bars with the keyboard and record my lyrics over it, using some samples of Bob Marley, John Lennon, Wayne Dyer, and all of the wise ones. I have a lot of amazing quotes in my songs from great people, like the Buddha and Albert Einstein, and all of these enlightened people.

It's your birthday when I'm writing this, so happy birthday. I hope to get a call. Let me know if you need me to pay for it. I want to talk to you more. Our minds, body, and spirits are stronger than ever. We'll be thriving at a peak together on the solar plexus of the Earth soon. I love you and appreciate every minute you've put into getting us where we need to be. You did everything perfectly, and you have helped so many people grow. With your past and understanding, you will continue to help evolve others even when unaware of it. Love you. I'll be sending good vibes.

September 2

SCOTT: Kanyon boy, how goes it? How is Lahaina? What have you been up to? How is your mom? Have you been playing ball and or working out? Surfing, wakeboarding, or bodyboarding? Any damage from the storm a month or so back? Have Jasper and Tyler moved out there yet? Do they live close by? Have you heard from Kai? When is he coming out? Have you seen pics of Casper? Recent ones of Daisy? It's crazy that Casper and Tawni were born four days apart and were the exact same length and weight, huh? Are you still learning to blow glass? How is your dog? How are James, the kids, and Kandi doing? How is mom's new job? What else is new? What are you hearing from Kylie Dawn?

I'm doing well. I'm basically just sleeping, eating, reading, and working out. I'm almost done with the Harry Potter series. It has been good. I am also reading a Dan Brown book. He is the author of *The Davinci Code*. He is good. I also have two Michael Crichton books. He is the author of *Jurassic Park*. I like him a lot also. I also have the original *Sherlock Holmes*. I am still working out 6 days a week during the day. I do abs at night after lights out. I am getting too much stamina and strength though, for cell workouts. My chest workouts now take over 2 hours. My elbows have been sore the last week or two from so many pushups. Love dad

SCOTT: Keri, how are you? I'm doing well. I have my sentencing in two weeks, so I am just trying to stay positive for that. Hopefully, I get out that day and go down to a rehab in Payson called STEPS. Regardless of what happens, I will know the end game so I can settle in and finalize this chapter of my life and get on with LIFE. I want this to go out with the morning mail, so I will finish here. Read Kanyon's letter. It talks about what I have been doing and has a bunch of questions. I got some extra envelopes today, so I will send this short one and then write a longer one this week. Love Scott

September 2013

I GOT ARRESTED
BLOG POST

Holy Shit! Talk about a duality polar opposite day!!! I don't celebrate holidays anymore. I got my moles removed on Mother's Day, and check out what happened on Labor Day, my day off. Let us start on yesterday's note, shall we?

Yesterday, I happened to be reading a book that my dear sister brought my way right when I was desiring new reading material. The name, *Healing Love through the Tao: Cultivating Female Sexual Energy*. I am a healer, and I had been wondering about healing through sex. It's great exercise, and it opens chakras. I have heard that one can astral travel upon orgasm together with your partner. WOW!!! Who wouldn't want to reach that ecstasy?

Anyway, Dwayne, a friend at the harbor, swung by to return a book he had taken out of the book donation box at our booth. Finishing a thick one in no time at all, I recognized that intelligent being in Dwayne who shares qualities of that husband of mine. I like a man with a high IQ. Dwayne tossed the book on my booth and suggested maybe I have this as my next book to check out. His recommendation was, "*Not bad, not great. Interesting, but disappointing. I thought it would have more facts about the actual murders.*" I guess the book was a true story about some scandalous murder.

I declined the offer, "*I'm good. I have a book that has landed in my hands.*" And with that, I whipped out the book I was reading.

Dwayne immediately took the book from me to check it out with a smile on his face. He was amused reading a part that spoke of an egg and a woman's vagina. Right at that moment, I had customers that came up, so Dwayne respectfully stepped out of the way, book in hand, over to the booth on the left of me, where Lois happened to be hanging out. Folks, let me fill you in on Ms. Lois. Lois is a great sistah friend of mine at the harbor. Lois is the one that used to work my job for nine years. While I was employed with Mark Robinson in slip #8, Lois was the West Maui Parasail girl in slip #15. Lois was brutally honest, which I adored. Lois could hang with the toughest truckers you can find. She is a badass. With that said, allow me to continue...

Dwayne stepped over to No Problem's (fishing boat) booth, speaking out loud his findings, right where Lois was sprawled out comfortably.

After finishing up with my customers, I heard Lois say, *"Dwayne, I do not want to discuss my vagina with you. Go back over to Keri's booth and talk about her vagina with her. It's her freakin' book!"*

Hearing this, I found myself very amused and I hollered out to Lois, *"Lois, I love you. This is so entertaining for me. Is Dwayne making you uncomfortable?"*

Right before hastily exiting the booth to remove herself from this situation, Lois spurted, *"I'm not uncomfortable. Why the f*** would I want to discuss my vagina with Dwayne!?"*

Dwayne then moseyed on over, returned my book, and informed me that I needed to be purchasing me an egg for future chapters.

Folks, this scene played over and over in my head and left me with perma-giggles all night long, and gave me an amazing ab workout, and a joyous release of tears. No joke, non-stop... I even drifted off to sleep with giggles. It fueled me with a high vibration and, most definitely, was my happy thought, lol. Literally.

Anyway, while I giggled at my repetitive thoughts, I checked out Madonna's new CD, *MDNA*. I had recently noticed the powerful manifestations that her last album, *Confessions on A Dance Floor*, brought into my life. I played it over and over in 2006, adding thoughts of desires and wants into my vortex, while dancing to that powerful CD, not realizing that the amazing Madonna would be taking me on an amazing journey that was still to come.

I was currently seeing the manifestations from *Confessions on A Dance Floor* in my life. I listened to each song, understanding the journey, applying it to my life, and helping me understand the cycle she was singing about AND in the order she sang it!!!

"Hung Up": *Time goes by so slowly... I'm tired of waiting on you*

"Get Together": *It's all an illusion, There's too much confusion... Do you believe in love at first sight... If it's bitter at the start, Then it's sweeter in the end*

"Sorry": *I've heard it all before... I don't wanna hear, I don't want to know... Please don't say you're sorry*

"Future Lovers": *I'm gonna tell you about love, Let's forget your life, Forget your problems... Let me be your guide, Cut inside your pride, Future lovers hide love inside their eyes*

"I Love New York": *I don't like cities, But I like New York, Other places make me feel like a dork... Los Angeles is for people who sleep... If you don't like my attitude, Then you can F off... Just go to Texas, Isn't that where they golf?... If you can't stand the heat, Then get off my street*

"Let It Will Be": *Now let me tell you about success, about fame... Don't it make you smile that it will be?... Let it will be, Just let it be*

"Forbidden Love": *Just one kiss on my lips, Was all it took to seal the future, Just one look from your eyes, Was like a certain kind of torture, Once upon a time, There was a boy, And there was a girl, Just one touch from your hands, Was all it took to make me falter... Forbidden love, are we supposed to be together?*

"Jump": *There's only so much you can learn in one place, The more that I wait, the more time that I waste, I haven't got much time to waste, It's time to make my way, I'm not afraid of what I'll face, but I'm afraid to stay, I'm going down my own road and I can make it alone... All work and no fighting, I'll find a place of my own, Are you ready to jump? Get ready to jump, Don't ever look back, Yes, I'm ready to jump, Just take my hands, Get ready to jump*

"How High": *How high are the stakes? How much fortune can you make?... Does this get any better? Should I carry on? Will it matter when I'm gone? Will any of this matter? It's funny, How everybody mentions my name, But they're never very nice, I took it, Just about everything, Except my own advice*

"Isaac": *Wrestle with your darkness, Angels call your name, can you hear what they're saying? Will you ever be the same?... Remember, remember, never forget, All of your life has all been a test, You will find a gate that's open, Even though your spirit's broken, Open up my heart, Cause my lips to speak, Bring the Heaven and the stars, Down to Earth for me*

"Push": *You push me to go the extra mile, You push me when it's difficult to smile. You push me, a better version of myself, You push me, only you and no one else, You push me to see the other point of view, You push me when there's nothing else to do, You push me when I think I know it all, You push me when I stumble and I fall... You push me, only you and no one else... Only you, and only you, and only you*

"Like It or Not": *You can call me a sinner, Or you can call me a saint, Celebrate me for who I am, Dislike me for what I ain't, Put me on a pedestal, Or drag me down in the dirt, Sticks and stones will break my bones, But your names will never hurt. I'll be the garden, You'll be the snake, All of my fruits, Is yours to take, Better the devil that you know, Your love for me will grow, Because, This is who I am, You can like it or not, You can love me, Or leave me, 'Cause I'm never gonna stop*

WOW!!! Right? I was so living the last of the CD. I wanted to know what was next!

"Girl Gone Wild" was song number one for the next part of my journey! Upon first hearing it, I had to have it! The new song of Madonna's was one of the first songs I downloaded when I arrived on Maui.

Knowing that I was on my way to the next "Station," I had a strong desire to know the rest of the ride. I got familiar with the next song on the album, "Gang Bang." It had great beats! I loved her voice, and I loved everything about it. Not fully understanding the message of what was to come or how this pertained to my journey, I just rocked out to it and loved jiving to it a few times before I went to bed.

"Gang Bang": *Like a bitch out of order, Like a bat out of hell, Like a fish out of water, I'm scared, can't you tell. Bang, bang. I thought it was you, And I loved you the most, But I was just keeping, My enemies close. I made a decision, I would never look back... Bang, bang, Shot you dead, Bang, bang, Shot you dead, Bang, bang, shot you dead, shot my lover in the head*

Let me fill you in... Besides really digging Madonna's deliverance of the beats with attitude, I connected with the song hugely.

For those of you that haven't heard, in the end, I stabbed my husband three times with my favorite Cutco scissors and choked him out with a crowbar. The cops arrived to haul my husband of **23** years off to jail right before I moved to Maui.

So, I woke up that morning with a strong desire to go and find a Madonna *MDNA* CD ASAP!!! After waking and baking, I headed over to the other side blaring "Confessions," rocking out with full understanding, excited to obtain *MDNA*.

In my blissful state of elation, I missed the turn to Walmart. Oh well, I would just go to the mall instead. Of course, they would have a CD store at the mall...

On the way to the mall, I remembered I needed to go to Green Lotus in Wailuku and pick up some business cards. I was drawing out maps to show others how to get to the store on a daily basis. I was being asked where I had gotten my amazing pendant pretty much every day I was at work.

I entered the store, and Mary was on the phone going on and on about how business hadn't been great in the past, but it had mysteriously been busy that day as if business would be picking up again.

I originally planned on just running in, getting the cards, and then running out. Since she was preoccupied on the phone, I took that as a sign there was something that I needed to get. I slowly browsed the store and waited for her to finish her call.

I browsed for 20 minutes before I set my eyes on some small egg-shaped stones. This brought me to laughter instantly. I had to check them out. There were five different little eggs that only cost $3 each. I instinctively picked up the egg on the end. As soon as I did, Mary got off the phone. I took that as a sign that I had the *"chosen one"* and proceeded to the counter. I got the business cards and paid for the egg.

I asked her, *"What stone is this made from?"*

"Jasper... let me look at the meaning for you."

Jasper: The ancient Egyptians wore Jasper scarabs as amulets as the stone was believed to increase sexual energy. According to the Bible, Jasper was a direct gift from God and would be the first foundation stone of the New Jerusalem. Also, both Indians in Asia as well as Native Americans see Jasper as a magical rain stone and also a powerful healing stone.

After she read it, I asked, *"Do you have time for a really funny story?"*

I shared the Lois and Dwayne story splitting my gut with laughter while telling it. We had a great laugh and had fun with the amazing connection of it all. I left Green Lotus and headed to the mall. When I arrived at the mall, I heard entertainment going on at the center stage. I made my way over and saw with delight that the keiki (children) were performing their Hawaiian dances. I LOVE this culture. They were dancing to live beautiful, fun Hawaiian music.

I am a sucker for performances. Especially children... I am a mother. I am also an excellent audience member. I am one who appreciates the talent, art, bravery, etc., it takes to perform, and I am not shy about showing it.

I stood near the front, enjoying the show to the fullest. First, the girls with props and singing, then the cutest little boys (3-6 yrs. of age) in long board shorts, no shirt, and a string of kukui nut lei. These little men were beyond a delight with the way they owned the stage with confidence, style, and manhood. Their Hawaiian dance was performed with the greatest hip moves that brought claps and laughs galore. Following the boys' performance were the beautiful young women who danced so gracefully to a beautiful Hawaiian song with words I did not know. They brought me to tears before the end. I excused myself and proudly showed my tears of gratitude for such a great, moving performance.

I continued to the information sign to try and find the media store that would have the CD and found... *one did not exist.* Wow, I *was* on an island. I headed to Walmart.

I was still touched by the performance and shedding tears of joy and love for those girls who were my daughter's age when my daughter called on my phone. Of course, she would have gotten a feeling to give me a call divinely perfect at this time. I answered with love affirmations telling Kylie how amazing I thought she was and telling her how proud

I was of her.

"*Are you crying?*" Kylie asked, annoyed.

"*Yes, I am crying, but they are tears of joy and love for you.*" I continued to tell her about the wonderful performance I had just left.

Kylie, uncomfortable with emotion, said, "*You're weird. I'm gonna go.*"

I again told her I loved her and hung up.

As soon as I hung up, I was at the light where you turn for Walmart. Without thinking, I pulled a total haole mainland move, and impatiently moved over to the lane that was not a turn lane, then saw that a cop had parked himself in that spot just to catch people like me who were not thinking.

Oh shit. But o'wells... sent him love. It had been a year since I had dealt with those men in blue.

I hurried for the turn as smoothly and quickly as possible, hoping I slipped by unnoticed to get to a parking spot so that he could not pull me over.

I got to my parking spot. It was the first one available upon entering the lot. You know, right there where everyone pulls in and out. Like the intersection when entering the Walmart parking lot.

Seconds before I slammed the gear shift into park, I heard the siren!

WTF ever... hang on for the ride and see where this takes me. I instinctively reached for the glove box... silly me. I had been pulled over many times and was trained to get my registration and insurance papers.

"*GET YOUR HANDS ON THE STEERING WHEEL!*" I heard in a tone of panic-stricken fear from the officer who was approaching from the passenger panel behind me.

Oh my, WOW. This guy was scared that little ole me was going to blow his brains out. "*It's okay. You have no need to fear.*" I softly, kindly spoke to him as if I was talking to my little ones. Gently bringing one hand off the steering wheel in a motion of surrender, I said, "*It's okay. I'm not going to hurt you.*" I continued speaking similar things with my gentle soft gesture, which just amped him up with more fear, and he screamed even louder and freaked out, *"GET YOUR HANDS ON THE STEERING WHEEL!"*

Oh, my heck, this guy was tripping.

The next thing I knew, he freaked out before he even got to my rolled-down window, *"I SMELL MARIJUANA. HAVE YOU BEEN SMOKING? DO YOU HAVE MARIJUANA IN THE CAR?"*

Softly, innocently chuckling to myself, I gently replied, *"No. I have just come from the mall where I witnessed a beautiful performance that brought me to a bit of a cry. I don't know why you would smell marijuana. I have not altered my state while being in this car today."*

The officer continued to get all razzed like a K9 about some scent that he assumed was flowing heavily out of my car. Not once had he even told me why he had pulled me over.

I was starting to get a little nervous because of the way he was treating me like a hard-core criminal when all I wanted was the new Madonna CD. Are you serious!? Finally, I told him, *"Dude, you're tripping, and if you need to search the car to help you feel better, go right ahead. Do what needs to be done so I can get on my way. I have nothing to hide from you."*

Immediately, backup was called, and I was asked to get out of the car and ordered to sign papers stating that I was allowing them to search the car. Then they searched me and all of my belongings. During all of this, the officers were asking questions left and right as if I was Nancy from the show *Weeds*, smuggling pounds of marijuana in from the border. Finally, the officer who was called for backup, asked, *"Do you have kids that could have been using the car, and do they smoke?"*

Well, folks, I am an honest person, and if you ask me a question, I don't care who you are, you get my honest answer. I stated, *"Well, actually, yes. And let me tell you something... My son has Tourette's, and we have tried those legally prescribed prescriptions, and they don't help as much as marijuana. So yes, my boys smoke weed, and I pray you don't follow me home to arrest them and pursue anything that might take my kids away!"*

The officer asked if I would like to sit in the shade.

Totally aware of the hot dark suits they were sporting, I quickly declined the offer stating, *"No, thank you. I love the sun. I love the heat, I work at the Lahaina Harbor, and I am very good being in the sun."* I loved my confidence, the power of my truth, and my lack of fear for these men in blue. I am not easily intimidated, and I am someone who was used to being a spectacle and being on stage. So, let's do this thing for all to see. That was the attitude rocking in my brain... **bang bang**.

I read the papers and realized I had a minute amount of weed in my purse for those occasions. I was calm but still a little nervous. I played it off and said, "*You know what? I am sick of playing this game. I have decided I just want my CD, and I don't think I want to allow you to search me and all my shit. This is turning into such a headache, and I am feeling violated for doing absolutely nothing. I've had a beautiful day, a bit of a cry, and just want my freakin' Madonna CD. So, if you could site me for whatever the f*** it is that you even pulled me over for, and maybe write me up for not having those registration and insurance papers that I could not find for you in the glove box, I will bring them to court because I know I will be able to find them at home.*"

I was then informed that if I did not consent to this search, I would be detained, my car would be impounded, and I would be taken into custody.

"*So, what I am hearing is that there is no choice, really. Either I can voluntarily allow you to violate my space, or I will be forced to, and it will be more unpleasant in the end. Hmmm... well, this sounds like that adoption game that I played when I was 16 years old and 'voluntarily' signed my firstborn away to adoption.*" Yes, I did say that out loud.

After hearing my point-blank honest answer, the backup officer got soft, but still supported his haole left-brained mother f***er coworker that had given me papers to sign, "*allowing*" the officers to violate my space. The backup officer realized I may have had some personal weed on me and whispered to me while the cop got new papers for me to sign because I had scribbled out the other one, "*You are in Maui. marijuana is no big deal.*"

Hearing his message, I bucked up and hung on for the ride to see where it would take me.

I signed the papers.

The men in blue proceeded to search my car thoroughly while I paced comfortably and watched them as a mother does, when her children were trying to find something that she knew wasn't there. The only words that were not spoken, *"Cold, Colder, Colder."*

I was extremely helpful and treated them like silly children that were trying their best to find fault. They asked about the broken trunk that could only be accessed from the back seat. I gladly showed them, like the famous Vanna White showing a letter, stating, *"My car is pretty beat up. I'm just a single mother, and my son has Tourette's, remember."* Not that my son broke the trunk, but I was capitalizing everywhere I could, being totally aware and present in the Now to win this game. They proceeded to the windows and tried to roll them up but found two busted out. *"Remember, my son has Tourette's? Those windows are busted out."* **"Bang bang"** was singing in my head.

Time for my personal belongings to be searched. The officers opened my purse and started snooping. That haole officer showed his fear, asking, *"You don't have any needles in here that I will poke myself with, do you?"*

"No, darling. You really need to work on all that fear you have in your space. But I will tell you what you will find (**bang bang**) *in this bag. I have medicine in that prescription bottle, so I guess you'll get what you wanted. So now what?"* **Bang bang**.

Well, then they needed a woman cop to come and frisk me and grope me so that I would feel more comfortable with it... whatever. **Bang bang**. Just had to hold on for this ride. It would soon be over. **Bang bang**.

Tita came on the scene ready for groping. I lifted my arms up and out sensually and spread my legs apart, ready for wherever she wanted to touch me. I was ever so grateful for living in Maui this past year to get me ok with myself... having had the year to get accustomed to the Hawaiian culture of love and aloha with hugs and kisses on the cheek and mouth; something that took me a full year to get used to. I had come from a place where I was like Rapunzel in a castle, not used to hugging even my cousin because of the insecurities my husband held. And seriously, no joke... Those that know me know that yes, I stated all that out loud to the three officers with love and humility, yet with an edge of Madonna sensuality. **Bang bang**.

Tita didn't like it and got a little gruff with me. But those boys were speechless as she roughly guided me to the hood of the car to bend me over with my hands on the hood like all those sexy music videos, I have seen many times... **bang bang**. I smiled sexily at those men in blue, keeping contact with their eyes hidden behind their lenses during the whole spread 'em and grope for all customers to witness at Walmart. It was quite a sight and a scene that I did get thrills on... **bang bang**.

They continued to handcuff me, and yes, I was in shock but kept my cool for them to see. They roughly grabbed my elbow and roughly hauled me to the back seat of the cruiser where they shoved me in my seat belt and ordered me to sit back. For those of you that know me, I am a very graceful, light-footed, fairy-like, loving caring person who is extremely obedient. I proceeded to inform them, in a soft loving motherly voice, "*I am being cooperative. I will walk this way gladly. No need to be so rough. I am very obedient, even so much so that I lost my firstborn to adoption. Well, I guess I am not a hundred percent obedient after all. I guess I did have sex before marriage, which wasn't so obedient. Yeah, I guess I am a criminal.*" I was killing them with kindness with my sarcastic, realistic humor.

Driving over to the jail as a prisoner, I could not help but think of that dear husband of mine and that night... **bang bang**. I often wondered what it was like for him. I hated that I had to call the cops on him. I sat humbly and confidently, holding good posture, holding eye contact through Officer K. Pieland's sunglasses in the rearview mirror with a sensual loving smile directed toward him the entire time. I only left the sunglasses to look directly at him, reading him, reading me, reading the situation, fully aware and present in the NOW.

Officer K. Pieland started texting while driving. I confidently kindly stated, "*I thought texting and driving were illegal.*" **Bang bang**.

"*Not for us officers. It is part of our job and how we communicate.*"

Proceeding to the jail, Officer K. Pieland raced up through the intersection, hitting it at 60 miles per hour... obviously very uncomfortable with his prisoner. "*Wow, you officers get to break all of the rules.*"

"*I'm sorry, what?*"

"*Speeding through an intersection, texting... Wow, I never do that.*"

Officer K. Pieland decided to turn up the radio. Even better... I love music and totally have a testimony that music speaks to the soul, and the angels and the Universe always send the right tune... **bang bang**.

I instantly started dancing to the song that was playing because that is how I am. It was a song I had surprisingly never heard before. A song that sounded like the Ting Tings... total punk flavor. The lyrics were something like, *"You need to work on making a girl smile."* I burst out with a soft laugh and said, *"This is good music for you to be listening to. I pray that you continue to listen to such uplifting music to help you on your journey."* I kept dancing and singing and jamming sensually to the tune... **bang bang**.

Shortly thereafter, we entered the bat cave so the officer could unload this criminal without inflicting harm on the public. I got the same rough-grabbing treatment. Again, I stated calmly and softly, as a kind, good mother does, *"You have no need to fear me. I am cooperating. You don't have to be so rough. I won't hurt you, and I am very obedient. It's ok, you're ok."*

We got to the Sarge and the local boys. The looks on those fella's faces when they saw the purple-haired, drug-addicted, hard-core menace to society, criminal Officer K. Pieland brought in... priceless.

I was taken to a room for the paperwork. Officer K. Pieland was fumbling to get my cuffs off in front of his Sarge. I stood still as glass, confident with excellent posture and no fear, while he was starting to dig the cuffs in my bony little wrists. I gently stated in that motherly soft voice that I had gotten so good at, *"You are hurting me."* Officer K Pieland softened his grip and got the first cuff off, swinging himself onto his knees in front of me to unlock the second, ironically taking the position of some engagement proposal. I gazed at him with love and kindness, keeping my solid stance. He continued to fumble, trying to unlock the key, inflicting pain on me once again. I kindly stated, *"You are hurting me,"* while I kept my wrist outstretched to him and stood still as glass.

Keep in mind, the Sarge and the boys were all watching with hot interest.

Officer K. Pieland then handcuffed me to a chair. A little taken aback and shocked, I stated, "*Really? You guys are that fearful of me? This has been the craziest day of my life. Lots of love to you all. I cannot imagine living in such fear on a daily basis. So glad to be me and not you. I will gladly be in handcuffs today.*"

Next came the questioning from a new officer. Well, let me tell you about the questioning. God bless my dear sister Kandi, who had shared with me her experience from when her babies' daddy called the cops on her because she was trying to get her kids back from him when he did not return them to her. Kandi was put in lockdown in an insane asylum because she did not keep her cool well enough. And those questions they ask, to trick you into I don't know what, somehow "prove" you are mentally insane and need lockdown. I was also aware of many stories from the Mothers of Loss chat group where answering those same questions got them locked up and shock treatment. Cops were always looking for the insane, even creating it on purpose. And they preyed on weak innocence, such as when a mother loves her children like the lioness that she is.

The questioning started, first with the easy ones. I answered delightfully and sweetly like I always did with my customers all day long.

"*So, your last name is Stone?*"

"*Like a rock, or however you would like to remember it,*" I answered with a wink. Because, after all, they did find a pinch of ganja on me.

"*Where are you from?*"

"*Salt Lake City, Utah. Home of the Mormons.*"

"*Oh yeah, you Mormon?*"

"*Hell yeah, born and raised! Aren't we all? Did you not hear, Salt Lake City, Utah? I am a good little girl. I was a Boy Scout leader, a Sunday school teacher. I am a very obedient girl. Remember, I gave my firstborn up for adoption because I am so obedient. Oh, but oh yeah, I guess I'm not that obedient. I did have sex before marriage.*"

"*How long have you been on Maui?*"

"*One year. Maui has received me well. God bless Maui. I have made it.*"

"*Where do you work?*"

"West Maui Parasail."

"What do you do there?"

"I'm a booth girl. I get them loaded, so they can get high, all day long, interesting enough."

"Oh yeah... Is that the one with the smiley face?"

"That it is. You know, the one that has the awesome shirts that say, 'I got high on Maui.'"

They were brought to silence with my ever-so-truthful innocent answers.

"What brought you here?"

"Well, remember, that baby I lost? Well, that baby found us in 2006, and it's not what they promised. It's not anything you expect. My husband had a harder time with it than I did. He started medicating with prescribed pills, on top of his occasional drinking, which escalated to heroin. I had to flee with my children from the man I had been married to for 23 years."

Now for those trick questions.

"Have you ever been suicidal?"

"Well, hasn't everyone?"

"Have you ever followed through with an attempt to kill yourself?"

"Hasn't everyone willed it with their thoughts on many occasions, wishing life would be over soon because life does suck on many occasions?"

Stumped, that sweet local boy, Officer Rodney, continued with the questioning. "Has anyone in your family ever contemplated suicide?"

"Well, doesn't everyone have someone in their family that has contemplated suicide?"

Stumped by my every answer, he gazed deeper into my eyes with each question. Officer Rodney continued, "Are you under a doctor's care?"

"No."

"Are you taking any meds?"

"Absolutely not. I don't believe in prescription drugs. Pills kill."

"Have you been in counseling or professional mental help?"

"Of course. Remember, I lost my firstborn to adoption... Post Traumatic Syndrome. A no-brainer."

"Well, are you still under mental care?"

"*No, I would like to think I have graduated.*"

"*Graduated? How do you mean? Graduated from where?*"

"*Graduated from others being my healer, and me becoming my own healer, helping others heal themselves. How do you think I have been able to handle this whole day of violation, probing, and groping so well? I am very grateful I am clear and good with myself because I can only imagine the trauma this day could have inflicted on my soul if I had not been clear. Have you not witnessed my calm, my cool, my ability to share with such solid truthfulness without any triggers of upset?*"

After passing the exam, I informed them, "*You may want to change your questions. I bet everyone that is asked those questions, truthfully would answer the same, including all you men in uniform. I don't know what you are digging for, but you may want to get clearer on what you are looking for and ask better questions to find what you really want to know.*"

Time for pictures and fingerprints. Officer K. Pieland let Rodney know that he didn't think Rodney needed to search and grope me again because that female officer had already done that.

Rodney took the cuff off that had me attached to the chair, and gently walked me through the finger and palm printing process of having them scanned into the computer. I gratefully acknowledged his kindness while he was cradling my hands and thanked him, "*Thank you for being so kind and gentle. I would have much rather had you do the search and groping. That other lady was a bit rough, bringing fear in my space that she was going to go for a cavity search right there at Walmart.*"

They told me I was going to need someone to come and bail me out for $100 because I didn't have cash on me. They asked if I knew someone that could come get me. I pondered with much thought and spoke out loud as I am known for doing, and said, "*Well, my sister is at work. My son is watching the children, and my boys are at work. Do I only get one phone call?*"

Officer K. Pieland answered, "*I'm sure Rodney will allow a few if you make it quick. You have five minutes to finalize the details of who is coming. Is there anything more that you need?*"

"*May I have some water?*"

He handed me a pixie cup and pointed to the sink.

I pulled a disappointed face and asked if I could just take a sip from my water bottle, please? And he proceeded to tell me that the plastic bottle was worse for me than the water from the pipes. I then proceeded to tell him that I would take my risk with the bottle because I was very protective of my pineal gland. Confusing these men over the top by now, the Sarge asked, "*What?*"

I informed these men that I recognized their soft acceptance of right-brain thinking, but Officer K. Pieland was very left-brained and should stick to bottled water.

Well, that got Officer K. Pieland wondering, and he asked, "*What do you mean left-brain?*"

"*Lacking in spirituality, lacking in creative thinking, lacking in love energy, not trusting your heart, being a robot to the man and logic. Not trusting intuition or the higher power/Source that we all have within... God bless you. I wish you the best. I pray that this day has been divine for such a left-brain to run into such a right-brain. God bless you.*"

I felt and recognized Officer K. Pieland's throat chakra knot up when he said, "*I am finished with you.*"

"*I am so glad you are. I did not enjoy you much at all. Good day.*"

I called my sister, and God bless Kandi; she dropped everything to drive straight to me. When I got off the phone, Rodney asked, "*So, you have a sister here?*"

"*Yes, but she is the husband's sister. When I was back home, I had financial abundance and was the stay-at-home mom that helped everyone to nurture and raise their children. A side effect of losing my firstborn means I am quick to see a mother in need and I help raise all children. Kandi is the youngest of her family of eight siblings, with Scott being the second oldest. When I had to flee after my husband got addicted to heroin, I told my dear sister, 'Once a sister, always a sister. You will always be welcome in my home, no matter where I live. I will continue to be here for you and your children, ever and always.' Well, Kandi contacted me two weeks after I arrived, asking if my offer was genuine because she had no money and had four mouths to feed. I answered her, yes, dear sister, together we are stronger. And my dear sister has joined me on this journey ever since. It makes for a great story. I have written four books about it. Because I get it; my father is an adoptee, I am an adoptee, I am a Mother of Loss, and I also am a bonus mother to many that I nurtured and loved without having to have any ownership papers. I get it... thank you, Maui... It's called Hanai.*"

Rodney seemed very moved. I sensed he was connecting in more ways than one, but he held back with a bit of a wrinkled chin, cleared his throat, and asked, *"So is this going to be in the book?"*

With that, I chuckled and said, *"Indeed it is, dear Rodney. I thought I was finished, but I now realize I have not written my final statements. And this definitely makes for a great final statement."*

Sarge and the boys continued booking this delicate fairy princess and noticed I had a beautiful pendant that I would, unfortunately, have to remove. Sarge took a better look and asked while looking into my eyes and holding my pendant in his hand, *"What is this? It is beautiful. I'm sorry, but we are going to have to cut it off your neck."*

Holding his gaze, I replied, *"Rose quartz for my heart chakra, and peridot, a stone that heals the healer."*

I loved the unanimous silent ah-ha's, and admiration the Sarge and the boys let slip out. They all were so cute. I stood with no fear and absolute vulnerability while these four men took turns gently working to remove my crystal pendant that was tied to my neck with hemp string.

They finally resorted to cutting it off with scissors. None of them could successfully undo the knot, and believe me, they all gave it a gentle try.

Sarge then asked, *"Do you have underwire in your bra?"*

At this point, I was inches away from all four men in blue, real comfortable with myself and with them in my space as if they were my brothers (which is what we all are to one another). I looked into Sarge's eyes while I reached around my back to slip off my bra right there, in front of them. *"Are you serious? I am so glad for bottled water and that my pineal gland is clear because I rarely wear a bando over my bra. "*

When Sarge and the boys realized that I was stripping right then and there, Rodney and Sarge both said, *"No, no, not right here. Are you sure you have the underwire?"*

"But of course. I have no boobs and utilize all of Victoria's Secret's tools."

After waving the wand around me and gently touching me here and there for a light search, I turned to face them once more, pleasantly and comfortably informing Sarge and the boys before entering my cage, "*Ya know, this has been quite an interesting day. I have to say, this experience, especially right here and now, has mirrored so many things to me... even currently right now. What happens when one gets ordained to enter the temple? They touch you here and there, having garments removed. Thank you for the experience. I was never accepted into the LDS temple, which I do not mind a bit. Do I get a cage by myself or will I share it with other inmates? Which... never mind. You know what? It doesn't matter. I will go where you want me to go. I will enjoy the journey and welcome all who are meant to be in my space to hear what I offer to say.*"

And with that, Sarge said, "*Put her in cell three by herself.*"

I was given a blanket, and I made the best of it. I folded the mattress and made a great sitting chair for meditating. After a good 20 minutes of chuckling to myself and thinking, "*WTF? I am a f***ing Rockstar. Bring it!*" I owned my truth. I am who I am, and I am solid with who I am. With that, I affirmed within myself to never again be ashamed of who I am or behave differently to accommodate others.

I easily and happily went into a meditation only to be woken by Rodney repeating, "*Ms. Stone? Ms. Stone, your sister is here.*"

Sarge and the boys had changed their mind about my needing bail and informed me that I was free to go with no charges, but I would have to attend court for the violations.

What a trip! Who knows what will come of this, but I have a pretty good idea. After my sister and I got a bite to eat, and she took me to my car, I headed straight to Paia to High Times. I needed to replace my hide-a-toke that was confiscated.

And p.s., I ordered *MADONNA MDNA* from the internet, and it will be here on Wednesday!

October 2013

Scott Gets Sentenced

SCOTT: Kanyon boy, not sure if you heard yet, but my sentencing did not go so well. I got sent to prison. I will be here for at least a year. It sucks, but I will use my time wisely. They have a 9-month drug and alcohol program here called Conquest, so I signed up for that. I can also get a college degree while I am here. I am thinking I will do computer-aided drafting and graphics design. That will keep me busy while I am here. They also have weight rooms here, basketball courts, and grass in the yard. The food is also way better. So as much as this sucks, I will be able to handle it.

Right now sucks 'cause we only get out one hour per day. I think this phase lasts like six weeks unless I get to Conquest ASAP.

So, are you guys coming to Salt Lake to visit or what? If so, when? I am super excited to see you. I miss you tons. Are you getting tall? I like being able to have a pen instead of that stupid pencil in jail. Those pencils were only like 2 ½" long.

So, it is Wednesday the 25th now. Yesterday I went to the school and took some tests to see where I will be placed at school, even though I have my GED. I only need a few credits for my high school diploma, so they will have me take the classes I need to complete that. I will do that while I am doing my college classes. I should be getting a book soon that shows the different degrees available and about them with the required classes soon, so then I can finalize my plan. Between that program and working a little bit, my time should go by quickly.

I guess on commissary, we can get a TV in our cell, we can buy a Walkman, headphones and batteries, t-shirts, wife beaters, shorts, sweats, and basketball clothes. All kinds of things. That way, I don't have to wear these stupid prison clothes the whole time. Right now, we are in bright orange jumpsuits, but I guess once we get to the general population, we will be in white two-piece scrubs. So those aren't too bad, but I would rather kick it in a T-shirt and basketball shorts.

So, you can write me here at the Utah State Prison.

So, I got your guys' letter last Tuesday, the night before I came here. That's crazy about Mom getting arrested. Flipping cops. So, it sounds like it is working out okay having Jasper there, huh? How come Tyler didn't come? Kylie says that Tyler is doing really well. How is James doing? How is Mom? I miss you guys terribly. How are Kandi and the kids? Are you still watching the kids a lot while she is working? How is that working out? How is your garden doing? How is your glass blowing doing? Are you doing anything for school? Packets or anything? Make sure that you keep yourself in a position to do well. Society is tough these days. You have to have a plan and follow through on the steps that your plan needs to succeed.

Have you been playing hoops? If you get two more nephews out there with you, you will have your own team. Have you guys been working out? Oh yeah so when I got here to the prison, I weighed 225. That is the lightest I have been since about the time you were a baby. I might be moving today from the first spot they put us to where I will be for the next 4-6 weeks. Then hopefully I will get into that program, Conquest, so then I will be busy instead of being in my cell 23 hours per day. It sure makes time drag when you just read, eat, work out, and sleep. I am ready to listen to music, watch some football, work out with free weights... the same old cell workouts start to get old!!! Then as it gets boring and redundant, it gets harder to work out every day. I also wanna play some hoops and hang out in the yard, touch and lie on the grass. See the blue sky.

Well, I better get this in the mail so you can find out what's up with me. Oh, for me to be able to call you, I need a copy of the front page of a phone bill that has a name, address, and the phone number on it. It can't be a prepay or any of those kinds. Does anyone out there have a phone like that? Jasper or anyone? If so, I will need a copy of the bill that has that info, then I will try to get some money on there so I can call you. I love you tons and miss you more. Dad

P.S. Tell your mom I love her and miss her every day. Kiss her for me. I will talk to you soon.

KERI: My dearest Scott, Life is hard. I miss having a best friend, even though I feel you weren't a friend that treated me how I deserved to be treated. Obviously, that is all that I allowed, and if it weren't you mistreating me, it would have been another, because obviously, I am an extremely intense person that most people can't handle for too long.

I like who I am. I feel I love and serve others, staying true to who I am.

Thanx for being my friend. Obviously, we did not appreciate all that we had. It was too much focusing on what we didn't like, and boy, did we create more of that.

I'm struggling with being alone... I have lots of lovely acquaintance friends. I have lots of friends that come for advice, but I guess why I don't have more close-knit friendships is because it seems everyone just hangs and gets drunk around here in Lahaina, and I just would rather be home smokin' a bowl than hanging out drinkin', acting like partying is the bomb. I have never had fun drinking and being stupid.

Plus, I feel I gave you the best years of my life 100%, with you being the only one for my thoughts and desires. It is extremely hurtful to know that it was not reciprocated.

I'm finding I have a strong desire to be desired as much as I desire. Obviously, I don't feel desirable... I'm 43. Everyone thinks I'm 30, and then it seems when they find out how old I am, the desire is deflated. I am so not interested in anyone. There has got to be someone out there for me that will love and appreciate my intense self, and I won't settle for anything less.

I may be a lonely old lady forever. I guess I should have ended our relationship a long time ago... God knows you were constantly wanting out. Too bad I only want to have sex with good-looking men that are over 6' tall. That right there is keeping me virtuous.

MONEY... Well, let's move on to money. Still having a rough time of it. Your sister is getting more and more help from Phil and makes way more money than me these days.

The landlady told Kandi she wants Keri and the dog gone. The landlady hates dealing with me because I kill her with kindness, and she doesn't have any control or power over me. And she gets nowhere with me when she is wanting to complain about something, like us painting the walls, because I turn it back on her with such maturity and intelligence, reminding her of the hell hole we are living in. So do you know what that sister of yours did???

Kandi told me that she told the landlady that she will just kick me and Kanyon and the dog out!!! While she renews the lease without us. Can you believe? I was a bit shocked being that it is the end of the month. I have no money for rent or for food for that matter, plus I have taken her in so many times, always choosing family over money and others.

I'm looking for a 2nd and a 3rd job. I am adding "flower girl" to my job title. I walk around Lahaina and Kaanapali with a basket of flower leis, trying to sell leis like Dawn did when she sold roses. It made me think how ahead of the game Dawn is. She kept her baby and was walking my shoes in her teens, and here I am, 43, walking those shoes much older.

I love hearing your positive thoughts in your letter. For it is our thoughts that create our reality/illusion. I'm using every ounce of energy to keep my thoughts positive, clearing energy, meditating, and I am so thankful I smoke marijuana. I am seriously realizing for the first time, I have PTDS... whatever it stands for, but basically, I am traumatized from my life, and marijuana helps quiet my negative thoughts. I hope for a better future, I pray for a happy life. I desire comfort, friendship, love, happiness, loyalty, honesty, abundance in all good things, having no worries if I can afford to eat, and such.

I want to be able to have the freedom to travel and see all I want to see, especially my family that has been ripped apart, which was the furthest from my desires. I want a beautiful home, a nice car with windows. I want a place to call my own (I don't even have a closet). I want close relationships/friendships. I want nice clothes. I want a washer/dryer. I want a dishwasher. I want a nice fridge. I want a nice, beautiful yard, and ultimately, I want peace and serenity filled with unconditional unquestionable love.

PS. I can't afford a phone that complies. Kandi doesn't have one. James has no phone. Jasper is never here. I need money and lots of it.

Love always, Keri

First Days of Incarceration

October 6

SCOTT: Hello Kanyon boy, Happy birthday! Big 17. Do you feel a year older? How is Hawaii? Are you staying busy? How is it having Jasper out there? How is Mom? How are James, Kandi, and the kids? So, Tyler never came out.

I am not at the prison anymore. I am now at the Beaver County Correctional Facility in Beaver, Utah. which is 230 miles south of SLC and 100 miles north of St. George. You have been here. When we would be driving through here, we would stop and get squeaky cheese. It is really cool here because it is a minimum-security jail. Most of the people here are non-violent and non-crazy people. They only have charges like drugs, DUIs, fraud, and stuff like that. I guess it is rare that I could come here with my gun charge, but at the prison, all the counselors said I was so mellow and nice that I got to come here. So instead of being in our cell 23 hours a day, we are only in our cell from 10pm to 6:30am, so that is super nice. Also, the TV is on from 6:30am to 10pm, so I get to watch sports. In the section that I am in, there are 28 people. I think 20-22 of them are between 19 & 26. So, a lot of kids like Jasper and his friends, so that is ok. Not a lot of swearing, bullying, and other criminal behavior.

They have a program here called BRT that I am down here to do. It is a drug and alcohol 9-month program. I am on the list and just waiting for a bed. I am excited to start that.

One of the main reasons that I got to come down here to Beaver is because a bully punched me in the face, and I just laughed at him and walked away. He cheap shot me in the chin, and I said, *"Dang, boy. As big of a bully as you are, I thought that you would be tough."* The guards wrote a report on that, and a week later I was here. So, I am glad I didn't drop him. I am out full-time; I can order food and stuff on the commissary. I can use the phone and have visits. If I was still at the prison, it would be another 15-20 weeks before I could have any of that stuff. I am glad that I am here instead of there also, so you don't have to worry about me. Oh, I do have five stitches in my chin from that guy though, but no biggie. His hand was split worse than my chin. I get my stitches out tomorrow. I hope I have a little scar, so I can say I have a prison scar. Haha.

In our section here, there are a couple hundred bottles: Sprite, Coke, Mt. Dew, water, peanut butter, coffee, etc. Some of the boys here sewed handles onto their pillowcases. Then we put water bottles into the pillowcases, and those are our weights. So, I should get really yoke now. There are like 18 of the 27 other people in here that work out hardcore, so I don't want for a workout partner. I only spent sixteen nights at the prison, so that wasn't so bad. I go see the board in March, then, like 10 days later, I will know my release date.

Down here at Beaver at the commissary, we can order protein powder, vitamins, amino acids, all kinds of stuff to get yoke. We can also buy gym shorts, gray sweats, sweatshirts (no hoodies), so no stupid jail clothes. Also, we get the *East Bay* magazine, and if we want a pair of shoes from there (80% has to be white), we can get the shoe approved, then we can order those, so that's nice.

Oh yeah, they have a yard we get to go to one hour a day. They have a jungle gym out there, so I can do pull-ups, dips, calf work, etc. I really like having pens instead of those stupid golf pencils that we had to use in SLC jail. My hands are way too big for those little things. I am trying to get permission to get a calculator and some construction rulers in here so that I can start doing a ton of take-offs. If I can do 2-3 a day, I should be able to make good while I am here. So hopefully, they approve that. Even if not, I will do take-offs. I will just have to add it in my head and on paper. Which will be slower, but it will make my mind super sharp and fast.

Have you been playing ball? Have you met any nice girls? You should study for and take your GED, so you have that. Have you played any ball over at the church? Is it still super-hot? Or is it cooling down a little? How 'bout your garden? I love you tons and can't wait to see you. Love, dad

October 9

KERI: Scott, I hate the limitations on communication. Thanx for the effort you put forward to call on Kanyon's birthday (I was at work). I sell leis at night. I get them loaded so they can get HIGH all day, and yeah, now I sell leis at night too.

Good thing the landlady wants us out. Who knows what's going to happen from here? It's Kanyon's birthday... time for eviction. I asked Kanyon, what gives? He says it's time to move forward to bigger and better.

I hold no fear in my space. I hold anticipation for something amazing and magical to happen. I am just focusing on having control over my emotions, keeping positive, happy thoughts, living each day in my vortex for as long as possible. In my vortex, I drive a white Jeep. I live in a big, beautiful home with plenty of room for others and plenty of room for a garden. I am a professional traveler who spreads Aloha worldwide.

We hated hearing how you got punched and had to get stitches. Good job holding your actions and staying in your power. So happy to hear you are somewhere better. Is this going to be your permanent residence for a while? At least you have no worries or stress about providing a roof over your head or food on the table. It can be bliss living within your means. It's crazy how little it takes to exist on this planet. I am grateful I have survived and have learned this bit of truth, but I am ready to thrive and get back to some luxuries of life.

Just missed your call! F***! I brushed my teeth and missed it. Kanyon is annoyed as well about the absence of communication. Dang, by the time you get your freedom, I'm sure you will be very good at checking in... a trait I was always praying you would get better at.

We are getting ready to go to Longboards for dinner. All-you-can-eat crab legs and prime rib for Kanyon's birthday. Just him and I... I always thought we all would be together forever. How silly was that? To think one would be so content clinging to the rocks living the SAME life with the SAME people. I miss all those people... I do, but I was getting bored with it and those characters in their roles surrounding me.

Kandi is asking what Kanyon and I are going to do. I know Kanyon needs the dog and the ganja, and I know the Universe/God/Source knows too. I know I have already lined it up as to what is to happen, but it all looks bad in this 3rd dimension reality. I have court and tons of fines for seriously a pinch of weed and failing to register my f***ing car. I loved how you always took care of those things, so I didn't have to worry my pretty little head. Because look at me, *"this hard-core criminal, threat to society."* Yeah... threat to society! I am an example to own your truth, be who you are, don't give a f*** what anybody else thinks, and rock it like the great ones did, such as EINSTEIN, Nostradamus, Madonna, John Lennon... the list goes on. All the "misfits" who truly got it and owned their uniqueness and trusted in who they are/were. I cannot wait to see what awaits behind door #2, but it's gotta be great!

October 13

KERI: Scott, So I have been babysitting like a teenager for the flower lady... you know, the lady I get the leis from to go out and sell at night. She lives in a beautiful home in a beautiful neighborhood with a beautiful yard. It feels so good to be in an environment I am so accustomed to living in. It helps with manifesting!!! It definitely keeps me in my vortex, living as if this is my beautiful home but wording it as such with gratefulness, *"I love this beautiful home I am in. I love this beautiful yard. I am enjoying it. I love this beautiful neighborhood I am always in. I love this beautiful park that I enjoy running around with kids in. I love, love living like this."* There are three boys - two from a rich daddy that lives on Lanai and is on vacation to Paris. So, the two older boys that usually stay with the dad, are staying with the mom for a while.

November 2013

West Maui Parasail

My days at the harbor were ending once again. Parasailing would be shutting down December 14th, closing for the season, and will open again in May. What a great job I had, that allowed time off to travel the world... or go to Utah and visit the family I fled from.

I hadn't originally planned on cashing in on the bennies of working this seasonal job. I had been chasing jobs, seeking to fill in the whale season. The combination of missing calls, landlady wanting, *"Keri & the dog out,"* Kandi opting out of, *"Together we're stronger,"* lack of finding a new place, Kanyon's predictions, Kai's visit, my mother's financial and emotional support & assistance... along with Lois & Barbara's strong, wise words of comfort... I shifted from resistance to allowance, and life was flowing smoothly, like a river. Everything was falling into place for Kanyon's return to Utah, and my VISIT to escort him there. It makes perfect sense that Kanyon needed to be with his older brother at this time. I had been hugely blessed to have Kanyon hold my hand along with his cousins to get me to my home in Maui. Now it was Kanyon's time to graduate to manhood and face his fears of being on his own without me.

I was thankful for all the family I had in Utah to support me and my children with their desires and dreams. I could not help but be thankful in some way for the healthy, stable, successful fine young man Kai had become. I give a lot of credit to that Papa Sanderson.

We all need to face our fears... no one is excluded from that. My biggest fear... being on my own, supporting myself. Scott's biggest fear... serving time in prison/jail.

It's crazy... there was a time when my biggest hopes and dreams were to keep my family together FOREVER, with Kai included in that statement.

I finally was able to, *let go and let God*, moving on from those hopes and dreams. A year and a half later, those hopes and dreams were falling into place just as I had desired (with Kai reclaiming me, wanting me to come home, meet his kids, be Grandma, live with him, whatever I desired, etc.). But guess what? I didn't have those hopes and dreams anymore. I moved on to living for me instead of living for others.

I was always accused of being codependent, a title I never understood. What was so wrong with serving and loving others, so we could all be happy? Right???... wrong. I finally got what codependency means. My whole life, I did what everyone else wanted me to do... for once in my life, other people's happiness was not a deciding factor for me.

For once in my life, I felt I had found true happiness. I was living in a sanctuary that stayed warm year-round. My job couldn't have been any better with the ocean's edge at my back while I greeted visitors, spreading Aloha, and receiving love from my harbor family on the daily.

I, for once in my life, felt a sense of belonging. I, for once in my life, felt I could truly be my authentic self. And I, for once in my life, was going to honor my feelings and return to my home Maui, even if I returned childless.

Messages through Dreams and Nature

I must mention a reoccurring dream I just had the other night. It was a migration of tons of beluga whales clearly seen thru the top of the water... I was peering down from the top, wanting to get as close as possible, holding on to a mast/pole with a strong grip. I felt unsteady, and I had a fear of falling in.

Whale: The power of song, creation, awakening the inner depths. It's time to show the magnificence and power of your creativity. Do not hold back.

Barbara was a great friend who worked the booth the opposite shifts of when I worked the booth. The problem was we never saw each other at work, so we were always making plans with one another. One time we went to the beach by her house to discuss our dreams and desires. We had the most interesting experience with this big seagull-looking bird. The bird perched itself right in front of us on a rock, almost as if it were enjoying our conversation. It sat and "listened in" for a long while (Barbara and I get pretty chatty). Anyway, this bird flew off just to circle back around to hear the rest. Noticing the odd behavior, Barbara confirmed, "*I come here almost every day, and I have never even seen a bird of that nature, let alone have one behave in such a way.*"

Gulls: Responsible behavior & communication. The gull is associated with the element of water, as well as the air. It knows how to work in both kingdoms, and it knows the behaviors appropriate to both. This teaches you how to behave and work in dimensions other than that which is normal. The appearance of a gull usually indicates lessons or abilities in proper behavior, courtesy, and communication. It may reflect that you need the lessons or that you may become the teacher of such. They can help you read between the lines and understand the body language of others. They hold knowledge of the techniques of psychological communication. The young are fussy eaters. They have to be stimulated to eat. They have ties to proper eating behaviors, stimulation of diet (physical & otherwise), and more.

Love it! Life is easier to live when you get cheat sheets, so to speak, of what the energy is in the space. Like attracts like... I saw the attraction! I needed to make eating healthy a priority. AND it just so happened that Barbara and I had communicated about those lessons and how to learn from them to fully receive our desires.

The seagull incident was such an amazing experience. I totally looked it up pronto. I went to work so high on life and pumped to share with Barbara... we wrote notes back and forth. It was an amazing day. I had many days that had magical moments, *but that day*... a Spanish romancer guy approached me, complementing how beautiful I was, inside and out. He was very respectful and gave me a strong message that a lover was on his way, with sweet regrets that it was not him.

BARBARA: Aloha beautiful, that is so awesome about the Spanish man. See, he was feeling what I'm feeling for you too! When you love yourself and allow love and healing to flow, that is when things happen. I believe he is right... in the next few months, when you let go and make all your amends, then your man will come. Yay, so exciting!!! I'm just feeling so blessed these days. I feel at peace, and I am happy to just be me and to be able to have such a beautiful life. Anything above and beyond what I have right now is such a blessing! Have a great day! Muah. Love, Barbara

Heart to Heart

November 1

KERI: Hello darling (Scott), How goes it? Fish (my harbor buddy) would say S.O.S.... same ole shit. I imagine that is what your answer could be. Never S.O.S. for me... seriously, you cannot make this shit up. I understand we wanted a great movie, but this movie is kicking my ass. Your sister has been unbelievable. She woke Kanyon up (while I was at work) screaming, bullying him to get up, *"Pack your shit up so you guys can get out of here."* This was the morning of Halloween. Well, thank God our son has Tourette's. He jumped up out of bed and gave her a piece of his f***ing mind.

I guess it was after this that Kandi called my mom to involve her to kick us out, telling my mom that she was just going to pack up our shit and start throwing it out. My mother proceeded to let her know that if she did, *"Keri could call the cops on you. You have no legal right to kick Keri out. You best be moving out yourself so you both can be done with the lease."* Damn, so glad she thought to call and involve my mother. I would have been so f***ing pissed if she had done that.

Well, in the midst of all this, Kai called unexpectedly and said he misses us and will be flying out on Tuesday. Interesting... but I must say his timing really couldn't be better. I have no idea how all this madness will turn out. I am not liking my journey AT ALL.

Thank God for the harbor and my love for my harbor family!!! Kanyon and I got into it, shouting the blame game for this f***ed up part of the journey. Yep, my fault for calling the cops on dad. Or we can take it further... yep, my fault for having sex with him in 1986 to begin with... oops. Well, let's take it further... it's all a reverberation from my ancestors, so let's f***ing curse them all for this f***ed up part of this journey. He then called me f***ing crazy with more names with it. F***ing kids throwing that shit in my face blaming me for your f***ing choices and the repercussions from such. Well, I am still waiting for the reverberations from my actions of loving and serving unconditionally to all!!! It's hard to believe how unsupported this mother is... which only brings more awareness in my space. **LOVE ONE ANOTHER** *'ADOPT'* **THE MOTHER.**

I don't know if I filled you in, but after Phil, Kandi's kid's daddy, never showed, his friend Kyle came by because they had made plans to meet up at the house. Remember, that was the whole reason Kandi started saying let's go our separate ways. She wanted to play house and be able to be a full-time mom, and that was what started all this.

Kyle was something else... I actually enjoyed his company for the most part. He was pretty comical. He reminded me of Lenny off *Laverne & Shirley*, except with more smarts and a bit of an Al Bundy flair. Except this guy is not married, nor does he have children. Kyle just left this morning, returning home from a very different vacation than he had expected on Maui.

Well, when Phil never showed, Kandi went back to Jeramiah, the ex-boyfriend who she had filed a restraining order against to keep his trip ass at a distance. I don't know where to begin to process all this madness, so is where I started... God bless Kandi for having to play this role, obviously to get the ball rolling for me to get to a better place. I would much rather play my role in this scene than her crazy ass role. I am so thankful I am the same person, no matter how much money I have in my wallet or bank account. I will always love and serve others, whether I am rich or poor, and I will never sell out!

November 4

SCOTT: Keri, I received your letters this morning. Thank you for writing. Firstly, let me touch on your comments about wanting to be desirable. You have no problem there. You are the most desirable woman that I know. You are desirable in every aspect and category. You are amazingly beautiful and sexy, your body is perfect, your eyes are amazing, your smile warms me and makes me feel loved, and your compassion and love for everyone is amazing. Your personality is perfect, you are the perfect lover. There is nothing about you that I would change. You are the perfect woman for any man. If I could go back and change my demons and addictions before I killed your love for me, I would do it without hesitation. I love you dearly, and I always have. I daydream about you all day and dream about you all night. Thoughts of you are what is keeping me strong throughout this hellacious time in my life.

I am doing everything I can daily to change who I am, to defeat my demons and addictions so that I can be free ASAP. I pray for you daily to be able to be successful and be able to cope with being dumped into the role of provider after so many years. I pray for you to be extremely happy. It is hard for me to accept you not being with me, but I want for you whatever gives you the most amazingly perfect life that the most wonderful woman that I know deserves. I find myself carefully selecting my words because you have made it clear how you feel, so I find myself in the conundrum of trying to be your friend and be supportive of you without crossing any lines that you do not want me to cross, so maybe you could clarify what is and what is not ok to tell you and share with you.

You will not be a lonely old woman. You are way too amazing for that. I know that I have not been there for you in the past, as I hobbled along as a broken man with a broken little dude inside of me, but the more time I spend here in this daily treatment setting, I feel my façade cracking and falling away and the real me coming out stronger every day. I want to be here for you in whatever role you would like me to be. I must admit, I am confused about what is what because when I simply think about you and sharing space with you, my heart pounds, I get short of breath, and I get lightheaded. I'm not sure what that is, what emotion, what feeling, etc.

I know that when I see other women or see pictures (all of these young boys in here have tons of pictures of women), I find myself comparing them to you. The problem is none of them come anywhere close to the bar that you set - so that is a conundrum.

So, later in this letter, I will try to walk you through logging onto Turbo Tax and finalizing the last of your taxes. I don't remember which email address I used. It will only take you a couple minutes once you are able to log on.

Ok sorry. So, as I was saying, I am trying to be a support to you because I am unclear as to what role you are playing. I know that it is not in my best interest to think about you physically or sexually because just the simplest and most innocent or maybe not-so-innocent thoughts or dreams about you get me crazily worked up. So, I hope things are better at the house with that sister of mine. Somehow, I am not surprised that Kandi was going to try and get you evicted when she thought Phil was coming.

So, Jasper and James got their own pad? How are they doing? Kanyon said you were looking for a place further away from the water.

I am starting to do estimates again and will start sending you all of that money as soon as it starts coming in. I will send it all to you. I was all set up in Salt Lake County jail and was just getting started when I got sent to the prison, and they don't let anything come with us, so that was a process.

As horrible as this whole deal has been, it has been super eye-opening, and I continue to learn lesson after lesson. Patience, tolerance, generosity, tolerance, acceptance, tolerance, etc. So, I have been in the BRT program down here in Beaver, Utah. I think BRT stands for Behavior Remodification Therapy. I am learning so much. I am losing my snobbery, having to live side by side with all types. People, that nine months ago, I would have been horrified by, and not given the time of day.

Sorry about my handwriting right now. I am in class and am not supposed to be writing to you. Supposed to be paying attention. The seminar is on rational recovery. So, in this program, we are in a dorm setting. I am up in what you could call a loft. It is about the size of our master suite at our Farm Circle house, where eighteen of us spend our nights. There are nine bunk beds, two sinks, two toilets, and two showers, as well as a square table that seats four. So, it is definitely close quarters. We program Monday-Friday from 7:30 a.m. to 4 p.m. We have an hour off for lunch from 12:00-1:00. We learn about different drugs and their effects, alcohol, etc. We learn about addiction and recovery behavior, life skills, etc. We have either AA or NA for an hour each day. We go to a class called criminogenics, which is criminal behavior and its relation to drug and alcohol use. We have group therapy and individual therapy. So, I am definitely using my time wisely. I am learning a ton of skills and useful information that I have been too stubborn to digest as I have heard them over the years.

I recently heard the quote, *"You can give up one thing for everything, or you can give up everything for one thing."* I understand that applies to me and my addiction and drug use/alcohol. I know that I am an addict, and I can't use or drink at all. I have to get those warm fuzzies from family and loved ones.

Material wealth, money, drugs, and alcohol are not the way to get the attention that little Scott needs. It is sad to me that I couldn't learn these lessons that you and others have tried to teach me all my life, but I guess 45 is better than never learning them.

So, I hear that Kai is coming out there tomorrow. That is awesome. I am excited for you to spend time with Daisy and Casper. We have beautiful grandchildren. We breed beautiful lineages. You are going to be so amazing with them. I am excited for you to be Grandma Keri and develop that bond with these special angels. I also pray and hope that it helps change the dynamics between you and Kai from "birth mom" and adoptee to more of a special unconditional bond. I am excited and will be looking forward to hearing how the visit goes. I am praying that the whole week is amazing and that there is no drama. I am warned that weed (marijuana) will lead to a diminished effect on the visit. I hope not Keri. I am not saying that in a chastising way at all, my lady. I just know that you are both strong-willed, and I want you to have a special experience this week. I hope that you did not read, "I hope not Keri," and hear your mom's voice, because I only said Keri, instead of baby or darling because I am trying to respect your boundaries.

Starting next week, I will have to start teaching and preparing seminars and presentations. The first presentation that I am going to do is the power of positive thinking. I am really looking forward to preparing that and presenting it to the community here. There are 34 people in my pod. One guy is like 52, there are maybe seven or eight that are 40-45, and the rest are between 21-35. There are quite a few that are Kai's age or close to that.

So, Keri, my darling, I am really really glad that you were comfortable enough to share your letter with me and to feel safe enough to be open about your feelings and insecurities with me. That means a lot to me, and I hope that I can reciprocate and be a support and a good friend to you. I care deeply for you. I love and adore you, and I hope I can be a strength and a positivity in your life.

What I have written in this letter is true life. There is truly nothing about you that I would change. I love how open and honest you can be. I think you are the most beautiful and sexy woman I have ever met, and you are an amazing wife, mother, aunt, friend, sister, daughter, granddaughter, niece, example, sister-in-law, teacher, etc. Be who you were meant to be, and don't let anyone tell you to change. I love how passionate you are in life, and in the bedroom. I can't even think about your/our passion without getting light-headed. Be the amazing woman that you are and do it proudly. I put you in the same category as Madonna and those other strong women that you mention, darling. You are amazing in every way. I love you and always will, and I will always be here as a rock or stone for you in whatever role you need/want me for. I will close and mail this, then will start another. Love always, Scott

November 9

SCOTT: Keri, so how are you this week? I'm starting to feel the holiday blues that I get this time of year, but I am working through it and trying to keep myself from getting down. I am taking what I am learning in this program to heal and reading other self-help books to work on myself as a man and a human being.

I am currently reading *The Voice of Knowledge* by Don Miguel Ruiz. It is really good. Some of the things it says on the cover are "A Toltec wisdom book" and "A practical guide to inner peace." It talks about all the lies that we learn as children. That we must be a certain way to be successful. Success looks this way or that way. That we are not good enough. I know that I have a lot of these lies and BS in my head. I am learning to recognize them and to reprogram myself. I don't want the demons from my childhood and teenage years to run my life now. I want to break free from these chains of bondage and recognize the amazing man of light that I truly am and achieve the things that I know that I am capable of.

You have taught me a lot my dear, and I love you for all you have taught me. You have always been an amazing example to me. You are a strong and amazing powerful woman of light, and you are perfect in every way.

So, tell me about your visit from Kai. Was it just him, or did he bring Mai and the babies? Did you guys have a blast or what?

Was there peace in the space, or was there contention? I hope it was peaceful and that you guys had an amazing visit. You deserve the best, and you deserve peace in your heart. It kills me when you are hurting over the whole Kai/adoption situation. I wish I could take the pain and hurt from you and fill you with pure light and happiness. I also pray that your relationship with your mom will align and that you guys can have an amazing mother and daughter relationship and friendship. Always remember that she has strong opinions and beliefs, but they are simply those... her opinions and beliefs. There is nothing you can do to change these so you can battle with her and not enjoy the goodness and sweet times that you guys can & should be having, or you can resist against it/her and have turmoil and conflict in your life with your mom.

I love you very much and want the best for you. I want you to be happy and have everything that you have ever wanted, hoped for, and dreamt about. Let me know what I can do to help you achieve and acquire all your dreams. Love Scott

November 15

KERI: Scott, It's a week until Thanksgiving. I'm supposed to be out by Dec 1st. I haven't found the place I'm supposed to be at. Kanyon thinks it's in Utah with him and Kai. Utah is the LAST place I want to be. Kanyon is obviously having to face his fears and live without me.

The kids don't understand why I wouldn't live in Utah, especially with them all there. I have raised all the kids. I have devoted myself to them and others so much that I have seriously lived my entire life for others, sacrificing for others my life thus far. For a first, I am living for me. I love my life in Maui, I love all my friends, and I love the weather. I think of even visiting Utah, and as much as I love my daughter and Kai, and as much as I am interested in meeting my grandchildren (not even Kanyon moving there could get me to stay there), the thought of Utah does not bring me happy thoughts. It feels suffocating.

I have lived that life and fought for that life. That life obviously is NOT for me. As much as I thought that life was for me, I feel I have definitely graduated from that homemaking, codependent, self-sacrificing life I have lived! I have been enlightened to live my life for me, and I, for once, am living it and loving it. Keri

November 25

SCOTT: Keri, how are you? I am doing well. I'm just doing the program. It is good I am learning a lot of new skills and seeing how messed up and crazy a lot of my thinking patterns have been. I see how hard it must have been for you to deal with my crazy self all of these years, so sorry about that.

There are a bunch of things in the program that I thought were ridiculous at first, but I am starting to see now that they all have a purpose. One is that we have to do facilities for the first 30-60 days when we come into the program. So, we have jobs to do six days a week, twice a day. Like, two days a week I have to clean two of the four showers, one day a week, toilets. So that has been humbling for me and taught me to be more aware of cleaning up after myself and being careful not to miss, and to watch where my hair goes when I shave. Things I never paid attention to. Also, we have to hold people accountable and give them tickets for stupid and/or incorrect behavior. This has really helped me to pay attention to my behavior and to stop and think before I act. We are also learning a lot about drugs and addiction, alcohol, etc. I had to do my first presentation this week. I did it on *The Voice of Knowledge*, which is the little voice in our head that tells us all of the lies and BS about ourselves. We are not good enough, we can't do this, etc. It went really well. I utilized a lot of the information from Don Miguel Ruiz's book. It is really good. He also wrote *The Four Agreements* and *The Miracle of Love*.

I think combining all these Agreements and utilizing them in my daily life will help me to be an amazing man and be the person that my family needs me to be. I wish I would have grasped these concepts earlier, but I guess it wasn't time yet.

So, how was the visit with Kai? He said it was awesome. Was that healing for you guys? I hope that it was good for you. You are the most amazing person that I know, and you deserve to be super happy. I pray for you daily, and you are always on my mind. You are in my dreams. I miss your beautiful face, your amazing smile, your sexy body. I miss the way you look at me. I know that you can do anything that you set your mind to. You deserve all of your hopes, dreams, and aspirations, and you know how to get there. Just always remember who you are and the amazing, honest, powerful woman that you are, and you will be more than fine. Step out of the past and into your future. Live every day like it is your last. You have always done that better than anyone that I know. Just keep that up. Maintain your selflessness, compassion, and how you care about others. It is a special gift, and it makes you the angel on earth that you are. I am working on some deals to get money flowing again and will get you money as quickly as I can.

So, it is Monday, November 25, 2013, and I am having a horrible day. Tired of the program, tired of prison/jail, tired of going to bed when I am told to, tired of not seeing or talking to you or Kanyon, tired of hanging with punk-ass criminals all day. I am ready to be done with this experience and to move on with life. My temper has been short all weekend and today. Thursday is Thanksgiving, and I am not real excited to spend that day here. I know that this is my consequence for my behavior, but it is still shitty. I want to finish this program and go home. I don't know how I am going to handle another year.

So, I hear you and Kanyon are flying back to SLC, then you are going to head back to Maui. I hope I see you while you are here. It would mean a lot to me. I miss you tons and will always love you. Love Scott

P.S. Hey, I need an impact letter from you, if you could... a letter that discusses how my addictions have impacted your life. I would appreciate it. I have to read it in front of the group. Thank you

Kai's Visit

Well, Kai's visit was an eventful one. It seemed to have gotten off to a bad start. Kai arrived right at the peak of the landlady and Kandi kicking Keri and the dog out.

I was stressed, needed money, and panicked. I took Kai's surprise visit as a gift from the Universe, with him showing up as some sort of "man of this family," showing up as a mentor for Kanyon, and showing up maybe, for financial assistance and to help me figure things out. Which was wrong for me to have assumed that because he felt the pressure of SOS when he came out because he was missing his mommy. I get it. Anyway, things worked out. My mother gave me the money I needed after she heard from Kai that I was a functional adult. Whatever? (Which makes what I will be sharing later, even more hilarious.)

Kai had rented a car and showed up late at night. I gave him a genuine hug and received him with open arms. It was late, and Kanyon was very excited to see his brother. I figured I would chat it up with them/him in the morning. Well, I guess he misread the part where I received him with open arms and felt neglected because I went to bed and left them to chat it up, just the two of them.

After an eventful day at Costco, Kanyon brought Kai's neglected feelings to my awareness, which opened up a conversation so he could better understand that I was very happy he was here.

Kai and I had a great time getting *"high on Maui,"* with West Maui Parasail. It was a memorable trip. During the trip back to the beach in the zodiac, a wave crashed onto the boat and drenched us all, including my camera. So, unfortunately, I did not have a camera to take pics for the majority of his visit.

I loved the memory it created. Kai, a very strong and handsome muscleman, was able to put them muscles to use and rescued all the people on the raft. He lifted me immediately and whisked me to safety first and foremost. Then, immediately went into rescue mode, and lifted some women out of the water to safety. We all loved it. All three of us ladies ruined our phones and cameras, but we had smiles on our faces after the eventful damsel was rescued by a prince.

While I was at work one of the following days, Kanyon and Kai had a memorable time. The boys had planned on leaving Lahaina, but with a roadblock heading north and a roadblock heading south, they decided to jump off the rocks at Cliff House when Kanyon cut his foot open. As soon as they made it back home, Kanyon had him some toast with a big ole slab of ganja butter, and Kai followed suit, stating he had a sore shoulder. Kanyon warned him he would get high, but Kai claimed Kanyon was talking too technical with big words such as cannabinoids.

Long story short, I went home to boys higher than a kite. Family from the Utah zone was mad at Kanyon for *"feeding Kai ganja"* and mad at me for not taking Kai to the hospital because he was tripping balls and thought he was dying.

Kanyon was awesome, held his ground, and didn't take the rap for Kai's choices. I loved it... We went out to eat at Aloha Mix Plate, and they had quite the heated discussion about their consumption of marijuana that day. It was kind of a loud conversation of who was right, with Kanyon not taking the rap for Kai getting higher than a kite ... and how ridiculous it was when he thought he was overdosing and dying. He would have been the first in history.

There were other heated moments during Kai's visit... There was mention of who I had been with in an intimate way. Kai had a very hard time with that because there was an age difference of 3 years between Kai and that someone, with Kai being the older one. I am a very youthful person who does not act or look 43. It was something that I had to get real with and be okay with because honestly, I can't see myself with any dude near my age.

KERI: My dear Kai, Thank you for your visit. Thank you for your understanding. Thank you for your love. Please forgive me. I'm sorry to disappoint all of my family, but honestly, I am the happiest I have ever been. And if that disappoints y'all, oh wells. I am not ashamed of receiving Ben's love. No one knows what he and I have shared except for him and me. Call it carnal - which, yes, that was nice too - but only Ben and I and God know what transpired between us. Just like people judge how you and I hold one another... a lot of people think it's creepy. But again, I am not ashamed of receiving your love. I am thankful for the love I am shown, and yes, I will reciprocate that love, reflecting right back the love I have to show.

I do not, nor have I ever, considered myself a whore. I feel I am very connected to God and Mother Earth, and this Divine Universe we exist in. I do have a strong love for Jesus the Christ. My most favored ancestor/brother/leader/example, etc. I need not explain to others the love I hold in my heart. I am unconditional love, and I have worked very hard to get here, allowing my light to shine. I could never go back to Utah. Being around everyone, including you, dampers my light. Yes, it was in the past. I wish I could be as successful as you (sarcasm) at being able to forget and be so Christ-like without sin. But I unfortunately suffer from PTSD. Yep, that event in 1986 affected me like it does every mother who loses a child. What is your biggest fear? You say to lose your children and Mai... Well, welcome to my world. Shit happens, and life goes on. And again, here right now, living in Maui and smoking weed is THE HAPPIEST I HAVE EVER BEEN. Think what you want of me. Because bottom line, I like who I am, and I am not interested in changing anything. I have been an excellent mother to my children and raised them well. NO REGRETS. And I am looking forward to finally living for me. Love, That lady

On the last day of Kai's visit, we went to the bamboo forest in Hana with the boys. We met a great soul who welcomed us to park our car on his property. We all shared wisdom, fruit and vegetables. Then we went on our way to the hike.

We had Kanyon's "service dog" with us and had a great hike. We made it all the way to the top before dark and headed back just as the sun was setting. On the way down we were met by the park rangers. Come to find out, there were some cars still parked in their lot, so they were out looking for the owners. Taken by surprise, the rangers informed us that there were no dogs allowed. I informed them that we had just gotten the dog registered as a service dog, and I had left the papers in the car. I felt the rangers were leaning towards a ticket, so we booked it down the mountain to the car with the rangers following us at our heels.

One of the rangers kept up with Kai and me, and the other rangers stayed back with Kanyon and the boys. The ranger was running out of breath, and he hollered out, *"Why are you moving so fast?"*

Gracefully, Kai and I bombed the path and raced, as we practically skied over the rocks and obstacles. I shouted out, *"I'm a Utah girl. I know how to get off a mountain fast and quick, especially when the sun is going down."*

"Utah? I used to work at Zion National Park."

"Well then, you must know my dear good friends, the Degroats. Amanda is practically my sister." My dear friends have worked in Zion as rangers for years, and come to find out, my friend had been this fella's boss. After we discussed my relationship and know-how of the Degroats, Kai and I made it to the bottom of the path and split, leaving the ex-Zion ranger in the dust. We figured we could run to the car, hop in, head back to pick up the boys, have them jump in, and then we could just take off.

Well, the boys were escorted slowly by the other rangers. For some reason, Kanyon didn't have shoes and did the hike barefoot, which slowed him down. God bless Jasper and James, who stayed by his side while Kai and I took off. When we flipped the car around to have them jump in, the rangers had already called for backup and two vehicles pulled up on the scene with their lights rolling. After playing blonde, we convinced them that we were truly in a hurry to get Kai off to the airport. After they ran my name, they saw the whole *"I got arrested on Labor Day"* thing, and the rangers became a little escalated about marijuana and developed fear in their space because I was listed as some kind of marijuana criminal in the system. But after all of that, they let us go, and the ex-Zion ranger said, *"This has nothing to do with you knowing the Degroats, but I am going to let you go."* Well, we all knew that it had everything to do with my knowing the Degroats! Lol. Love my dear sistah Amanda and her husband who have served our national forests their entire grownup life.

We got Kai back to Kahului, and he made his flight on time. Kai and I ended on a good note. We had a great moment on the hike where he acknowledged how much I drove him crazy to the point of being his least favorite person. But as crazy as I drove him, I was one of his most favorite people at the same time. I'll take it.

December 2013

Utah...

December 2

KERI: Scott, so hey, life is working out as always. No money is flowing in yet. But my mother bought Kanyon and me a plane ticket to Utah, one way. I figure the state of Utah is loaning me money for such things because they are suing me for child support and getting ready to garnish my wages. Unbelievable how this mother in need, along with mothers for centuries, are not supported and provided for. I plan on flying back to Maui without Kanyon. Kanyon needs this time to spread his wings and fly. He needs a male mentor to prepare him to be a provider. He is an amazing nurturer, and it's time for this momma to cut the apron strings. As life would have it, I'm not being supported in raising my children, but like my daddy always said, *"You can only teach them until they are 14, and then they are in the driver's seat."* I'm looking forward to the Utah visit, but I am looking more forward to my return to Maui. Love, Keri

December 8

KERI: Hey darlin' (Scott), So, I found some letters that I guess I hadn't mailed to you yet. I am busy finalizing all the details and getting my stuff boxed for storage at Jasper and James' apartment.

I will be returning and living with Rachel and sharing a bed with her for $350 a month. I'm getting packed for my VISIT to Utah and helping Kanyon get his stuff packed. I have been taking the dog, Stoney, to work with me at the harbor. I have to get this "service dog" ready.

We got the harness and paperwork for $200 so the landlord couldn't kick us out. It has been totally divine to have the landlady freak out and have Eric as my friend and example at the harbor of how to get around things. It is saving me money to have the dog fly to Utah with Kanyon, which is what needs to happen. So, the dog gets to ride at our feet or on our lap. We get preloading and pre-unloading... way cool... FOR FREE. But I'm a little nervous. He behaves a bit like a dog, but a good dog. So, I have been taking him everywhere with me, training him, getting him used to being around a lot of people and indoors. No barking or acting like a dog. I have 9 days. Speaking of... I only have 9 days. That sister of yours... I am glad I have the wisdom and clarity I have and have my chakras as my focus to clear because this situation could be a whole lot worse. You Stones can be BULLIES.

I'm so glad I have great friends at the harbor to remind me of such things. As Capt. Tiff would say, *"Don't let others' actions and behaviors change who you are or how you behave."*

Kanyon overheard Kandi telling Jeramiah that she was going to tell the landlady, that it is not working out, and I guess, try to get the landlady to kick us out 'cause Kandi can't stand the 9 days we have left to get out of here. She is unbelievable... I continue to wash her dishes and clean up after her, which she seems to be getting better at. I have, like, three boxes in the living room that I live out of and put away on the bar. I make my bed before I need to lay my head and take it away after, so there is no evidence even as to where I sleep. I leave no trace, and Kanyon stays in his room. They use our things, get into my stuff, help themselves, eat all, ruin all... which I should not say "all." They are getting better, I think, because I continue to be who I am, and not eating their food, never going through their shit.

The kids have been bullying the dog lately, that got me to realize I need to take Stoney to the harbor with me to better train him and prepare him for the plane ride. So again, thank you, Universe, for getting louder so that I do what I need to do, and thank you, Kandi, for having to be the villain to get me to do the things I need to do.

Which brings me to your request for a letter about the impact of your behavior and how it has affected me... Well, for starters, thank you for the lessons. Your behavior has made me one wise, wise woman. But bottom line, it was an energy match. I was messed up from my childhood and abandonment issues and messed up from the whole adoption shit. I am so grateful I had you through it all. If it weren't you, it would have been someone else helping me identify who I am, what my truth is, and what my true desires, wants, and likes are.

I thought all I ever wanted was to be a mom, a grandma... I thought I would be with you forever to share our children's and grandchildren's lives. There was a time when that was all I wanted.

My true belief... You can live happily ever after with anyone. I have since acquired more desires. I now have a desire to live in the moment. I now have a desire to be happy in my every moment. I now have a desire to surround myself with others who appreciate and love all I do. I now have a desire to be with a lover who adores me and is my best friend whom I can trust. I also have learned to love lightly because nothing lasts forever. Everything is just a steppingstone to the next level of understanding.

Obviously, we were destined to travel the path we have traveled... facing our fears... yours being confinement, mine being on my own providing for myself, losing my children. Well look, here we are, facing our fears that we needed to clear.

Our life together seems so long ago. I have no regrets. I loved you, I hated you, I grew up with you.

Thanks for providing a lavish lifestyle which I prefer. Thank you for working as hard as you did to provide the great lavish vacations and all the kids' classes and activities. It truly compensated for your lack!

Our union caused me a lot of heartbreak, but bottom line, it was my doing as well. Obviously, I was fearful of unconditional deep love and didn't feel I was worthy of it. For my truth, as horrible as my life has been, I created it. I endured till the end. And I am excited for my new life. Thank you for forcing me on my way to bigger and better. I'm having a hard time writing about *"the impact your behavior had on me."* I guess I could say it definitely was not fun seeing all we had to offer you, and then being rejected and not valued. It was scary having to stand on my own two feet, relying on my 14-year-old son for support, sanity, companionship... creating a slightly dysfunctional relationship between us, creating quite a codependence, which is why this is perfect that Kanyon moves in with my mother or Kai. He has developed into a fine young man ... 17. This is the age the father is around to transition them to a man and introduce them to the work field and working out. It is also the time Kylie needs her father to show her how she should be treated. No worries... because again, after all, everything is perfect, and Kai is stepping up to fill your shoes. I don't know how long I will be in Utah, but I do know this... I have lived that life, and that life is so far ago. I have a new life that I absolutely love. I spread Aloha all day. I love having the sun year-round and wearing shorts year-round. I love all the friends I have, and I love the lifestyle. Ultimately, I thank you for contributing to who I am and contributing to getting me here. Many Mahalo's. See you soon. Love, Keri

January 2014

Telling Scott All about It
A Letter from Keri

Dearest Scott, sorry it's been so long since I have written. Since our visit to see you, not so much has happened, if it makes you feel any better. I don't celebrate holidays, even Christmas. I would even go as far as to say I dislike the Christmas holiday season the most.

Yep, this year really wasn't any different as far as the Kai thing. I thought this year would be the year that it would come full circle, and I would be spending his birthday, Christmas Eve, and Christmas Day with him. After all, I stayed at his house up until those exact days.

We came to see you on the 22nd. I thought the visit went well. Kanyon wished he had been able to have alone time with you and still desires as much. I thought I was very loving towards you, showing you complete forgiveness, holding no bitterness. But upon exiting the jail, all three kids gave me an ass chewing, saying that I didn't shower you with love and affection, and then proceeded to treat me like a whore because I made it real clear to them that you can never go backward. And if I were to go back to being together with you, I would not be honoring my truth, nor would I be respecting me.

They all should be grateful I hold no bitterness!

And with that, I rummaged through my bags and pulled out my sneak-a-toke, demanding to be let out of the car on the side of the freeway because I had had enough of those three kids treating me in such a way... telling me how to act, how to be, how to feel.

After Kai wouldn't pull over even with the insanity building in the car, I lit up, which got him to slam on the brakes so I could get out. Kai freaked out that I was doing "illegal drugs" in his car (so dumb how marijuana is illegal). I jumped out of his car on the side of the freeway. He has so much fear toward the miraculous herb he even pulled forward twenty feet to leave me and my sinful self crouched on the freeway.

Kylie is a sweetie. She didn't like how the boys escalated their disrespect for this chicki because, after all, she is a chicki too, and chicki's get one another.

Kylie jumped out of the car from the twenty-foot clearance mark, walked to me, and crouched beside me to help calm me down and walk me back to the car.

Then, I don't know if you recall, but we had the family party to go to at Jenn & Clark's. They have a beautiful new home in Herriman that's just a few streets south of where we had lived. Yeah, it's all developed with neighborhoods now. I bet those Hamilton, Butterfield, and Mascaro families are enjoying the wealth. But anyway, it was great seeing the fam. Everyone lined up for hugs and kisses. It felt good to have everyone so excited to see Kanyon and I.

But back to the Kai thing... he had said he would have me for the holidays because he knows how it is, and he had said he would work it out so he could see me on those three important days. Well, we all know how Kai is. He tries to please everyone, telling everyone what they want to hear, saying yes to everyone, making plans with everyone. After overhearing there was no room in his plans to hang, I took the initiative to pack and planned to stay at Tabi's and not plan on seeing Kai because, after all, Mai, him, and the kids were staying at his folk's house. I'm sure Kai was relieved that he wouldn't have to juggle this family with that one. And I was grateful for the four nights I stayed at his house meeting his kids.

There again, Kanyon started chewing my ass because I *"sabotaged my happiness"* because I don't like raining on other people's parades. I don't need to see Kai that bad for those three days of the year. Yes, those three days brought me sorrow and grief but, PEOPLE! ... allow me to grieve those f***ing three days. I wasn't being hysterical until Tabi and Kanyon both were again telling me how I should, act, be, and feel. By Christmas Eve, the behavior of others towards me totally pissed me off. I ran away to Helen's. Once I got to Helen's, I was great. No pressure on how I should act, be, and feel. And Helen totally gets it. *"I don't have to be joyful on these days."* Those days are not great days for me, nor do I think they ever will be. Understandably so!

So, on Christmas Day around 10:00 a.m. I called my mother and let her know where I was so she could come pick me up to take me back to Tabi's to see the kids.

I guess Kanyon had gone to his friend Santiago's for Christmas Eve. Kylie had a great Christmas. Tabi is so good to her. She got Kylie a laptop and gave Kanyon and me both a hundred bucks. She said she wanted to buy Shanae a big-screen TV, and she was able to get one of ours out of the storage unit from Julie so she could "buy" it from us. I thought that was great.

I think you should allow Julie to let us sell all of our stuff in that storage unit. It's just accumulating dust and incurring debt, with the monthly payments Julie is wasting on storing it. You could buy all new stuff when you get out and use the money from selling all our stuff now at a time when I need it. Plus, everything is going to be so outdated, and if you wait too long, no one will want to buy the stuff you have in there. Can you even remember what you have in there?

Anyway, my mother came and picked me up from Helen's house, and on the way back to Tabi's, she tells me, out of love and concern and the only way she knows how to deal with upset, I guess, *"I'm concerned about you. Keri, we may have to hospitalize you."*

"WHAT?!" You know I flipped the f*** out on that. Do you realize that is what society has done throughout history? *"Let us take babies away from their mothers, and if the mothers show grief and sorrow, then let's lock them up in the insane asylum and drug them up and give them some shock treatment!"* I was livid. I told her if she is so f***ing worried about me, she should help me get a ticket back to Maui! And I insisted she promise she would never threaten me with such a thing. *"I would never lock you up in an old's home and leave you to rot in your old age, so I can't believe you would even think of such f***ing nonsense,"* I yelled at her. Well, when I say the F-word, it freaks them the f*** out, and they want to sedate me with their choice of drugs... pills that kill.

So that was the Christmas season. Except, I forgot to tell you that part of the reason I called him out about the plans to forget about Kai for his birthday and Christmas, was because your sister Eva had called Kai and informed him that the Stones were getting together the day after Christmas and asked if he was going to be there. I witnessed Kai acting all cheery, as he does with everyone, telling her, *"Yeah, yeah, we will definitely be there."* Then, as soon as he hung up with her, he said,

"*Yeah right, not going to that.*" Well, I immediately asked Kylie and Kanyon if they wanted to go to the Stone party because if they wanted to go, I would go, as much as I didn't care to go. Upon those two saying yes, they wanted to go, was when I decided to give Kai this time with his adopted family, once again separate. Obviously, this year was not the year.

Well, after the Christmas Day blowup of everyone attacking me for *"sabotaging my own happiness and allowing those Sanderson's to take away those days that Kai was supposedly wanting to spend with us."* NOT. My mother, Tabi, Kanyon, and I decided that Kanyon and I needed to be separated.

Kanyon and I had been warned before we came here by Kristi, the Hawaiian healer, that those cords needed to be cut. It's normal to unite with the oldest child in the house to survive what happened. My spouse got addicted to heroin, and then everything went down, but I needed to take back my power. So needless to say, when Zila texted to ask when we would come for the Stone party, I told her no in so many words, excusing my behavior, saying something to the effect of, *"I'm not in the mood for your security law-loving mother anyway."*

I don't know if you heard that we were greeted at the SLC airport baggage claim by airport security. They came right up to me, asking if I was Keri Stone. *"A family member called to inform them that they needed to search my bags for marijuana."* Yeah, ridiculous, all right. Boy, is my family lucky nothing came of it. Well, airport security let this CRAZY woman go because right before I left Maui, I randomly had an interview with some fellas on, *"How do I feel about legalization?"* And with that, they sent a strong message my way. *"When asked to search me and my things, say NO."* After witnessing the pathetic scene of this skinny purple-haired marijuana-medicated woman hanging on to Stoney, the "service dog," with her daughter, Kylie, running up like it has been years since they saw each other, they thanked me for my time and wished me a happy holiday season and bid me a good day, after I gave them that big NO as my answer when they asked if they could search my bags.

So, I went to stay at my mother's while Kanyon stayed at

Tabi's.

At my mother's, I was able to go through six boxes of stuff I had there that had been gone through, by the way. I found NO shoes except for one of my combat boots. Not one pair, one boot. Whatever... Barbara, my dear friend at the harbor, had said, *"You don't want to be walking in those old shoes anyway. You have already walked that walk. Time to have new combat boots to walk your new walk."* I liked that, so when food stamps hit, I was able to buy Tabi some groceries, and she bought me some new boots.

I didn't last at my mother's house for long. She was treating me like a 16-year-old. Both she and my dad were checking in on me all night, past their bedtime, making sure I wasn't sneaking out to toke, making sure my eyes weren't red. Whatever. Well, the second night there, I didn't sneak. I left for a walkabout and didn't air out long enough, and my mother freaked out as if I had snorted a line of cocaine.

It's crazy how much fear people have for "Mary Jane." My mother basically threatened me, telling me I needed to go to Jean's because she can't have illegal substances in her house (just a cupboard full of prescription pills that kill are allowed in her house). Well, fine by me. I was lookin' forward to Jean picking me up. I don't trust my mother to NOT call the po-po. The blue medical card only works in Hawaii... whatever, such nonsense.

Had a great New Year. Loved hanging with Mama Jean. She is a busybody like me, moving from project to project. That intelligent bipolar wonder woman is outliving the death sentence the doctors keep trying to get her to own. She firmly says, *"I'm not owning that illness. I have to live till I'm 60. I have put money into my retirement, and I will collect!"* Gotta love it. That is one great trait of those with bipolar. Once they set their mind on something, it's on. Just like changing the color of your eyes, right babe...

Well, I don't think my mother thought I would be so quick to say, *"OK see ya. I will be at Jean's."* My mom called me on New Year's Eve day to make a date with me to go bra shopping. It has been five years since they cut her boobs off, and she was not looking forward to finding inserts and bras that could make her feel more like a woman.

Upon getting off the phone after arranging our "date" for bra shopping, Jean informed me of a prosthetic bra place just down the street. I called the place to ask how late they were open, being New Year's Eve and all. They would be closing at 1:00 p.m. I called my mother back to tell her to get a move on, be early to her Dr.'s apt, and not get chatty with the Doc, so she can hustle over here.

I have never witnessed my mother move so fast. She arrived at Jean's house at 12:45 p.m... But Jean being so military-minded, because after all, she is a retired Air Force chief, sets all her clocks 15 minutes fast to never be late. When my mother pulled up, Jean announced, "*Well, you might as well invite her in. She's missed the boat.*"

Before I could even get to the door to invite my mother in, she was already there, rushing, saying, "*I think we can make it. We have 15 minutes.*" It was a sight I will never forget, my mother, moving so fast, bouncing in such an excited way. Once in her car, she sped up, putting the car in reverse and putting the pedal to the medal.

The prosthetic bra place was the best time I have had with my mother. For $40 each, which my mother paid, we were gifted four donated inserts with our bras.

We both left feeling like sex goddesses, which is a great way to feel. We are women, hear us roar! I love the idea of being able to choose how busty I want to be every day. So much better than the permanency of a boob job, plus much cheaper and pain-free!!!

I had a great stay at Mama Jean's. I turned her onto the Steve Harvey movie that my dear friend Barbara had been coaching me on all season long, *Think Like a Man*. My sister Ashley came over, and we had a great movie night. It's a movie that I recommend all women, especially young maidens, to watch.

Jean also gifted me a reading/healing session at Rainbow Gardens. It's at the mouth of Ogden Canyon, across from the Dinosaur Park. I was gifted extra time from the healer lady. It is $35 for a half hour, and not only did she hang with me for almost two hours, but she also gifted me some bath salts that have some special thing for the solstice moon??? Not sure.

But anyway, I knew this woman would be a good one when she

immediately picked up on my chatty Great Aunt Edna, who is always thick in my space for the gifted sensitives to pick up on. I guess I am so used to her presence, that I'm not aware of the all-knowing information she is constantly downloading to me.

She gave me a great read, confirming all the abundance and desires that were being delivered right now. I have no need to even worry about getting back to Maui because it is here, and I just had a few cords that needed to be cut.

She said I had cords in my crown area from beliefs that have been programmed and passed down from generation to generation, and I had cords to cut from past trauma. She cleared some things that were in my space/aura that were keeping me from opening up my heart. Seriously, upon leaving, I felt my heart feel open and free to receive. And yes, it's a vulnerable feeling. It felt like a heaviness had been lifted.

For New Year's Eve, Mama Jean and I got all dressed up and went out to an R&B party at a fancy steakhouse. This was the first time for both Mama Jean and I to bring in the New Year out on the town with no kids. She had always stayed home playing games with friends or family.

We had a great time playing up the mama and daughter act, with us only being four years apart. We had a story... She is 50, and I am 30. I am the rebellious daughter who ran away to Maui to be a beach bum because she is a military Mama. We had a fun time entertaining ourselves. Mama Jean taught me the people-watching game with a twist to improve my observation skills (everyone knows how oblivious I can be to my surroundings). Being military-minded, Jean is very good at the game and was able to teach me the importance of being aware of my surroundings. For example, there was this guy that had asked me to dance right when we got there. Every time he would turn into me to dance, I would turn out to create distance. I thanked him for the dance, and upon returning to our table, Mama Jean brought to my awareness what that body language really meant. Boy, was she right. As we watched this player, he found himself three other women throughout the night that immediately after dancing with them (with the women welcoming him in their space on the dance floor, unlike I was), they would leave the club out to the parking lot and return shortly with the player ignoring the lady/ladies for the rest of the night after he got what he wanted. And then the ladies were in a bitchy mood all of a sudden for the rest of the night.

I was blown away that this goes on.

Mama Jean also taught me to always order a fresh glass of water when I leave my glass. The things that go on... CRAZY SCARY. I am so virgin at clubbing.

Anyway, I had a great time. Noelle, the receptionist from the ortho, was there. It was great seeing a familiar face and to talk story.

So, New Year's is over. Kai took Kanyon and me skiing. We had a great day. I forgot how much I love to ski. I was kind of not looking forward to it because of the freezing cold that is exhausting me, but when you dress warm... and it was a beautiful sunny day. We had a great time.

I have been living like a nomad, just like Crystal and the others had predicted. I go from house to house wherever the Universe guides me. I rotate from my mother's, Mama Jean's, Tabi's, Helen's, Kai's, and even my new baby sister's house.

Yeah, that's right... I finally met my baby sister on December **23**rd, Kai's birthday. Shae is 22 and more amazing than I ever dreamed her to be. She is very gifted. Like Kanyon, she reads minds and is so full of love and unity.

We all went to the Hogle Zoo for the zoo lights event, and guess what? I took that Stoney dog as a service dog to the zoo!!! Love it. I had to sign papers that even being a "service dog," he may act up, and if he does any damage, I am responsible. And then they made it clear that I did not want to walk through the big cat exhibit. I wasn't ballsy enough to do that but thought it funny they expressed how not a good idea that would be.

Shae drove me down to Kai's to spend the weekend with me when he blessed his baby boy at church. Seriously, I had just run through my mind, *"I wish Shae could come this weekend so I felt like I had a friend by my side for an event that I would really feel alone."* You know how ostracized I always am, especially without having you there. As soon as my wishes danced in my thoughts, Shae asked if she could come!!! So glad, because yep, without saying a word, that dear sister picked up on the vibes that go on that people are so oblivious, or shall I say ignorant, too.

But hey, you will be happy to hear that Kai got up and bore his testimony, mentioning only his birth father, who is in prison, but bearing testimony of how the scriptures are bringing you comfort while you serve your sentence.

Plus, I must add my highlight of the day... When we were back at their house for the feed, Kai's best friend approached me, asking, "*So... you are?*"

"*Whatever you want me to be,*" I interjected with sarcasm and a smile.

Kai was standing nearby and shook his head with a chuckle because we all know how sensitive I used to get with this bullshit verbiage.

Well, after my response, the friend caught on that this was awkward but not, so he continued with, "*Well, you and Kai look just alike, and oh my heck, Daisy has your eyes.*"

Well immediately after that compliment, I chuckled and said with sarcasm, "*Oh really now. Funny you should say such a thing.*"

I loved it and needed to say no more. I left Kai and his friend to further the conversation on their own, with me telling Kai how much I adore that friend.

Life is good.

I love not needing Kai to honor me as his mother. I love not needing validation because DNA is a beautiful curse that runs thick. I don't have to fight for who I am because guess what? I AM.

I had a lovely time visiting with Mai and the kids. Mai is great. She is the best for the job. Moscow has prepared her well. She is a badass in whom I see many traits of myself. Which Kai would disagree.

I am so thankful that you know, the kids know, my friends know, family knows, but most of all, GOD knows what an amazing mother I have been, serving all God's children 100%, dedicating my life to my family in such a way, and sacrificing more than my own happiness for others.

I have nothing to prove. I don't need to explain, justify, or defend.

I have come to realize through all of this that you cannot skip out on any phase/stage of your life. I never experienced being on my own and "dating," even though I "gave" my baby away at 16. It changes you to have a baby, whether your baby dies, is kidnapped, or is lost to adoption. I was a mother and began using my nurturing instincts on anyone who needed it. I went from my mother's rules to my Daddy Randy's rules to you.

So now I get to live the 16-year-old to 25-year-old phase/stage of being on my own.

Look at you. You were robbed of your childhood and were never taught consequences or how to play, if you will, because of the grownup dysfunction you had to live. And here you are, incarcerated, learning to play, being nurtured, so to speak, being taught healthy behavior, having to stick your nose in the corner for being naughty in dodgeball... loved hearing it. We need to live each phase/stage of life.

And honestly, I love hearing that you are able to live without stress. Not having to work hard to provide a roof over your head or any others for that matter. And I love hearing you are able to live such a carefree life. People may not think of prison/jail as a carefree life, but compared to the life you have lived... This is the best closest thing.

Enjoy focusing on you. Don't worry about me and the kids. We are blessed with an abundance of family who are blessed with abundance to help care for Kanyon and Kylie. As for me... Tiffani (my hoodoo voodoo adoptive mother friend from Waterford) has informed me of an adoption conference she wants to attend with Kai and me in tow. We will see. Lots of love darling. Keep up the good work. Many Mahalo's, Thank you for the lessons, Aloha, Love Keri

February 2014

Kanyon Stays in Utah & I Go Home to Maui

KANYON: Hey dad, how are you? I've been staying with Grandma most of the time. I got into the storage unit a few days back and got my dressers, guitars, and what not. I didn't get the keyboard, pictures, or anything in the smaller unit. I want to get your stuff out of there so that we can store it in Grandma's garage. All of your stuff is being sold to pay for the unit bill. I've been telling Julie she needs to sell what she needs to pay herself back, and then she needs to give me what's left. She won't listen. I've been telling everybody that it's stupid to pay the storage bill with the stuff you're storing. I'd rather sell it all and buy a car if it's all going to disappear anyway.

Grandma and Grandpa keep saying to just let Julie have all of the stuff or sell it all and keep the money since she was the one that stored it. But that's nonsense. They just didn't want to store it in their garages. So, I told them, *"Fine. I'll keep it in Kai's garage."* Then they said I should just let Kai keep it all, which is more nonsense. I'm the one that's been pushing and communicating with Julie to get into the damn unit. I'm the one trying to keep the shit from getting sold. So just let Julie know what's up. She needs confirmation from you about me taking the Noah's Arc and elephant picture and the monitor. She said she has to wait until the flood damage is fixed. I'm going to keep track of what she sells and how much we still owe her. Then I'll get the rest of our stuff and keep it safe, rent-free.

I've been writing a lot of lyrics lately, blowing glass, welding, playing ball, and working out. I've been talking to the Utah work department, and they gave me a placement test, which I tested college level and above, so I don't need tutoring. My new card just arrived today! It's taken so long since you registered as me to get benefits with my identity, haha, but it's all good. I straightened it all out. Imma be getting the card about Thursday, and then we can figure out when I can go pass the

GED. I'm too cool for school fool, haha. Then they'll pay for two years of college, so I might take welding classes or psychology, but that's like eight years, so I don't know about that.

Plus, I'm hella smarter than the damn psychologist I've been forced to be seeing. I've been the one teaching him about marijuana, CBD, THC, spirituality, over-firing neurons, and hyperactive minds. He agrees that "Mary Jane" brings me to the neuron-firing pace of a normal person. Upon our first meeting, he really noticed that I talk and think at a much higher pace than most people. The intake, which usually takes half a session, took two sessions because of all the shit that's gone down in my life. Today was just tests and resolutions of my hyperactive mind and my medicinal marijuana. I already quit weed though, so I'm done being labeled. I'm just a Crystal Child. Grandma has been labeling me as a schizophrenic, psychotic, selfish, and indulging person because I focus on my music instead of playing ball with a bunch of clowns. She shuts me down so much with her labels and negativity. My chi has been so drained since I've been here. I wish you were out so we could live the bachelor life together. That will be perfect because we're so much alike. Yeah, with our hyperactive minds, we'll create great things. We are like the mathematician in A Beautiful Mind.

I've been really changing our family's perspective on God, alpha and omega, Jesus, the power of the mind, and all kinds of biblical/spiritual aspects. Grandma always compares me to Professor Nash in *A Beautiful Mind*. We watched it the other night, and I related so much! So, I got kind of sketched when I saw that he has schizophrenia, haha, but it's all about equalizing and balancing out the over-firing neurons when that superpower called our mania isn't necessary, but our neurons are over firing for a reason. I believe it's just the new children coming and being hyperactive because of the quickening. Time is speeding up, and the frequencies are rising. Our extensions of Source consciousness are returning back to the center point after this veering out like the flower of life. Life is all about expansion and contraction... Duality to unity.

Some are trapped in the illusion of separateness and are so corrupt. We heard Earth's call for help, and that's why we Indigo, Crystal, and Rainbow children came here. To help the full essence of our Source to return back home. It is the end of days, the last dispensation. It's the Golden Age, the age of enlightenment, the second coming, Armageddon, the apocalypse, whatever you may call it. We have gone through cycles of consciousness to evolve. The veil gets thicker at times, bringing more darkness. Then, Jesus, Noah, Enoch, Abraham, Moses, and Joseph Smith bring back the light. This time, all of the ascended masters, divinities, ETs, and any high-frequency souls are coming to radiate love and unity to help people come together again and remember who they truly are and what is in their hearts past the distraction of the man through the media like the mark of the beast. It's a battle of good against evil, and that is why we have hyperactive minds so that we can think more out of this reality, more in the cosmos, getting revelation, creating new patterns to manifest the New Earth and our kin's ascension and resurrection.

I love you so much, Dad, and I am so excited to see you again and feel accepted, supported, secure, and at home again. You have to come to Maui with me! It is so amazing there. I'm so excited to see what we will create for ourselves in the future! Our foreordination is miraculous, and we are going to change the world for the better.

I'm so glad you're doing so great in jail, and your trinity is so clear and pure. Keep up the good work, and I'll be coming to visit you soon. Even if I have to ride with Julie, I'll do it. She's not that bad. She has a good, nurturing heart, and she's in touch with reiki, Source, and spirituality. I just wish she wasn't so damn flaky, haha. Alright, much love, peace, and tranquility to you.

Aloha, Namaste

Back in Maui!!!

KERI: Scott, hey babe, how are you? I am doing fabulously! I am back in Maui and back at the harbor! I love it so much that I seriously would show up and work for free!

I am happy, whole, and complete! I unpacked some of my boxes and found the Serena in me... my jewelry, socks, hats, scarves, fairies, etc. Little bits of me that I had boxed up for two years... Well, I am back at the harbor with my Serena on. They only saw Samantha (you know, *Bewitched*... the sitcom series I owned and watched nightly along with *Gilligan's Island*, and *I Dream of Jeannie*. We are what we watch... remember me telling you, you Mr. Soprano, *CSI* guy, haha, j/k... I love you). Anyway, I have jumped out of my closet, and am OUT OF MY CLOSET. Yes, dear... Keri at her mostest. You know the look. I will send you a pic...

Kanyon has been back with my mom. That has been such a rollercoaster ride... one minute, my mother is accepting of Kanyon smoking weed for his medicine, and then the next, she's not. She flops like a fish on it. Kanyon does really well on it. He isn't smoking nearly as much as he was. I honestly don't see the logic in making him quit using his marijuana as his medicine. Especially when we have already got him okayed by a doctor telling us he can see why marijuana would help Kanyon so much. But that was a Maui Dr., and marijuana isn't a medicine in Utah. They want Kanyon to quit his "Mary Jane" and replace it with pills that kill just so everyone in Utah can feel good about it because of the bullshit legality of it, which makes no sense to me. How can it be legal in one state, and then you cross a border, and you are a criminal for taking your medicine? And Grandma, who ultimately just barely paid Kanyon $200 to break the bong I had bought right after she was telling me how expensive it is to have Kanyon. I am going to be sending my food stamp card to help feed Kanyon. The world is so messed up, but I am grateful for the help I can get to raise these kids of ours.

Kylie seems to be doing great, as always. She does so well at Tabi's. Kai, I believe, is full-on ignoring me. I have called and texted, leaving messages. Obviously, he is purposely avoiding and ignoring. Mai says he is all bent that I left Utah and went back to Maui. I cannot imagine being anywhere else. I know I am to be here. I don't know the direction I am going until that very moment. I love riding the current of life by the seat of my pants and going with the flow without many plans for the future, just trusting that the future is already planned for me. To be in a state of allowance, to receive all that is intended (good and bad), to be the character I am to be.

My brother Travis is flying his sister and mother out in March. I am lookin' forward to that. And Kylie wants me to fly her out for her birthday, which I will be able to do as soon as my taxes hit my account. Yes, I filed my taxes this year, and because I am a mother who made too little to live off of, the feds are gifting me $6000 on my return. It is saving my ass. I am going to try to buy a car that has windows.

My new place is in Kahana, and it rains every night, and I do not have covered parking. I really lucked out on my living arrangement. Jennifer, the flower lady I was working for, is my new roommate.

When my mother loaned me the money to buy a ticket back to Maui, Rachel (the chicki with the soul mate birthday of June 26th, like all my other roommates in my life), informed me that her landlord was already pitching a fit about having someone move in with her. We were going to share a bed in her studio apartment for $300. So, I called Jennifer. She was just barely moving out of her baller house into a baller condo and was thrilled to rent the room to me. We haven't fully worked out a price (she literally let me move in with no money. I gladly helped her with her move, and she is waiting for my funds to hit. God bless her). It's somewhere around $550, with some babysitting here and there. It's her and her 2-year-old from her present husband (relationship is on the rocks).

I am so grateful for everyone in my life who is helping me along the way. I am finally happy, whole, and complete. Now I'm ready for the gravy! I desire a friendship, aka boyfriend, with someone I can fully open my heart to. I don't regret any of my time with you. All those years have made me who I am, and I love who I am. I am a wise, happy, joyful person. I have fallen and risen out of the ashes as the phoenix has. It is such an incredible feeling to have a knowing of so many things because I have been there and done that. And ultimately, whether you have someone in the space to love or not, it does start within.

Having someone in the space to love is just a mirroring of what one has in their own space and I cannot wait to experience a friendship/relationship on a whole new level. I already am so happy and know when that relationship comes along, it will feel so right on that whole new level. Lots of love to you.

The kids, even the nephews, always talk so respectfully about you and honor your greatness. I love that I was married to such a badass. Imagine what's in store for you once you arrive with the freedom to choose your path on the outside. Coming out a new man with love for yourself, loving others on a whole new level. I'm excited for all of us. Again, lots of love to you. Aloha, Love Keri

March 2014

Making the Best of Our Situations

March 1

SCOTT: Hey baby, I got your letter this morning. Thank you for writing and sending Kanyon's letter. I really enjoy hearing from you. I love you and miss you tons, and I am glad that you are happy. You are amazing, and you can have any man that will make you happy. I am getting discouraged here. I want to be done already and get on with life. I am nervous to see the board, but I want to get it over with and know my release date. I'm excited to graduate from the program so that I can work and earn money so that I am not mooching off of people. I am glad you figured out your taxes. Love you

March 5

KERI: So today you see the board. I love that Kai made sure to be there for you with Kanyon. Kanyon wishes he could see you more often. I am so very grateful that Kanyon is closer to you. I am so thankful for Kanyon escorting me to get me where I needed to be... here in Maui.

I look forward to hearing what's up with your near future. I received your postcard. I couldn't help but notice that your prime reason to get out of there is, *"I can work and earn money so that I am not mooching off of people."* You deserve to be taken care of. Think of all the people you have taken care of. *"Work and earn money..."* you deserve a vacation from working. Think how hard you have worked your whole life.

What is your passion besides working and earning money? Pretend money had no value, and we lived in a world of communal living with people serving others by living their passions. When my millions hit, I would love to still work at the harbor. I love my job so much, I would volunteer. I love interacting with people, spreading Aloha.

What would you love to do with yourself, serving and loving

others, participating in this illusion of our life, if money was not part of the equation?

Ultimately, you are in a perfect place to be gifted the time to meditate on what makes Scott happy. If you were on an island, or in the mountains, what can you see yourself doing? Are you surrounded by your kids? Are you visiting others on the island, talking story? Maybe reminiscing of your crazy times, but instead, retelling the stories this time with wisdom obtained from the path traveled. It's helpful to share wisdom with others. You are an extremely intelligent man. After this stint in prison/jail (you lucky bastard), you are going to be that much wiser. You have been humbled. Now you just need to work on loving yourself.

Energy is moving fast: learn the lesson asap... thank the lesson learned... shift happens... awe... back on track with desires... raise the vibration and watch the manifestation.

Speaking of raising the vibration and watching manifestation... Kanyon and my mother don't know yet, but I traded my car with no windows in for a... Jeep!!!

I prayed and said, *"Lord, if it is meant to be, it will be. If they are able to finance, I will not say no, and I will trust the Universe is focused on me and the Universe will provide abundance for me to pay my bills."*

Well, for $3500, along with my car as a down, I pay $520ish a month! @#$%

I know... but I told the Universe if they said yes, I would too.

In the end, I am paying 24% interest for this 2007 Jeep Wrangler, which if I kept for the entire loan, I would be paying $37,000ish for this fun ride of mine that I have always wanted and pictured myself in.

I needed a car with windows... and I'm not going to buy just any car with windows.

Anyway, life is good. The state of Utah garnished my taxes...

yeah, they were trying to sue me for both the children. I am a mother in need on Hawaii assistance with Kanyon, but when my mother reported Kylie needing a cash benefit while living with her, I guess the state of Utah thought they were paying her for Kanyon also, even though it was the state of Hawaii paying for Kanyon. Anyway, I had brought it to my mother's attention to rectify the problem because I don't believe in the bullshit way of The Man ways of doing things. After all, I have always helped mothers in need without any expectations or "pay me back," and when the state of Hawaii asked me if I wanted cash assistance, but they would sue you for it, I declined. I knew that you were not in a financial position to be sued for that. I figured I would just do my best to provide for our son, and assumed my mother would do the same for our daughter... it takes a village to raise a child.

Anyway... The state of Utah was notified of their mistake in suing me for both the children a month prior to me filing for my 2013 taxes, and they garnished my taxes and took more than half of my gifted funds from the Feds. I was annoyed but stayed calm, notified my mother of the bogus bullshit, then called the state of Utah and calmly told the over-defensive female that hates her job, "*I just wanted you to know how wrong this is. You stole from a mother in need. I hope you sleep well at night.*" Well, before I told her those last words of mine, she had said they would return my money in 4 weeks. I got my check 2 days later. ATTITUDE... it gets you miles... good or bad... whichever way you aim it.

Tyler works at Ululani's Shave Ice with James. James has been promoted to manager ice shaver dude. Jasper is flying out of here on Monday the 10th to go back to Utah for a bit. We all are going to drive to Hana before Jasper's flight.

I am flying Kylie out here from March 17th to April 2nd for her birthday. I am very excited for her to come and to fully focus on her without having any other offspring around. Total GIRL time!

My brother is flying out at the end of March as well!!! I will totally send you pics.

My mother has filed to get child support from me through ORS. It has infuriated me. It took my power away. It dictated what I was to buy. It dictated what I was to spend on my child (when, in all reality, I was planning on sending more, but towards things I felt were more important). Which ultimately took my power away as to what I wanted that money to go towards. But most importantly, it took my interaction away from my child... The gift from me, the mother... The deciding together on where and what we were going to do with the money. It takes a village to raise a child, and all that we can do as a village is pull together, offering our strengths without living in fear of lack, and focusing instead on all the strengths one is contributing, and supporting me and each other.

JC Checks In

JC: How u Ms. Keri? How things going?

KERI: Oh, my dear JC! How the heck are you? I couldn't be better! I have never been happier. I needed a break from the kids living with me. I could not do it by myself. It doesn't matter if the mother in need is 16 or 43, I do not see how single mothers out there do it. You cannot, well, at least I could not, work full time and continue being the over-the-top amazing homemaker, tentative mother my kids are used to having. Nor could I provide the lifestyle they were accustomed to living. God bless Scott. I have realized how henpecked one can feel to "pay for this, pay for that." It seemed that's all the focus was a lot of the time. I understand how my behavior contributed to Scott's sorrows. Thank you for the lesson. But when one is so giving, it's hard to say no firmly and hang on to your money for what you feel is the right way to spend it. I hate how money has so much power... power that we ultimately give it. I am learning lessons about money. I have never provided for myself, and it is a great lesson to learn.

When are you going to come see me? Kylie is flying out on St. Patrick's Day! I can't wait. Kanyon is going to be going with Kai to New Jersey on April 5th. Kai is ignoring me... he is angry. He thinks I am the worst mother ever because I chose to come back to Maui instead of taking responsibility for my kids. But my kids are where they want to be, and Kai needs to focus on the blessing it is... that Kanyon is in his space instead of focusing on how much it costs to feed him. But my dear JC, how are you? Lots of love

JC: Yeah, I'm good Ms. Keri. Still coaching and started a lil business with my friend. Yeah I'm glad u happy at this point in ur life. You deserve it. I know ur not custom to living how u are now. But money's not everything though. I feel u and Scott were together for so long and been so much, it's only a matter of time for someone throw in the towel. And that u was hanging on because of the kids. Which, y'all still can be good parents to Kanyon and Kylie (my stinker), even though she is almost as tall as me now, lol. I'm sure Scott has time to reflect on the situation as well. Kai is gonna be alright. Probably a lot of pressure to take care of his family and Kanyon at the same time. But that's what Scott did for him, tho now he sees now. Yeah, I'm coming there. I just don't know when yet. Love u, Ms. Keri. Take care

Last Letters from Scott

March 4

SCOTT: So, I heard a story about a boy who asked his dad what to look for in a woman, and his dad told him to worry about being a man that a dad will tell his daughter to look for, and everything will fall into place for him. I realize how true that is, and I'm sorry I didn't spend more time understanding that concept. I'm sorry that I didn't have a father figure who taught me how to treat a woman, to treat a wife, to treat and respect a best friend, a co-parent, and especially how to treat the mother of my children. Thank you for being amazing at all of your roles. Sorry it took until it was too late for these lessons to matter. I love you just the way you are and hope you find true happiness and love.

March 19

SCOTT: So, I got your letter yesterday morning. That was nice. Thank you for your words. I really value your words and your praise. It really makes my day when I get mail from you, so thank you for that. I'm glad that you got your taxes. I hope that helped. I saw the pic of your Jeep. It is awesome. I am so glad that you were able to get it. At that interest rate though, I would pay it off as quickly as you can. I'll bet even paying an extra $100-$200 a month when you can afford it would drop it a lot.

So, I have not got my date yet. I am a little worried about it, but mostly because it is the unknown. I'm sure I will be out between February and August next year, my original date, and that is before any time cuts for completing the program. People have been getting between 30 days and 6 months. It would be nice if my date was February of 2015, and I got a 3-month time cut because that would get me out before Thanksgiving and Christmas next year, which would be awesome.

I understand what you are saying about taking a break from

work and taking care of myself, but I have been locked up for 401 days today, and enough is enough. I realize what's what, and I am ready to use it in the real world.

I'm excited for Kylie Dawn to spend some time with you. I have been worried about her not having her daddy. I want to get out of here and be there for the kids and the grandkids.

Thank you for everything, darling. I love you tons and want the best for you. I will talk to you soon. Love, Scott

April 2014

Last Letter to Scott

KERI: Hey darling, Kanyon was sad that he hadn't heard from you... he has a new number, so you don't have to go through Kai. I told him to write to you, and he said, *"Just tell Dad to call me."*

Which brings me to your comment, *"I'm ready to use it in the real world."* Let's start living "as if" right now. You need to call your son once a week (his request). I would write Kylie at least once a week. Take this time to continue to father and develop your relationships with your children. Even reaching out to Liah and Braden. Even if they are letters not sent, but letters that you write even if only to send the loving thoughts their way, which brings you in a better relationship with you in that area as well. Kai was enjoying the weekly phone calls. Keep it up... start there and do what is most important to you Now. Now that you are free to choose what you are doing... almost a blessing that there aren't so many distractions so that you can focus on your children.

Thank you for the lesson on that darling. Thank you for teaching me how to occupy my time with productive actions and thoughts within my walls of freedom. Everything is a choice of how we are going to get through things. I have struggled with patience. By always having to wait for you, I got really good at making the choice of what I am going to do while I wait... sometimes being hours. Which, compared to a prison sentence, is so minute. But you do receive tenfold what you put out, and you have made a lot of people wait for Your Highness. Speaking softly darling... but as I would think, what would Jesus do?

I remember being taught, that if Jesus was to show up at your doorstep right now, would you be ready to go? Well looking around my house, I would want to offer him a clean house to host him in, so that is why my house was always clean and my chores were always done, with time to spare... in most cases waiting on you. But I was available for so many to stop by unexpectedly and offer so many stories from my experiences, sharing my wisdom with those that Jesus has put in my space.

Darling, prison is on a much lower flying disc than Farm Circle, that fairylicious home you provided for us. But truly, you have a choice as to what you are spending your time doing and what you are focusing on. Who is in your space right now??? I'm sorry that your vibration has gotten that low that you are now amongst others who are matching your vibration. Look at those around you as the blessing they are to you... the lesson to learn... Who is the teacher??? Who is the student???

I just finished reading Elisabeth Smart's story... she wrote it with Chris Stewart. If you can receive books, I would love to send you it. It was so amazing to hear how she survived it... kidnapped at 14 out of her parent's window by knife... starved, tortured, and raped every day for 9 months. How does she go on? How did she deserve this? How did she survive it? Well, she tells you... 9 months of pure torture doesn't even compare to all the glorious months she has had and continues to have. She was able to keep her thoughts positive, focusing on the love of her mother, God, and family. And you know what else she admits to? She admits having a conversation with God to be an example to others and to really be someone of importance. Well, dear darling, your son Kanyon told me of his similar conversation with the Universe. He said life was always given to him and he wanted to make a difference in this world, and knew he had to experience something pretty gnarly, and he is so grateful for the ride.

Thank you for so many lessons. Take the lessons you have learned and apply them ... love yourself, love others. By loving others, even fellow inmates, you are loving yourself. You are no better than them, darling. Even I had to get my royal highness ass humbled. I used to fear homeless, dirty people just as much as you feared inmates. We are all one and let's learn from our journey, ditch the f***ing programs that our parents and others have programmed into us, get real with yourself, dig yourself, embrace yourself... and in doing so, you will get real with others, dig others, and embrace others.

I sent a picture of Lahaina Larry wearing a shirt saying all in bold, "YOU MAD BRO?" to Kai because that kid was still ignoring me because of his upset about me leaving. His abandonment and rejection issues in his face are hard-core, I get it. But please... I finally got a response after this one. He was able to vent, and I was able to send unconditional love regardless.

The boys are great! Tyler has arrived, and Alek arrived as Jasper departed. I love having them here. I am very thankful for the love they all shower on me. Me and the boys are always on an adventure!

Picked up Kylie on... St. Patrick's Day!!!! We had a great visit. At first, it was pretty gnarly. We had to share a bedroom, and you know how I like to make my bed every day and how Kylie does not like to make her bed every day. We shared a bed and a room... Fine-tuning at its best. Thank you, Kylie, ... I did not lose my temper ...much.

By the end of the stay, she had bonded with my dear friend Barbara who speaks my language, and by accepting it with Barbara, she was able to shift and accept it in me and also within herself.

Had a great visit... To sum it up, we both shifted in a beautiful way. Kylie was able to see me through new eyes. And I was able to stand strong with who I am, owning who I am, owning my truth with everything down to my style. It felt good to not care what anyone thinks and was a great example for her to find love for herself instantaneously as I myself shift. Energy is energy, and it is just like your mother taught me... by healing and shifting my energy within, it heals ancestors of old and generations to come in that instant. Much love, Darling. Aloha.

April 2015

Final Words

As I sit in Kona for my 45th birthday, I reflect on what has transpired over this past year. It has definitely been a year of fine-tuning. Life for me is not much different. I still work at the harbor. Both my kids live with me once again. I am still a single mother striving to make ends meet. But the difference in awareness when living in a state of allowance, consciously focused on the NOW, makes the ongoing ride of this thing called Life make a lot more sense.

I finally understand what groundhog day means. Cycles will continue to repeat, and energies will continue to spin. I am riding this wave as an audience member in a state of allowance, observing the pattern of groundhog day. But this time, I am going to follow my heart instead of my head. I'm not going to force what I desire. I am going to trust that my desires are known and be in a state of allowance, watching the Universe deliver all my desires in a better way than I could ever imagine. I am going to continue the ride, loving everyone that enters my space. I have come to the understanding that love IS all we need... My new "*aha.*"

I really do believe this world is stepping into feminine power with nurture and love. Let us all get over the past. I am grateful for the lessons. From here on out, I am stepping into my feminine power. I am here to love all unconditionally. After all, we can only lead by example. To know the end, we must know the beginning... the chicken or the egg. The other day, my dear cousin was asking for advice on keeping her young hottie, and I told her, "*These men, no matter the age, are just looking for nurturing and love. As long as you keep it fun and all about nurturing and loving them... no nagging, you can keep a man forever.*" This is what it is. These men are no different than our own boys, who we are raising, nurturing, and loving. Then these boys start dating girls who are just like their mother, who have daddy issues, and who don't feel safe being vulnerable to love. So, when we get together with these boys and our daddy issues come out... then there you have it. Cycles have repeated like groundhog day. So, get vulnerable with love and always look at the man in your life as if they are the boy in yours now, behaving the best they can in the moment. And when they misbehave, ignore them and act happy whether or not they are in your life. So, if they are naughty (doing something you don't like), you ignore them while still being happy and nice. Because ultimately, I am not going to give anything outside of myself so much power over my happiness. Love yourself. Everything about yourself... the good, the bad, and the ugly. And by loving who you are, accepting who you are, owning who you are, and embracing who you are, you will empower us all to live in a state of acceptance and unconditional love so we can focus on our passions and contribute to the village without keeping track of who is better than who. All of us just living peacefully together, enjoying this physical experience to the max.

If you enjoyed *Healing at the Harbor*, please consider leaving a book review by scanning the QR code below.

To learn more about the author and join her email list to receive announcements about new book releases, sales, or special events, please visit www.keridangerfieldstone.com

Other titles by Keri Dangerfield Stone

Life Goes On by Keri Dangerfield Stone is a moving memoir about her journey as a birth mother, from teenage pregnancy to the emotional reunion with her son. Exploring themes of sacrifice, identity, and resilience, Keri's story highlights her advocacy for change in the adoption world and her personal evolution.

Four years after reuniting with her son, whom she lost to adoption as a teenager, Keri shares her emotional journey during her son's mission to Mexico. Through heartfelt letters, Keri delves into her motherly love, insecurities, and spiritual journey, offering a raw and introspective look at her struggles with identity, forgiveness, and personal growth.

Mothers of Loss delves into the emotional world of birth mothers within an online support group, exploring themes of loss, identity, and the intricacies of adoption. Through personal stories and advocacy, it reveals the group's shared experiences and their push for transparency and reform in adoption practices.